# WHO OWNS AMERICA?

by Edmund Blair Bolles

M. Evans and Company, Inc.
New York

*To friends indeed.*
*Bruce, Clift,*
*Esther, and Pete*

*Library of Congress Cataloging in Publication Data*

Bolles, Edmund Blair, 1911–
Who owns America?

1. Property—United States. I. Title.
HB711.B65 1984 330.973'0927 84-13705

ISBN 0-87131-450-9 (pbk.)



M. Evans and Company, Inc.
216 East 49 Street
New York, New York 10017

Design by Lauren Dong

Manufactured in the United States of America
9 8 7 6 5 4 3 2 1

# CONTENTS

# INTRODUCTION

Who owns the prominent, the important, bizarre, or precious bits of America? After all, the things that shape our lives and culture do have owners. The Empire State Building is a worldwide symbol of the American talent for enormousness, design, and utility, but it also has an owner, a man whose real estate holdings are valued at $5 billion. (As you might expect, his lawyer is a shrewd fellow too.)

Or consider another unique product of our way of life, the giant roadside statues that stand in front of highway restaurants and other enterprises. Huge bulls stand before steak houses in the hope of snaring passing travelers; gigantic effigies of Paul Bunyan straddle wayside inns. They are as characteristic of post–World War II America as tavern signs were typical of Olde England. Some of these statues are rather handsome, but most seem desperately tasteless and unsuited to the scene. Who owns the most vulgar of them all? As a matter of fact he is a fellow you've probably heard of, Roy Rogers (born Leonard Slye).

To most of us, state songs are nice little ditties to be played on festive occasions, but to others the songs are bits of property. Paul McCartney of the Beatles, for example, has been loading up on American classics, and to him a state song such as "On Wisconsin" is a source of income.

This book surveys the materials at the heart of American culture and tells who owns them. The result is a series of facts whose individual value ranges from gossip to historical footnote to social significance. Taken as a whole, the facts display important patterns. Among the landowners, for example, we see a hard rivalry between owners committed to their property's historic position and owners whose only concern is cash flow. Surprisingly for the cynics, the historically aware owners seem to be slightly ahead of the game, but it is a close contest and many a millionaire Visigoth calls himself a developer.

A different pattern emerges from a study of the owners of the information media. There we can distinguish two types of owners—those who own the technology of communication and those who are concerned with the content of communication. There is no contest here. The technology is valued a lot more highly than the content.

Such patterns plot a detailed map of the routes to power, fame, and wealth in contemporary America. One way is through connections.

Another way is straight out of Horatio Alger: work hard, reinvest your savings, and think big. Following that advice, one man traveled a convoluted path that led from the atomic bomb to America's largest shopping center.

Inheritances are there too, as are crooks and con men. And then there is a category of person—the inventor Henry Kloss is a good example—who seems not at all interested in acquiring property. He has the soul of a poet and the determination of Hercules, a combination that almost inevitably generates a trail of purchasable things. Despite his best efforts to pursue ethereal pleasures, this fellow often ends up as a minor millionaire.

In short, this is a reference book that on one level can be used as a list of facts detailing the owners of the archetypal elements of America today. At that level it serves as a basic directory of owners, properties, and worth. On a second level, it suggests ways these distinct elements and owners link together. Then the book serves as a guide to how America's material culture works.

## The Roll

The first task in writing this book was to develop a consistent and accurate method of identifying owners. Ownership seems concrete and fixed, but upon inquiry it can often turn out to be elusive.

The only people considered for inclusion on the roll were those whose right of control is backed up by force of law. Sometimes the law recognizes a claim, but is of little help in supporting it. The apparently endless battle over the laser patent and the many successful piracies during the height of the Rubik's cube fad illustrate the limitations of ownership. In such cases the book lists the lawful owner, but reports the serious weakness that accompanies the title.

Ownership also requires at least a theoretical ability to transfer the right of possession; however, along with the transfer of things (old-fashioned selling), a person can transfer rights. By now this second kind of sale has become so lucrative that things are created just so the rights to them can be sold. The Strawberry Shortcake character is perhaps the most familiar example, but the arrangement turns up in everything from computer languages to designer jeans to syndicates controlling the sexual deeds of racehorses. In these cases ownership usually rests with the seller of the right rather than with the buyer. The original owner is free to sell rights over and over. Sale without loss of possession is the closest thing yet found to perpetual motion.

Properties can also acquire many claimants, some of them hidden from view. It is quite common for landlords to keep their names hidden from their tenants. Often they are so eager to avoid responsibility for things like heat and water that landlords turn over management of the property to a third party. Thus a single property can have an investor gaining an income, a renter in physical possession of the place, and a manager taking responsibility for the property's condition and use. In the case of apartment buildings, the issue has been settled by the courts—the investor is the owner. In other situations where responsibility has been finessed, much investigation and study are sometimes needed before the owner of a particular property can be identified.

In cases concerning public corporations, careful analysis was necessary. Shareholders of a company are repeatedly told that they are the owners, but theirs is usually an impotent form of ownership that brings no special right of access or sale or policymaking. Such a feeble claim is far from the powerful forms of ownership explored in this book, in which nobody, not even a corporation's chief executive officer, was eligible for the roll of owners simply by holding a few shares of stock. Large shareholders posed a different problem. The Securities and Exchange Commission says that investors with more than 5 percent of a company's shares are significant stockholders; however, such an investment does not always bring the powers of ownership and, for this book, all cases had to be judged individually. Sometimes owning 10 percent is enough to bring decisive power, while in other cases a 30 percent holding is too weak to be important.

A final problem concerns debt. Nathalie Hocq, the young woman who heads Cartier's jewelry empire, denies that her family owns Cartier, insisting that the banks own it. This may sound petulant or cute—and indeed this book lists Nathalie Hocq rather than her bankers as owner of Cartier—but Ms. Hocq is on to more than an old joke. Just at this moment much of the American economy is undergoing a radical change.

During the past few years a number of corporations have been "taken private"; that is, the stock of many investors has been bought by a few. The investors seldom have the cash to make such a purchase, so they borrow most of what they need. Of course, to borrow, you need collateral, but today's owners often use the property they plan to buy as collateral. This form of purchase is known as a leveraged buyout and, just like a mortgage on a house, it places many restrictions on the borrower. In this book the borrowers rather than the lenders are listed as the owners of leveraged property, because, if the investment goes well and the borrowers are honorable, their title is clear. But if the investment turns sour or the borrower begins looting the company's assets, then the ownership claim of the lending bank ceases to be the punch line of an old joke.

## Auctioneer's Price

Each listing begins with an estimate of what the item would bring if it were suddenly available for competitive bidding. This figure depends on a property's worth to investors, its prestige, and demand. It ignores the problem of whether the current owner would actually be willing to settle for the listed price.

Most prices were estimated with the aid of a computer programmed to evaluate assets, liabilities, and earnings. Since some properties would inspire bidders to foolhardiness while others would make people sit on their hands, the program also included factors to adjust each estimate in accordance with an item's prestige. The results were then adjusted according to various historical data: how the computer estimate compared with recent sales of similar properties; how it compared with relevant stock prices; etc. Finally, the figure was rounded. As is the way of computers, the program generated foolishly exact estimates, precise to the penny. If an auctioneer's price were given as $1,930,158,975.91, the reader might be tempted to take the calculation a little too literally.

Some years ago the author was involved, in a minor capacity, with an attempt by the Shah of Iran to purchase the Inter-Continental hotel chain from Pan American Airways. Of course, before a sale could be considered a price had to be determined, so an accounting firm was hired to decide what was fair. For months I read reports on the tax problems and management contracts of individual hotels. Next came several hundred balance sheets depicting hotel assets, debts, and cash flow. Only after all that was covered did anybody address the point of the inquiry and begin asking what this data added up to. For the Shah and Pan Am the whole thing was a waste of time and money; the sale never took place. But for me it was many educations: it taught me about the hotel business, international finance, and tax loopholes. It also showed me exactly what is involved in working out a price on a large complex piece of property. Needless to say, that kind of rigorous examination of company books has been impossible in the preparation of this study, so anybody thinking of actually bidding on an item is advised to do his own figuring.

The research for this book took many forms. The chief ones were the looting of libraries for previously published facts, searches through the many official documents companies are required to file with government agencies, and extensive telephone interviews with owners, public relations officers, and assorted experts. Once a fact was obtained, I had to be sure that it stayed a fact. *The Wall Street Journal* was especially valuable in keeping track of the changing details of ownership.

I have made a steady effort to keep all statements of fact up-to-date, but there seems to be no way of escaping the problem that a book about the things of this world is a book which contains few eternal truths. Deaths, sales, and taxes transform facts into history. For example, after this manuscript was turned in to the publisher, an offer to buy the A.C. Nielsen company was tendered by the management of Dun & Bradstreet. Whether the sale will be completed or aborted is for the future to resolve. In the same way Binney & Smith, makers of Crayola crayons, was bought by the giant, privately-held Hallmark empire, which is discussed in the book. However, because the possibility of change is inherent in the nature of ownership, potential buyers of anything listed in this book are urged to double-check the facts, to be sure nothing vital has yet changed.

As for the opinions in this book, they are mine. Assistance in this book in no way implies an endorsement of what is said. That point is especially important to keep in mind when considering the book's photographs, which are not endorsements of any facts or opinions presented in the book.

E.B.B.

# 1

# THE LAND

## AMERICA'S LARGEST CATTLE RANCH

**Auctioneer's price:** $851,000,000.
**Owner:** Kleberg family.

The 825,000 acres of the King Ranch in south Texas carry 60,000 head of cattle and use less than 600 employees. This combination of a few hearty souls and endless stretches of land is so in keeping with America's pioneer myth it is hard to credit that such a place could still operate in the age of multinational corporations and boards of directors.

Legally, the King Ranch is organized like a modern corporation and it is indeed multinational. Its foreign land holdings total over four million acres. In keeping with corporate jargon, the separate regions of the ranch are called "divisions" and the Texas operation has four divisions: Santa Gertrudis Ranch Division, Laureles Ranch Division, Encino Ranch Division, and Noria Ranch Division. The man in charge of the Texas operation is listed as a corporate vice-president.

But dig a little deeper and this corporate structure begins to look less like General Motors. That vice-president in charge of the Texas land is not yet forty years old. His great-great-grandfather founded the ranch. Then his great-grandfather ran it. Next his great-uncle ran it, followed by his father. Now it is his turn.

The presence of family history grows still more evident if you start to ride among the herds. The cowboys are called *kineños* and have been called by that name for 130 years, ever since Richard King persuaded an entire Mexican village to resettle on his land and work it. Many of the present-day *kineños* are descended from the original settlers. The foremen of the separate ranches were also born on them and their fathers before them were also foremen.

Under the guise of a modern corporation we have a family structure so old and intertwined that it could serve as the basis for a family-saga novel. Of course it has already turned up in Edna Ferber's *Giant*, but this story is rich enough for a James Michener–type saga, one in which the first few hundred pages describe the creation of the land and then comes generation upon generation of history-making family.

***First generation:*** In 1853 Richard King, a steamboat pilot on the Rio Grande, pays $300 for land around the Santa Gertrudis River and begins developing his ranch. An army officer posted in Texas, one Robert E. Lee, advises King, "Buy land and never sell." King follows the advice. During the Civil War, King makes a fortune shipping Southern cotton to Europe. During the 1870s he grows richer by sending his cattle up the trails to the railroads in the North.

***Second generation:*** One night, after losing a lawsuit, Richard King goes to see the lawyer who bested him and offers him a job. The lawyer, Robert Justus Kleberg, accepts, comes to the ranch, and marries King's daughter. King dies in 1886 and Kleberg takes over the running of the ranch. He develops the ranch's water system and founds the town of Kingsville.

***Third generation*** (the generation depicted in *Giant*): At age 22 Kleberg's second son, Robert, is put in charge of the ranch. Soon thereafter he meets the daughter of a Kansas congressman and marries her seventeen days later. When King's widow dies, at age 92, Robert organizes the ranch as a modern corporation. He develops a new breed of cattle, the

Santa Gertrudis, and persuades Humble Oil to search for oil on his land. They find it, and soon the King Ranch holds more oil wells than Saudi Arabia. The money is invested in ranchland abroad.

***Fourth generation:*** As Robert begins to concentrate his attention on the foreign holdings, he puts the Texas operations under the care of a favorite nephew, Dick Kleberg. After Robert's death in 1974 the family follows Dick's advice and elects Jim Clement as head of the ranch. Clement is the husband of Robert's niece. He is an Easterner whose father was chairman of the Pennsylvania Railroad, but he understands the business side of affairs and has lived on the ranch since 1947.

***Fifth generation:*** The ranching itself is not in the hands of business experts. The 825,000 acres of Texas land are under the control of Stephen Justus, Dick Kleberg's second son. He is a cattleman who knows the land, the herds, and the men. On the King Ranch these things still matter as much as the subtleties of the tax code.

The family now numbers over sixty shareholders in the ranch (all shares are privately held within the family).

The future of the ranch is uncertain. Its oil is expected to dry up at the end of this decade and oil profits can make cattle profits seem mighty slim. Still, each generation has been able to find leaders suited to the needs of the ranch. The Klebergs hold a broad view of what makes a family: in-laws are as acceptable as blood kin and order of birth imparts no priority of rank. Because the Klebergs have taken a narrow view of corporations—sticking only to family—the ranch has survived the pressure of the bottom line and may again.

At present the most famous ranch in Texas is the fictitious Southfork on the television show "Dallas." There actually is such a ranch, located in Plano, just north of Dallas. It is used for outdoor scenes in the TV series. The ranch has become one of

Dallas's favorite tourist sites, ranking just after Dealy Plaza and the Texas School Book Depository. Astonishingly, Southfork's owner really is named J. R.—J[oseph] R[and] Duncan. The ranch comprises 200 acres, which does not sound like a lot. Yet it is twice the size of the average ranch in Texas, and by the standards of Southfork's neighbors the ranch is huge. On the television show, Southfork always looks pretty isolated, but it is set in a development scheme. Just across the street sits a row of ordinary-looking suburban houses on ordinary-sized plots of land. Duncan gets a tidy income from the use of his house and has the right to market souvenirs with the name "Southfork" on them, but his neighbors have only an unending river of tourists parked on their street, gawking across a fence, and saying, "Looks just like on television."

## HYATT HOTELS

**Auctioneer's price:** $551,000,000.
**Owner:** Pritzker family.

Surely one of the most revolutionary American buildings of the past several decades has been the Hyatt Regency Hotel in Atlanta. Hotel management principles used to argue that a hotel should be crowded and cramped like a hive. Attractive public areas like courtyards and large lobbies were thought to waste space that otherwise could be rented out. Ugly tenement-style hotels were built throughout the 1960s. Travelers were dismayed by what was happening, but who cared what the customers thought? Not the financiers and not the architectural critics, who agreed that the tenements were rational and right.

One dissenter was John Portman, an architect/developer based in Atlanta, Georgia. He did both the work of a developer (commissioning projects) and that of an architect (designing projects). Portman liked this dual role because of the freedom it gave him. He avoided the architect's humiliation of bowing to the outrageous tastes of his client, and evaded the developer's anguish of depending on the whimsy of the architect.

Portman's first big project had been Atlanta's Peachtree Center, a wholesale merchandising mart that he designed and developed. Then he decided to build a great hotel for the city. He was so removed from the mainstream of hotel design that he did not realize most hotel designers expected the guests to be stoics. Instead he designed a flamboyant lobby that was 220 feet high and 140 feet wide. Glass-walled elevators gave an extra touch of showmanship to the atrium. When he tried to find partners for the project, he was laughed at. Sheraton and Hilton both turned him down. Their experts felt the extravagant atrium was a waste of space.

The scheme was saved when Jay Pritzker, owner of Hyatt Hotels, came forward with $18.9 million. And, lo, the hotel was a popular triumph. It turned out that many travelers preferred to stay in interesting environments and Atlanta's Hyatt quickly became more popular than the hives and tenements offered by rivals. What's more, instead of fleeing the hotel at their earliest opportunity, guests stayed in its atrium and spent money. Why, even the locals came over to the hotel to soak up the atmosphere and spend money. What the arithmeticians had thought was practical business wisdom was revealed as a great delusion. Profits come from giving people what they want, not from putting their wallets to the torture rack. Today new tenement hotels are restricted to interstate exit areas. Elsewhere, no matter how stingy the management, new hotels offer at least a nod to Portman's work in Atlanta.

The success of the Hyatt Regency transformed the Hyatt chain. It had started in 1957 with one small motel near the Los Angeles airport. (The company name came from Hyatt von Dehn, the real estate developer who sold the motel to Jay Pritzker.) The Hyatt chain grew, but persisted as a group of small, almost unknown hotels. After Atlanta the company took off. Today it has sixty-eight hotels in the United States and thirty-nine more around the world.

Most amazing of all, perhaps, is that the Hyatt Corporation is wholly owned by one family. Most corporations that grow to Hyatt's size feed on the capital provided by outside investors. Hyatt did grow with the help of other people's money, but the Pritzker family managed to avoid giving up any company control. Quite the reverse. They have bought out the few investors they once faced and now both Hyatt and Hyatt International (which is responsible for the overseas hotels) are completely owned by the Pritzkers. Compare that with Hilton (9,000 shareholders; Barron Hilton owns 29 percent of the stock), Holiday Inn (35,000 shareholders), and Sheraton (a wholly owned subsidiary of ITT, which has nearly 200,000 shareholders).

Of course it took a warehouse stacked with thousand-dollar bills to keep Hyatt in the family, but the Pritzkers are not troubled by such things. Hyatt is only one of their holdings. Another wholly owned Pritzker company is the Marmon Group, which sells over $1.8 billion worth of goods each year—everything from wire cable to poultry incubators to Hammond organs.

The basis of the family wealth is the fortune amassed by Jay's father. Patriarch Abraham Nicholas Pritzker made a fortune advising clients on real estate deals and then joining in on the ventures.

Company names like Hyatt and Marmon obscure the Pritzkers' role, but when you look at their holdings, the story never changes: Jay or his brother Robert is in charge, and the board of directors includes children, in-laws, wives, and trustees for the children. If stars sold for a buck apiece, this family could buy the whole blinking night.

Hotels are often a good investment, but they are so costly that usually the only people who can think of owning great ones need a sizable fortune to begin with. One person able to invest $350,000,000 without flinching is Caroline Hunt Schoellkopf, a daughter of the late oilman H.L. Hunt. Mrs. Schoellkopf is sometimes called America's richest woman, although her sister, Margaret Hunt Hill, cannot be far behind. Mrs. Schoellkopf's first hotel, Mansion on Turtle Creek, in Dallas, employs two staff people per guest. Even the bathrooms are luxurious. They include terry-cloth robes, marble bathtubs, and a variety of scented bath oils. Much of the styling seems cluttered and the restaurant is rated only so-so, but the smell of money is so strong it wouldn't be surprising to find five-dollar bills in the lamps. Mrs. Schoellkopf's company, Rosewood Hotels, is expanding and has luxury hotels in Beverly Hills (the Bel Air) and Houston (the Remington).

The most famous of all American fortunes has also found its way into luxury hotels. Laurence Rockefeller owns a hotel chain called Rockresorts. Laurence is the fourth child of John D. Rockefeller II. His older brother, Nelson, was the best known of that particular generation of Rockefellers. Rockresorts is for guests with Rockefeller-sized checkbooks. Its most attractively situated hotel is the Jenny Lake Lodge in Wyoming's Grand Teton National Park. A two bedroom cabin can cost as much as $400 per night.

When it comes to beach resort hotels the most famous is surely the Fontainebleau in Miami Beach. Built in the 1950s, it seemed an astonishing monument to laziness in the sun, but during the 1970s it fell upon hard times and was bankrupted. Now it has been refurbished and is called the Miami Fontainebleau Hilton. Its current owner is Stephen Muss, a real estate emperor in south Florida. The other great Miami Beach hotel is the Eden Roc. It too was bought out of bankruptcy and restored to life. The new owner is a Saudi Arabian diplomat, Sheik Wadji Tahlawi. In 1980 he paid $12,500,000 for it, a bargain.

## THE LARGEST NUMBER OF APARTMENTS

**Auctioneer's price:** $412,000,000.
**Owner:** Samuel LeFrak.

One of the surprising features of the Lefrak Organization is the way its real-life operation follows the same principles known to millions of Monopoly masters: (1) sell at a profit; (2) move from low-value property to higher-priced items; and (3) keep those checks and coins coming in. It's the steady income of rent money that keeps the Monopoly player solvent, not the fancy address. Samuel LeFrak has used this principle of cash flow to become America's number-one apartment landlord. According to the accounting firm of Kenneth Leventhal & Co., LeFrak has 85,000 units, most of them in New York City. (Note to spelling freaks: LeFrak is the spelling for the family name; Lefrak is the spelling for the company name.)

Most high-flyers in real estate development prefer to invest in office buildings and other commercial operations, but LeFrak has stayed with private residences wherein the operating rules are the most basic in economics. Ambitious developers are in too much of a hurry to fool with the conservative methods that dominate apartment management. Their plan is usually to risk all on a couple of quick throws of the dice—a spirit that makes a few millionaires and many bankrupts. LeFrak, however, slowly built up the family realty company—founded generations ago by an ancestor who served as an architect for Napoleon—and now he is one of the sovereigns of property.

Lately he has begun to chafe a bit at the dull image his family fortune inspires. LeFrak continues to prefer apartments to commercial buildings, but his projects have become more flamboyant. In the late 1950s he built a 40-acre complex, called LeFrak City, in Queens, New York. He is now developing, outside New York, a 10,000-apartment project called Newport City. This last scheme is so large he has taken on a partner, Melvin Simon, a developer who owns over 100 shopping centers.

Another sign of his restlessness is the way he groans to interviewers that he is not just a real estate man. In the 1970s he expanded into oil drilling. He has also gone into entertainment, publishing music. His daughter Francine is a Broadway producer with two big hits on her résumé, *Cats* and *Nine*. The Lefrak Organization publishes the music for both of those shows and for the television series "Fame."

The LeFrak family is without serious rival in the apartment empire, but it does not dominate its other areas. Music publishing is an especially tricky area because it depends so much on shifting popular tastes. Monopoly board principles are of little assistance there. The owner of the music from the most successful Broadway shows is Paul McCartney. The former Beatle owns the rights to the two longest-running musicals of Broadway history, *A Chorus Line* and *Grease*, and to the most recent smash hit, *La Cage aux Folles.* One of the most performed show songs of the past dozen years is the pseudo-inspirational "Tomorrow" from *Annie.* McCartney is co-owner of that one too.

## A CITY

**Auctioneer's price:** $236,000,000.
**Owner:** Ben Carpenter.

Binghamton, New York; Bismarck, North Dakota; Bridgeport, Connecticut; Dubuque, Iowa; Huntington, West Virginia; Providence, Rhode Island; Wilmington, Delaware; and Yakima, Washington—all have smaller areas than Las Colinas, Texas. Each of them has its large property holders, but Las Colinas is one man's personal spread. The town, 10 miles west of central Dallas and just south of the enormous Dallas–Fort Worth airport, straddles the geological line where the rich Midwestern prairie suddenly becomes the Western desert. Its population of 10,000 is supposed to grow to 50,000, although not even owner/developer Ben Carpenter can guarantee the success of the plan.

Carpenter got to be so rich by a shrewd choice of parents. His father, John Carpenter, parlayed a small stack of chips into many large stacks. First he built a number of Texas electric utilities, then he made even greater piles through insurance, which in turn was transformed into industrial wealth (steel) and real estate holdings. In 1928, before Carpenter entered the insurance world, he bought a spread west of Dallas called the Hackberry Creek Ranch. Nineteen twenty-eight was two years before the discovery of the stupendous East Texas oil field that transformed Dallas from a cotton town to an oil capital, so you might say the Carpenters got their Dallas property at the perfect time. During the '50s they expanded their holdings, buying up land adjacent to their spread. Then in 1968 came the announcement that the new regional airport would be built just north of the Carpenter lands.

At that moment most landowners would have sold out and taken their profit, but Ben Carpenter (his father had died in

1959) seems to have decided that if a city was about to rise on his ranch, he might as well be the one to build it. The ambition was not new, but it is usually limited to pharaohs, tsars, and great khans. Always the idea is a bad one. Cities get their life from the mix and contradictions of its inhabitants. Autocrats, even autocrats with the vision of a Michelangelo, can only stunt and repress the life of a city and, besides, autocrats never do begin with Michelangelo's eye.

In Carpenter's case we find the standard portrait of utopia. There is a communications control center where security guards watch the street activity on banks of televisions. Folks over in the limited-access residential area can tune their own TVs to the gate and eyeball any strangers profaning the site through their presence. Security like this, of course, is a big draw for all those who'd rather be safe than saucy. Careful landscaping is ubiquitous. Every year 400,000 flowers are planted in tidy rows that bloom with the spontaneity of graph paper. A million-dollar artificial lake raises surrounding property values. There is the Royal [*sic*] Tech Center, where high-technology companies are supposed to sprout. As is the case with most such areas around the country, not many high-tech firms have actually appeared, but there is plenty of room for them. In short, every cliché from this century's world's fairs is being offered as the paradise of Las Colinas.

Carpenter describes the place as a "free enterprise community," a boast that in America seems so redundant it can only be taken as a warning. When multimillionaires start reminding folks of their devotion to free enterprise, hang on to your judgment. A second warning light starts shining when the eye spots the advertising slogan of the Las Colinas resort hotel, the Mandalay Four Seasons. "It's what the world is coming to," boasts the ad. Behind every argument that we've got the future on our side lurks a jug full of castor oil that folks are supposed to swallow with a grin, all in the name of progress.

The free future of Las Colinas includes a weekly meeting of the Las Colinas Association to review all construction plans for the city. Ben Carpenter, of course, is president of the association and what he likes he gets; what he doesn't like doesn't get got. Even the McDonald's restaurant had to reduce its golden arches to a shy little logo. (Naturally there is a McDonald's in Las

Colinas.) For Carpenter to talk about freedom in Las Colinas sets one to imagining Louis XIV watching Versailles go up, exactly in accordance with his desires, and exclaiming aloud, "Ain't freedom grand."

Perhaps the most successful invented town in America is Lake Havasu City, Arizona. It is a more traditional type of residential development project than Carpenter's attempt to make a fully integrated city, but Lake Havasu's founder was struck by an idea of such whimsy that it amounted to genius. He bought London Bridge for $2,400,000 and had it transported, stone by stone, to Arizona.

The purchaser was Robert McCulloch, creator of McCulloch chain saws. When he bought the bridge McCulloch thought he was bidding on London's more picturesque Tower Bridge. Instead he got a perfectly ordinary thousand-foot span, built just before Victoria became queen. But the investment worked well. Nearly 20,000 people live in Lake Havasu City and London Bridge has become Arizona's second most popular tourist attraction. (Number one is the Grand Canyon.)

McCulloch died in 1977. His son, Robert, Jr., took over the property, but then lost it in a stock fight. The bridge was owned via a set of subsidiaries and stock arrangements that the younger Robert could not preserve. Shortly after Robert senior died an investment broker named Charles Hurwitz began buying large numbers of shares of stock. Initially he bought 13 percent. His holding is now almost 30 percent and Robert, Jr., has been forced out of the company. Hurwitz has made himself chairman of the board and has even removed "McCulloch" from the company name; the corporation now calls itself MCO Holdings. Hurwitz has also become the new owner of London Bridge.

The most valuable privately held block of property in a metropolitan area is thought to be the Irvine Ranch in Orange County, California. It is much larger than Las Colinas; in fact, it is much larger than Washington, D.C., and only slightly smaller than Atlanta. However, 60,000 of its 68,000 acres are devoted to ranching and farming. It was established during the 1800s as a ranch, but since then, thanks to Los Angeles and Disneyland, the place has been surrounded by urban and suburban developments. The principal owner (86 percent of the shares) is Donald Bren, a real estate developer who saw his fortunes rise with the Orange County boom. At the moment the auctioneer's price for the ranch is about $1,080,000,000. Who knows what it would be if the acres were turned into a city?

Country and western singing star Loretta Lynn owns the town of Hurricane Mills, Tennessee. As towns go, even in Tennessee, this one is small—a post office, some stores, plus some tourist attractions (dude ranch and theme park).

## THE EMPIRE STATE BUILDING

**Auctioneer's price:** $167,000,000.
**Owners:** Harry Helmsley and Lawrence Wien.

Although no longer the tallest building in the world, the Empire State Building is still the world's tallest attractive building. The Sears Tower in Chicago and the World Trade Center in lower Manhattan stand higher, but they are as exciting to the eye as a restaurant named Eat. More than fifty years after its completion (in 1931) the Empire State Building still holds the country's imagination as the premier skyscraper.

Harry Brackman Helmsley owns the giant. If feudal titles were still popular, Helmsley would be called something like the Duke of Manhattan. His real estate empire is valued at $5 billion and he has 100,000 tenants, including many of America's largest corporations. He is surely the richest landlord in America. There are richer people who, having made a pile elsewhere, turned to real estate for further wealth, but Helmsley's fortune is based entirely on buying the right property at the right time.

Co-owner of the Empire State Building is Lawrence Wien, Helmsley's lawyer. Wien is a tax specialist who, back in 1949, figured out how to organize a syndicate of investors without forming a corporation. The benefit of that idea is twofold: first, the avoidance of the corporate income tax and, second, increased power on the part of the major owners. Syndicate members have contractual rights rather than the privileges of a shareholder and are kept more solidly in check. Syndicate members gain an income, but have no say in Helmsley's running of the building. When they bought the Empire State Building, Helmsley and Wien formed a syndicate of 3,300 investors, most of whom put up only $10,000 apiece, not enough to lease a moderate-sized office in the building. When combined with other small investments, however, it works out to be a good sum. (The purchase price was $65,000,000.) The investment has proven a great commercial success and the 102-story building is fully rented.

Helmsley is unlike most other real estate kings. He pays attention to cash flow, all right, but he hardly ever sells. Especially, he never sells properties like the Empire State Building. He loves owning it, loves changing the colors of the lights according to the season, loves giving permission for whimsical projects like attaching an inflatable King Kong to its side, loves being the owner of America's most famous building. His ego is not small, but he is smart enough to know he will never build a monument more notable than this skyscraper. So he holds onto it.

The two other most admired buildings in New York City are probably the Flatiron Building, once the world's tallest building (1902–1904) and the Chrysler Building, briefly the world's tallest building until the Empire State topped it. Helmsley owns the Flatiron, but the Chrysler Building is owned by Jack Kent Cook, a Canadian-born demi-billionaire who has turned door-to-door selling, publishing, and cable TV into an Everest of dollar bills.

## THE LARGEST SHOPPING CENTER

**Auctioneer's price:** $69,800,000.
**Owner:** Guilford Glazer.

America's largest shopping center is the Del Amo Fashion Center in Torrance, California. Its developer/owner, Guilford Glazer, got his first break back East from the Manhattan Project. (Truly, almost anything brings opportunity to somebody.) Initially the creation of the atomic bomb was so secret that private enterprise had almost no role in it, but during the 1950s many aspects of the atomic race were put into private hands. When the change came Glazer was a young man in the right place.

He was born and raised in Knoxville, Tennessee. During World War II Knoxville's Oak Ridge suburb became the secret headquarters of the Manhattan Project. Later, when the security fences came down, Glazer was an active developer. Oak Ridge was converted from a makeshift barracks to a civilian city. Glazer built much of what is now downtown Oak Ridge. The '50s was not a time when developers were going to make their fortunes by constructing a string of downtowns and Glazer soon switched to erecting shopping centers. At first he continued working in the Tennessee/Ohio area, but for an ambitious developer who had built up a little capital, the big draw was America's fastest-growing region. By 1960 Glazer had reached California.

Glazer's Del Amo site began as two separate shopping centers. The first was the Del Amo Center, built by Glazer in 1960. It was one of the first shopping centers in the country to hold several big department stores. During the 1950s, the typical center had one department store and many smaller shops. A bit later developers discovered that two department stores brought more money than one monopoly. In 1960 Glazer's development opened with three such stores, Sears, J.C. Penney, and Broadway.

In 1972 Glazer began his second Torrance center, the Del Amo Fashion Square. The union of the two centers was completed in 1981 when an elevated walkway was built across the street that divided them. The walkway is lined with shops and merchants, like the Ponte Vecchio of Renaissance Florence.

Indeed, most people using the bridge are not even aware that they are on it. It seems like just another part of the two-mile stretch of stores.

The figures on the Del Amo shopping center promise megatons of dollars: parking for 12,000 cars (the parking lots in most large shopping centers hold well under 1,000 cars); 350 stores (the largest shopping center in the East is Boston's Faneuil Hall Marketplace—170 stores); it is spread over 145 acres (the Chicago giant is the Illinois Center Retail Concourse—83 acres); and the gross leasable area—the selling floor—is 2,650,000 square feet. At this point comparison breaks down. Shopping centers are considered super-huge when their leasable area reaches one-third of the Del Amo size. We can be thankful money never reaches a fissionable mass. Otherwise there would be a mushroom cloud over Torrance.

The world's largest *wholesale* mart is the Dallas Market Center, owned by a self-made demi-billionaire named Trammell Crow. There's an old joke about the rich Texan with a small spread he calls "downtown Dallas." Crow is the man that joke describes. His construction company, the Trammell Crow Co., is America's largest, and had $1.2 billion in construction projects under way in 1983.

The Dallas Market Center consists of seven buildings that are used for a continuous series of trade fairs and public exhibitions, such as an annual boat show. There are also a number of permanent merchandise exhibits. The market has been a key element in making Dallas one of the country's most important commercial centers. It is a major furniture, apparel, toy, and jewelry center. A high-tech mart is currently under construction.

Crow has also invested in other important marts around the country, including San Francisco's Embarcadero Center and Atlanta's Peachtree Center. He is currently working on a project to erect a giant mart near New York's Times Square.

## SANGRE DE CRISTO LANDS

**Auctioneer's price:** $32,000,000.
**Owner:** Malcolm Forbes.

In 1844 a sixteen-year-old boy named Narcisso Beaubien paid $30 for 1,038,000 acres of land in what is now Colorado and New Mexico. That price works out to under two cents for a square mile. Such generosity on the part of the Mexican government, which claimed this whole region, was born of desperation. In those days it was Mexico that worried about illegal aliens. American immigrants had turned Texas into an independent republic in 1836 and Mexico feared the same fate might befall other territories. Unable to stop this expansion, Mexico gave away enormous tracts of land to loyalists in the hope that these new landlords would chase out the suspect foreigners.

In Beaubien's case, he got a stretch of desert and mountain larger than Rhode Island; small if you are a state, but not bad for a teenage kid. There were bigger grants (Beaubien's father got one of 1,714,000 acres) but the Sangre de Cristo grant was unusually important for its strategic placement. Its heart contained the Sangre de Cristo Mountains, a branch of the Rockies whose highest point—Blanca Mountain (14,317 feet)—is greater than Pike's Peak. The many rivers running down from its slopes serve as headwaters for the Rio Grande. The Sante Fe Trail ran along the eastern side of the grant while the Old Spanish Trail, which linked Sante Fe to California, took travelers along the grant's western side.

Unfortunately for Mexico, the American government outflanked this whole land-grant maneuver by going to war. Sovereignty over the region passed to the United States; however, the legality of the land-grant titles was upheld. On June 21, 1860, Congress confirmed the validity of the Sangre de Cristo grant.

By now the original territory has been broken up, but the northwest portion is still a unit and in 1969 was bought by publisher Malcolm Forbes for about $4,000,000. His section covered 174,000 acres (272 square miles). The auctioneer's price above is for the Forbes portion of the original grant.

Forbes's initial idea was to turn his spread—now called Trinchera Ranch—into a posh hunting preserve, and he ordered a million dollars' worth of fence to surround his property. Colorado lawyers, however, seemed to have studied under Portia, the Shakespearean heroine who argued that Shylock was entitled to his pound of flesh but could not take one drop of blood. Colorado informed Forbes that it was his right to fence in his land, but not the animals on it.

Forced to think anew, Forbes decided to try to sell a little over one-quarter of his land in small (5-acre) bits. His price per acre was set at about forty times what he paid and this scheme has done quite well for him. He still owns well over 100,000 acres of the Sangre de Cristo land. Hunters cay pay him $1,000 to shoot an elk. He raises cattle on the land and has erected a lodge high in the mountains where he can survey what he owns.

## AMERICA'S MOST HEAVILY ADVERTISED TOURIST TRAP

**Auctioneer's price:** $20,600,000.
**Owner:** Alan Schafer.

Travelers along a 200-mile stretch of Interstate 10 in the Southwest see signs advertising a roadside attraction called The Thing. Up in the Dakotas other cars are passing ads for Wall's Drug Store, but no signs get more notice than those for the South of the Border. This combination motel, fireworks armory, souvenir stand, gas station, kiddie attraction, and restaurant lies beside Interstate 95, just below the North Carolina/South Carolina line. Almost all cars traveling between Florida and the cities of the Northeast pass this tourist stop. Of course those cars also pass hundreds of other restaurants, motels, and gas stations, but South of the Border is the one everybody remembers because its advertising covers a 350-mile swatch of the countryside. For three hours before a car actually reaches the place, travelers see signs saying things like "Fill Your Trunque with Pedro's

Junque." Even kids intent on their own exhaustion begin to ask what the signs are about.

South of the Border is the ultimate achievement along one of the roads-not-taken by American culture. Back in 1949, when Alan Schafer opened his hamburger stand, he appeared to be one more small entrepreneur in America's mainstream. His place was right across from North Carolina, a dry state, and he sold beer along with hamburgers. Thirsty tarheels came in, loaded up, and drove back home with their taboo liquid. Besides banning firewater, North Carolina also prohibited fireworks, so Schafer began selling them too. In 1952 he added a motel. I-95 was still twenty years in the future, but he was astride U.S. 301, the main blacktop road to Florida. The name of his place automatically suggested a Mexican theme for the motel.

In the early 1950s America appeared to be headed for a commercial architecture of great whimsy and unpredictability. Motels with log cabins or buildings shaped like tepees, sombreros, Indian pueblos, and other fantastic designs were strewn from coast to coast. In that world a pseudo-Mexican pseudo-resort was neither surprising nor remarkable, but by the end of the '50s the battle for America's motel space was being won by the great standardizers. Holiday Inn, Ramada, and TraveLodge were replacing fantasy with monotony. The difference between a motel outside a Sioux reservation and one in Vermont was becoming as trivial as the difference between a dime in Seattle and one in Miami.

South of the Border, however, thrived on the power and peculiarity of the '50s. Frequent billboards were a regular part of that era, but most of the signs were small and looked as if they had last been painted shortly before the fall of Rome. South of the Border takes its signs seriously. It has its own billboard company and every year it repaints all 250 of them. New slogans are written each year and the signs are kept large, colorful, and instantly recognizable.

Roadside attractions were also common in the '50s, but they tended to be cheap and dusty. Most of them appeared to be just what they were, commercial slums bound for bankruptcy. In most ways South of the Border is typical of all the old roadside draws, except that it is booming. It offers carnival rides, a miniature golf course, a 200-foot-high tower with a panoramic view of an utterly routine Carolina countryside, a steam locomotive, restaurants (four of them), gift shops (with 22,000 items, nearly all of them junk), a campground, and a huge sign that stands 104 feet tall and looks like a caricatural Mexican wearing a mile-wide sombrero. Its fireworks stand has grown into a supermarket of Roman candles and deadly explosives. This roadside draw has all the taste of hot pants at a funeral, but, let's face it, the old attractions didn't go bust because they were too tasteless. They were too dead. Bustle goes where bustle is, and South of the Border doesn't look like it's going broke.

Perhaps in some alternate reality there is a United States filled with whimsical motels, each run by a founder and his two sons. It didn't happen in the America we inhabit, but then it didn't entirely disappear either.

One of the most striking features at South of the Border is its huge fireworks store. A small stand for firecrackers and Roman candles has grown into an arsenal. Yet most people, thank heaven, still prefer to leave fireworks displays to people who know what they are doing. Two Italian-American families dominate the fireworks business.

New York Pyrotechnic Products is owned by the Grucci family (patriarch: Felix Grucci) of Bellport, Long Island, outside New York City. Seven family members work for the company, which specializes in great extravaganzas like the $150,000 display on the 100th anniversary of the opening of the Brooklyn Bridge. During a thirty-minute show, 9,600 rockets were exploded. Late in 1983 the Grucci factory was destroyed in a series of explosions, but the family has managed to stage displays since then.

Zambelli Fireworks Manufacturing of New Castle, Pennsylvania, is owned by the Zambelli family (patriarch: George Zambelli). Fourteen family members work for the company. It provides less dramatic but more frequent shows. Their biggest day, of course, is the Fourth of July, when they organize shows in towns all over the country.

## CASTLE NIXON

**Auctioneer's price:** $8,500,000.
**Owners:** Gavin Herbert and partners.

As the Watergate scandal unfolded, increasing attention was given to the $702,321 spent by the federal government to improve the estate known to the press as the Western White House and to its owner as La Casa Pacifica. In order to appease his critics, Richard Nixon promised to turn the estate over to the public upon his death. Five years after resigning, Nixon sold the estate to three land developers: Gavin Herbert, Donald M. Koll, and George Argyros.

Following the sale there was a brief furor over the president's having again lied and bilked the taxpayers. Nixon partially reimbursed the government, sending a check for $33,295. Many people shrugged and wondered why on earth anybody would want to hang on to a monument to America's least-favored president, but the estate is indeed beautiful. It has 20 acres and overlooks a beach reputed to provide some of the greatest surfing in California. (Try to imagine Mr. Nixon brooding on a surfboard.) Besides, people want to see it. Tourists still arrive every day in San Clemente to ask directions out to the house. They are disappointed when they arrive, for the house cannot be seen from the gate. You can, however, rent the house for an evening's celebration. With catering, expect to pay $300 or $400, depending on the size of your group.

Actually, Nixon was the second president to stay at the house. During the '30s, the estate was owned by Hamilton Cotton, onetime Democratic state treasurer. When Franklin Roosevelt campaigned in California he spent a night at the house, playing poker, it is said.

Current plans are to divide the property into sixteen lots and build million-dollar houses on the thirteen smallest, each of which will be slightly less than an acre. The Nixon house will be preserved and stand on a 3-acre site. Two other large houses will also be built on lots of a similar size.

The occupant of the Nixon house is Gavin Herbert, a businessman in pharmaceuticals.

## SANTA CATALINA ISLAND

**Auctioneer's price:** $2,150,000.
**Owner:** Wrigley family.

Eccentric men of property are common in literature, but in real life it is rare to meet anyone as set in his ways as the late Philip Wrigley (1894–1977). Even dukes and squires are seldom as opposed to change as Philip was. As heir to a chewing gum fortune he presided over the company for decades without ever introducing a new flavor and without addressing the challenge presented by bubble gum. His gum's TV commercials were so old-fashioned they seemed to predate television. Spearmint gum ads actually used inanimate cartoons. Wrigley's baseball team, the Chicago Cubs, never amounted to a damn and never got stadium lights. All home games are day games. Sure, this lack of night games cost thousands of fans in attendance, but Wrigley hated change more than he hated losing money.

Another property of his was Santa Catalina Island, off the coast of southern California. Philip's father, William Wrigley, bought the island in 1919 and began developing it as a resort. When Philip took charge, however, development halted.

Santa Catalina is much larger than the ordinary private island. It is 22 miles long, 8 miles wide at its broadest point, and 74 square miles in total area. The size is considerably larger than many other popular tourist islands, such as Bermuda, Block Island, Nantucket, and Georgia's Sea Island, all of which are parceled out among many owners. There is one town on Santa Catalina, Avalon, and it is possible to buy a small plot of ground there. Elsewhere the island is quite undeveloped and is great for hiking. The tallest point is Mount Orizaba, 2,130 feet above the beach. The desert landscape of the island is somewhat forbidding, although recent years of heavy rain have turned the place much greener than normal.

Change entered the Wrigley institutions immediately after Philip Wrigley's death. New kinds of chewing gum reached the market. Television advertising became avant-garde. The Cubs baseball team was actually sold, and the new owners began pleading for the right to install lights at the ball park. But

Catalina has been stable. In 1975, shortly before his death, Wrigley established a conservancy, turning 86 percent of the island into a kind of private national park. The plan had many tax benefits, but Wrigley was not a man to put money first among his considerations. His rule over the Cubs shows that. He wanted to fight change. The conservancy is directed by members of the Wrigley family. (Philip's son, William, is the new family patriarch.) Its creation has eased their tax burden considerably, but most notably the conservancy assured the continued preservation of the island as an undeveloped wilderness. The 14 percent of the island not owned by Wrigley's conservancy is held by the Santa Catalina Island Company, wholly owned by the Wrigley family. The income netted from the property is negligible, less than $20,000 a year. Obviously they could make a lot more cash by going condo, yet they choose not to.

The island is part of Los Angeles County and lies only 26 miles off the coast. The Los-Angeles-to-San-Diego land strip that overlooks the island is one of the most densely populated areas in America. The masses of people make even the relative wilderness of Yosemite Valley and Mount Whitney seem like city parks. But thanks to the strange mind of Wrigley, a promising resort location right next to the Los Angeles sprawl survives as a wilderness where a lost tourist can get into serious danger. Admirable unprogress.

Hawaii presents the opposite extreme from Santa Catalina. Its islands are convenient to nowhere and yet so thoroughly developed that there "conservation" usually means keeping the land for plantation, rather than resort, use. Most of the islands were bought at bead-and-blanket prices by the descendants of missionaries who, according to an ancient joke, came to do good and stayed to do well. After World War II the power of the missionary families was broken. The interlocking directorates of the great landholding companies were dismantled, the plantations were unionized, and, after statehood came, political leaders were subject to democratic accountability. By now the

Maui Grove. Photo: Maui Land & Pineapple Company, Inc.

stock of the original companies is divided among so many descendants that you'd expect that nobody could claim to hold much of the land. In the past few years, however, an outsider named Harry Weinberg has been buying up property.

Weinberg was born in Austria and made his first fortune investing in Maryland real estate. Later he began buying land in Hawaii and now owns a number of shopping centers and small resort communities. His real estate interests there go under a variety of names, including Honolulu Ltd., HRT Ltd., Gutman Realty, 3900 Corporation, and the 300 Corporation. More important, he has been buying huge holdings in the old landowning companies.

Maui Land and Pineapple Company owns 29,800 acres on

the island of Maui. One of its sections contains 23,180 acres, the largest contiguous plantation on the islands. It rises from the ocean (9 miles of beach frontage) to the 5,700-foot mark up the island's volcanic slope. Much of this land is unused, consisting of gorges and forest. The rest is planted in pineapple. Weinberg owns over 30 percent of the company; however, this holding is not enough to make him the owner yet. Colin Cameron, the company's chairman, and his family hold 40 percent of the stock and they see Weinberg as an interloper. (Cameron is related to the Baldwins, one of the original missionary families.) Weinberg still has to maneuver a bit before gaining control over that land.

Meanwhile Weinberg has also been investing in Alexander & Baldwin, one of the oldest of the Hawaiian companies, originally called the Hawaiian Commercial and Sugar Company. Weinberg owns 21 percent of the stock, just a little bit less than the 22 percent held by the descendants of the founders. Alexander & Baldwin owns 71,800 acres on Maui and another 22,000 acres on the small island of Kauai.

Together, the two companies' holdings on Maui alone come to over twice the size of Santa Catalina Island. Weinberg is believed to want to take control of Alexander & Baldwin. If he can manage it, either by a buyout or a stockholders' proxy fight, Maui Land and Pineapple should not be far behind. The land is all valued at plantation prices. If he can develop it into resort and residential land, it would be an even greater killing than the original missionaries made.

## SOLZHENITSYN'S RETREAT

**Auctioneer's price:** $560,000.
**Owner:** Alexis Vinogradov.

The Marquis de Lafayette, Winston Churchill, and Alexander Solzhenitsyn are the only three people for whom Congress has ever voted honorary American citizenship. It is a strange sort of honor because the commitment of all three men to their respective homelands is beyond doubting. Yet in each of them there lived a singularity of viewpoint which, for years, forced them out of the mainstream of the society they loved. In the cases of Lafayette and Churchill this combination of patriotism and doggedness finally served them and their countries well, and both died as great heroes mourned by all their countrymen. It seems too much to hope that the same end awaits Solzhenitsyn.

On February 13, 1974, the Soviet Union deported its most acclaimed author. At first he settled in Zurich, the same city where Lenin spent his exile, but in 1976 he moved to a house in central Vermont. Solzhenitsyn's wife, Nathalya, had a brother living in the same state and another Soviet refugee, an architect named Alexis Vinogradov, had bought a 50-acre estate outside the town of Cavendish. There Solzhenitsyn writes in privacy. The isolation of the house is well symbolized by its address—Windy Hill Road. Uninvited visitors are seldom allowed past the wrought-iron gate. Although his books bring him over $100,000 per year, it seems that Solzhenitsyn has not come to America to luxuriate in her great cities.

At first this move into Mr. Vinogradov's house puzzled Americans. We are used to exiles here, but exiles who have come to build new lives. Surely, people thought, Solzhenitsyn would do the same. Every morsel of information that hinted at his Americanization was snatched up by the press. "Solzhenitsyn Attends Cavendish Town Meeting" or "Solzhenitsyn Applies for Vermont Driver's License"—stories like these were presented, straight-facedly, as news.

Then, in 1978, Solzhenitsyn spoke at Harvard's graduation ceremonies and criticized the West for a loss of "civil courage" and a moral standard based on legalistic expediency. He irritated many in his audience by rejecting humanism, but the alternative he offered—a spirituality without religion—was sure to annoy any anti-humanists who were listening. He denounced both those who had opposed the war in Vietnam and those who like Henry Kissinger and his boss sought a foreign policy based on stability and the status quo. Just in case there was someone in the audience who smugly felt exempt from the criticism, Solzhenitsyn included this passage, "Should someone ask me whether I would indicate the West such as it is today as a model to my country, frankly I would have to answer negatively. Life's complexity and mortal weight have produced stronger, deeper and more interesting characters [in the East] than those generated by standardized Western well-being."

In Russia this kind of criticism of the regime had kept Solzhenitsyn in premanent trouble and, from time to time, brought long stretches in work camps. Ultimately it led to his banishment. In the West, of course, we don't treat people that way, and Solzhenitsyn is in no danger of being jailed or tortured for what he thinks. Yet in Russia Solzhenitsyn's forbidden words were treasured and circulated in crude copies so widely that even Khrushchev read them. In America few words are forbidden but many are ignored, and after his Harvard speech Solzhenitsyn ceased to be news. Another volume of his history of the gulag is always welcome, of course. But when it comes to explaining why the West no longer appeals to the best foreigners—well, perhaps the cows that graze on the green hills of Cavendish are interested.

An earlier famous refugee from tyranny who settled in Vermont is the Baroness Maria von Trapp. She fled Austria in 1938 with her family and, in 1941, settled on a 300-acre farm in Stowe, Vermont. The estate has since grown to 1,700 acres and includes a large hotel, the Trapp Family Lodge. The original lodge was built in 1952 and burned down in 1980. A replacement opened in 1983. The baroness, who was made famous by Rodgers and Hammerstein's *The Sound of Music,* is still active. Her husband died in 1947 and the children are now long grown and scattered. The lodge is run by a son, Johannes, who was born shortly after the von Trapps left Austria.

## THE OLDEST HOUSE IN AMERICA

**Auctioneer's price:** $75,000.
**Owner:** Christian Brothers.

Sante Fe, New Mexico, has an adobe house, that is thought to be about 800 years old. Santa Fe itself is a bit of a newcomer, founded in 1610 when the house was already 400 years old, but the Tiwa Indians had been there long before the Spanish arrived. By the 1600s New Mexico was the way we think of it today, rough desert. A few centuries earlier, however, the climate supported extensive agriculture. Less than 5 miles from the plaza of Santa Fe are the ruins of an important old pueblo called Arroyo Hondo. It was a farming settlement by A.D. 600 and began to expand with the good weather, permitting many settlements in the region. After the year 1300 the weather turned permanently sour and the population began to dwindle. When the Spanish arrived, they found the survivors easy pickings.

The Sante Fe house is now used as a curio shop and is owned by the Christian Brothers, who operate the nearby Mission of San Miguel. The mission, built in 1636, is the oldest church in the United States. Mass is still celebrated there every Sunday. The Christian Brothers are the newest part of this story, the order having been founded only in 1684. They arrived in Santa Fe in 1859—just yesterday by local standards.

The rather high auctioneer's price on the house has little to do with its historic interest. Technology has made the area again suitable to population concentrations and the price of land has soared. If it were not owned by a religious order, the house would probably have been sold and torn down by now.

# 2

# ENTERTAINMENT

## TWENTIETH CENTURY-FOX

**Auctioneer's price:** $483,000,000.
**Owners:** Marc Rich and Marvin Davis.

There will be some gaudy books written about Marc Rich, a Belgian-born trader who came to the U.S. during World War II, when he was a child. Rich is surely the most aptly named proprietor in this volume, for he is simultaneously extremely wealthy and secretive. The source of his money goes undeclared; he is just rich. As all Americans know, one organization that constantly asks "Where'd you get them bucks?" is the IRS. During the spring and summer of 1983, tax agents tried asking that question of Mr. Rich. His answers were considered quite unsatisfactory.

Marc Rich has two primary operations. One, based in Switzerland, is Marc Rich & Company AG. It was formed in 1974 and has subsidiaries in Panama and Switzerland. A second company, formed in 1980 and based in the Netherlands Antilles, is called Richco NV. It has numerous subsidiaries in Europe and America. Richco's work seems to be trading—precious metals, sugar, securities, grain, oil, and commodities futures. Mr. Rich also has other companies and holdings, all bound together through mutual shareholders, of whom Marc Rich himself is, decidedly, the largest.

Suspicious people grow even more suspicious when they see American citizens setting up secretive companies in Switzerland and the Netherlands Antilles, two places where laws make tax inquiries almost impossible. The IRS is, by nature, most suspicious. It believes that Mr. Rich has engaged in overly imaginative bookkeeping. Specifically, the IRS thinks Rich's Swiss operation charged an American company, also owned by Mr. Rich, absurdly high prices for its services. Since these prices were deductible as a cost of doing business, they lowered the size of the American company's tax bill. Of course, Rich himself didn't suffer as a result of these high prices. The money was simply switched to banks in Switzerland.

In 1983 the IRS brought an indictment against Rich and his partner, Pincus Green, charging them with evading $48 million in income taxes. As part of the inquiry, many of Rich's documents were subpoenaed. The subpoena was not completely obeyed. Eventually the judge held the company in contempt and imposed a fine of $50,000 for each day that delivery of the documents was delayed. These developments may not have ruined Mr. Rich, but they certainly complicated his life. He took up Spanish citizenship and disappeared from view.

It says a lot about today's entertainment industry when men like Mr. Rich are drawn to it. During the 1960s entrepreneurs sold the great movie studios to conglomerates. Lately, the trend has been in the opposite direction. Mr. Rich owns Twentieth Century-Fox. Fox was a public corporation for decades, but in 1981 a Denver billionaire named Marvin Davis offered to buy the company for $725,000,000. Davis and his attorney, Edward Bennett Williams, got all the attention, but when the details of the offer were spelled out it was revealed that Davis would get only half the stock. Under the purchase a new company, called TCF Holdings, was formed and became sole owner of the Twentieth Century-Fox corporation. Stock in TCF was divided into two types: class A, with voting power, was for Davis; class B, with no voting power, was going to an obscure Caribbean firm called Richco. Once Fox was sold, the class B stock was given voting power and then Davis sold half of his class A voting rights. All of this controlling authority (75 percent) went into Marc Rich's hands.

Mr. Rich has shown no interest in making a great movie. He has let Davis garner whatever publicity there is to be had from the movie mogul's chair. But there is a lot of cash in the entertainment industry. Many of Fox's assets have been sold off and the money transferred to TCF Holdings. This asset-selling is why the auctioneer's price for Twentieth Century-Fox is substantially below what Rich and Davis paid for the property. The opportunity for gaining control of great assets and a sizable cash flow has brought a new breed of businessmen into entertainment. The presence of businessmen is nothing new, nothing shocking, but in the past producers like Louis Mayer and John Heminge knew that success depended on being able to sense what customers wanted. Commodity traders think differently. Never in world history has the amusement business been more lucrative and never has it been under the control of people less able to discern what amuses the public.

The biggest bombs at Fox under the Rich/Davis regime have been *King of Comedy* (cost $19 million; earned $1.2 million at U.S. box offices) and a completely forgotten epic called *Megaforce* (cost $20 million; earned $3.5 million). The biggest success was a sleeper called *Porky's*. It earned $53 million at U.S. box offices and cost only a few million to make. The success of that film, a broad leering comedy, seems to have set the tone for recent Fox films. Low-budget slapstick was also the formula behind *Porky's II*, *Mr. Mom*, *Modern Problems*, and *National Lampoon's Class Reunion*. Twentieth Century-Fox also distributes the *Star Wars* films (q.v.), but that deal was made long before Messrs. Rich and Davis entered the scene.

By now Mr. Rich's tax problems have grown so large that he has been speaking to Davis about selling his holding in Fox, but the IRS has obtained a court injunction blocking any sale of Rich's share of TCF. It is expected to be many years before the issues in the Rich case are untangled.

MGM/United Artists is owned by Kirk Kerkorian. He is a Las Vegas financier (if you can imagine such a thing), who has put money into casinos, airlines, hotels, and entertainment. Since 1969 he has been the majority owner of MGM's stock. In 1983 he made a brief attempt to buy the rest of the shares. Apparently he found the price too high for he backed away from the deal; however, he is still the majority stockholder.

Smaller production companies continue to be owned by the old-type businessman who knows how to balance the books and considers the tastes of his customers. Particularly notable are two Israeli cousins, Menahem Golan and Yoram Globus, who own the Cannon Group. This Hollywood company makes about a dozen films a year, the same number turned out by the major studios. Their films are low-budget American-quality items made for the overseas market. Anybody who has ever seen the typical fare offered in Third World movie theaters knows that a Grade-C American film is far superior to the Grade-Z stuff turned out by foreign studios. The plots may not be better, but their technical quality is far superior. Cannon cannot afford to make American blockbusters, but it can use our craftsmanship to upgrade entertainment in the poorer parts of the world.

The smallest companies still tend to be run by people whose minds are oriented more toward entertainment than toward business. A notable example is the Brock/Trumbull Entertainment corporation, owned in equal parts by Douglas Trumbull and Brock Hotels. Trumbull is a special-effects genius who worked on *2001* and *Close Encounters of the Third Kind*. For years he has been touting a filmmaking process that shows sixty frames a second rather than the usual twenty-four. Everyone who has seen the process agrees that such films are dramatically more realistic and involving than ordinary movies, but no businessman is willing to invest the millions of dollars necessary to convert theaters, projectors, movie cameras, and editing equipment. After all, the appeal of these films might be only a fad.

The partner Trumbull finally wooed was Robert Brock, chairman and chief stockholder (30 percent) of Brock Hotels. Brock has a subsidiary restaurant chain called ShowBiz Pizza Palaces and plans to show high-speed films in these restaurants. So the cutting edge of movie technology is right back where it was at the start of the century—a combination of technical enthusiasts who just want to make movies and low-grade showmen who need something to show. If it works, a fancier grade of businessman will follow.

## NIELSEN RATINGS

**Auctioneer's price:** $445,000,000.
**Owner:** Arthur Charles Nielsen family.

We laugh at the Romans for studying the entrails of dead animals before going off to war, but think of their predicament. They had to decide upon action and had no way of knowing how things would turn out. Americans too must often act without having a sure basis for deciding what to do; however, it is not our style to rely on priests and seers. For us, decisions taken in ignorance must be justified by numbers, preferably decimal numbers that look precise, scientific, and unambiguous. Statisticians point out that numbers are not always as exact as they seem. "No matter," cry the faithful. "Say what you will, *23.623* is still bigger than *23.622*." "Not always," retort statisticians, but their voices are no more welcome than atheists at a revival camp. When ignorance is king we like to slit open a computer and read its numbers.

Chief goat slaughterer and entrail reader to the television industry is the A.C. Nielsen company. In 1923 Arthur Charles Nielsen founded a market research company that investigated consumer tastes and responses to products. This sort of research is not easy since people tend to be inarticulate and inaccurate. Nielsen's great test as a soothsayer came when he discovered that his marketing data were unreliable. People lied about their purchases, claiming, for example, to use a costly brand of soap when they really bought Ivory. Many another entrail reader has simply tried to gloss over this sort of weakness in his method, but Nielsen quit asking people what they bought and began measuring sales at grocery stores. From that turning point came Nielsen's empire. He started to rise in the 1930s, but the boom began after World War II, when television and advertising pressure brought a great need for auguries and readers of omens. In 1952 the Nielsen company began to compile television ratings and its money suddenly acquired the reproductive power of rabbits.

The founder Nielsen retired in 1974. He was succeeded as chairman of the board by A.C., Jr., who retired in the spring of 1984. The family still has voting control of the stock and A.C.,

Jr., is still actively interested in the company. Two other Nielsens remain with the firm—A.C., Jr.'s brother, Philip, and son Christopher. The power this clan has brought itself is amazing and nutty. No industry bases decisions on shakier numbers than does television broadcasting.

Surely sometimes Nielsen gets the numbers right. When the ratings report says that the Super Bowl was the week's most popular show, you can believe it. Who would doubt it when interest in the game oozes all over the culture? Nielsen's power, however, is based on its ranking of ordinary programs whose popularity is not so evident. Unfortunately the statistical methods used in developing the list are so weak that an accurate survey of the whole country might well rank the programs in quite another order. It is an axiom of mathematics that every survey contains distortions. To find the truth researchers should study as large a sample as possible and keep surveying new people. This method reduces the potential size of an error and, over time, distortions tend to balance out. The trouble is that this solution is expensive. Nielsen prefers to survey a small number of people and to keep surveying the same viewers over and over. These weaknesses are well known, but complaints never get any results. Fifteen billion dollars in advertising revenues are at stake each year, yet the success of any particular broadcast is hidden in the privacy of homes scattered across the country. Television executives must make decisions; if they were not able to use the ratings, they would have to rely on some equally shaky guide or, heaven forfend, their own judgment.

## THE GRAND OLE OPRY

**Auctioneer's price:** $250,000,000.
**Owner:** Edward L. Gaylord.

Back in the 1920s, when radio began, local stations provided a lot of their own programming. That didn't just mean having some in-town DJ play records; the announcer, musicians, and type of music were all local. Thus, almost from radio's first days, hillbilly, or barn dance, music was played on the air. This style of music had no prestige beyond its local audience and no professional performers. Its instruments—fiddles and banjos mostly—were laughed at by city folk, but country dwellers liked it. So radio stations with rural audiences played it.

Barn dance music was almost all instrumental. Much contemporary country music—characterized by a strong guitar beat, frank lyrics, and yodeling vocalization—was so unlike the original material that it wouldn't have been allowed on the barn dance shows. The music broadcast was what country musicians played at social gatherings, with one exception: radio performers tended to be more gifted than those normally found at a crossroads tavern.

On November 28, 1925, a Nashville radio station began broadcasting "The WSM Barn Dance." By then many stations had such programs. Nashville was slow because it thought itself too sophisticated for hillbilly stuff. Once begun, however, WSM's show was defiantly proud of its hick origins. In 1927 it took the name "Grand Ole Opry" as a boastful rejection of the classical music broadcast that preceded the barn dance show. But the performers changed and with them so did the music and its pretensions. In the early '30s the directors of the Grand Ole Opry began to notice that its young performers were dreaming of making a living just by playing music. In 1937 the show got its first star singing group, Roy Acuff and the Crazy Tennesseans, but the music's new image consciousness quickly forced a name change to Roy Acuff and the Smoky Mountain Boys. In 1943 Ernest Tubb brought two revolutions. His music was much more rhythmic, more suitable for dancing in places that weren't barns, and he made his record company, Decca, call him a "country singer."

In the early days of barn dance shows it was impossible to predict that the Nashville show would become the classic of them all. Atlanta and Chicago programs had much going for them. Little advantages began to mount up, though. The Nashville show got an unusually professional stage manager. In 1932 WSM became a 50,000-watt clear-channel station. With that kind of power listeners hundreds of miles away could tune in the Grand Ole Opry. WSM was affiliated with NBC, which in 1939 began carrying a half-hour of the Opry nationwide. This national audience, and the evolution of the music away from a barn dance style, created a distinct sound associated with Nashville. In 1945 Nashville's first recording studio opened.

Meanwhile other programs were in trouble. The loss of contact with barn dance roots cost these shows the more conservative members of their audiences. During the '50s, with the rise of rock and roll, the more avant-garde members of the audience also turned away. So by the 1960s Nashville's Grand Ole Opry was the triumphant survivor of the long competition.

Left to itself the Opry became a huge business. Its assets now include a theme park (Opryland USA), an enormous hotel-convention center (Opryland Hotel), two radio stations, and a cable TV channel (the Nashville Network) that provides continuous country and western music to subscribers. When entertainment companies get this big they attract buyers, and in late 1983 the company was bought by Edward Gaylord, a publishing and broadcasting millionaire based in Oklahoma City. He publishes both of that city's major papers, the morning *Oklahoman* and the evening *Times*.

The chain of possession works as follows: The Grand Ole Opry is a wholly owned subsidiary of Gaylord Broadcasting, which is, in turn, a wholly owned subsidiary of the Oklahoma Publishing Company, which is privately owned by Edward Gaylord. Before buying the Nashville industry Gaylord was already connected with the Grand Ole Opry. His company produces "Hee-Haw," a syndicated television show filmed at the Opryland theater.

At the same time that hillbilly music was first aired, black artists were composing another variety of minority music with strong local appeal. A classic piece from 1928 was "Basin Street Blues" by Spencer Williams. There were many other works as well. King Oliver wrote "Sugar Foot Stomp" (a great Louis Armstrong hit) and "Doctor Jazz." Fats Waller was writing pieces like "Keep a Song in Your Soul," "Why Am I Alone?" and "Keepin' Out of Mischief Now." Perhaps the most prolific of the black composers of the late '20s was Jelly Roll Morton, whose many songs included "Black Bottom Stomp," "Cannon Ball Blues," "Jersey," and "Wild Man Blues." The latter was written with Louis Armstrong. The copyrights on all the songs mentioned in this paragraph are now owned by composer/performer Paul James McCartney.

Mainstream pop music from the '30s was admirable too, producing many old standards such as "Sentimental Journey," "One for My Baby," "Stormy Weather," and "Prisoner of Love." During the '40s, however, mainstream pop seems to have lost its way and produced decidedly inferior "classics" like Mel Torme's "The Christmas Song," Bob Troup's "Route 66," and (the best of a weak lot) Walter Gross's "Tenderly." (The copyrights on all these songs are now owned by Paul McCartney.)

During the '50s it was the outsiders' music from the black and country traditions that revitalized the exhausted mainstream. Elvis Presley was the outstanding performer to find success by linking the black and country traditions. Presley, however, was no composer and wisely contented himself with singing other people's songs. The first great composer/performer who blended country and black music was Buddy Holly. His short career ended with a plane crash, but was long enough to produce "That'll Be the Day," "Peggy Sue," "Oh Boy!," "Maybe Baby," "Rave On," and "It's So Easy." The copyright on the entire Buddy Holly oeuvre is owned by Paul McCartney.

The entry of country and black traditions into the mainstream briefly made stars of black and hick performers, but it is in the nature of mainstreams to *be* the main stream, and soon white-skinned urbanites were back in command. At first they were no-talents like Frankie Avalon, but eventually true genius raised its conquering head. A series of songs like "Love Me Do," "All My Loving," "A Hard Day's Night," "Yesterday," "You've Got to Hide Your Love Away," "Norwegian Wood," "Michelle," and "Eleanor Rigby" showed such a range and musical imagination that the composers—John Lennon and Paul McCartney—swept their rivals away. Black and country music returned to minority status.

Copyrights on the Beatles songs listed above are owned by Robert Holmes a' Court. Paul McCartney has offered as much as $40,000,000 for those rights, but a' Court turned him down. Until they formed the Apple Corporation the Beatles music was copyrighted through EMI, a British studio owned by Lew Grade (now dubbed Lord Elstree). Grade sold his rights to a' Court, an Australian investor with television stations in Perth and Adelaide.

The most widely sung song in America is thought to be "Happy Birthday to You," copyright owned by David Sengstack. It may seem incredible to report that so famous a song has an owner, but it does. You don't have to send David a nickel every time you sing the song, but he gets a royalty whenever it appears in a movie or on a record or in some other commercial setting. The copyright runs through 1996.

The melody was published in 1893 as "Good Morning to All" and written by two sisters, Mildred and Patty Hill. The present version was copyrighted on December 27, 1934, by the music publisher Clayton F. Summy Co. (now called Summy-Birchard Music), which was owned by David Sengstack's father, John. The record of that initial application was lost and the song was copyrighted again on December 6, 1935. David inherited the company and is its president.

## MOVIE THEATER PALAZZOS

**Auctioneer's price:** $102,000,000.
**Owners:** Tisch brothers.

In the days when movies presented a fantasy world of spectacle and grandeur, it seemed only natural to build theaters in a mock-monumental style that imitated the sumptuous world of potent kings and fancy costumes found on the screen. Now that movie fantasies are colder and more mechanical, we no longer build such imaginative houses, but some have survived. Like the vision of glory they were meant to express, the theaters seem a bit dowdy, a bit foolish, but they are still charming. What must the world have been like, for anybody to think it would be a good idea to place a pharaoh's head above a popcorn stand?

When such tulips were in bloom, the film company that produced the most sumptuous movies was MGM, a subsidiary of the Loews Corporation. Loews also built a chain of extravagant multi-tiered theaters in the heart of thriving commercial districts.

In the 1950s, as part of an antitrust suit, the government forced production companies to sell their theaters. The Loews chain was bought by two brothers, Laurence and Preston Tisch. Their background was in real estate. They began with a hotel, Laurel-in-the-Pines, in Lakewood, New Jersey, and soon expanded into Atlantic City. (That was before the casinos, when the resort town was entering its long slide into oblivion.) With this background, the brothers were primarily interested in the real estate under the Loews palazzos, and fifty of the ornate baubles were torn down. But they kept others and built new ones. The new theaters continue to be first-run city theaters and, although the new designs are not as remarkable as the old rhinestone settings, they are better than the whitewashed popcorn stands going up in suburban malls.

Under the direction of the Tisch brothers, the Loews Corporation has grown into a gigantic conglomerate with hotels, tobacco interests, and a giant investment portfolio (auctioneer's price for the whole corporation: $2,400,000,000; the price above is just for the theater chain). The brothers have kept 45 percent of the firm's stock. Laurence is chairman of the board, Preston is the president, and James Tisch, son of Laurence, is a vice-president. Laurence is considered the investment genius behind the Loews portfolio. Preston is the more affable of the two; a big New York City booster, he is said to be the man who came up with the name "The Big Apple" for that city.

★★★

Movie fans who prefer to see old films in those old palazzos can turn to their local repertory theater. The largest chain of them is the Landmark Theater Corporation, privately owned by Kim Jorgensen. Kim is unusually cultured; he was born in Denmark, speaks eight languages, and has a master's degree in comparative literature. Normally such erudition would condemn him to a life of poverty, and indeed he started out quite unpromisingly, as a film buyer for a chain of theaters. Fortunately for him the chain folded and he lost his job. Forced to think anew, he got the idea that made him rich. He bought the Fox Venice, an old movie palazzo in Los Angeles, and he began showing classic movies. Now he owns almost forty theaters, stretched across the country from Los Angeles to Chicago. Each theater changes its program almost every day. His financial partners are Stephen Gilvla and Gary Meyer.

The most notorious group of old movie palazzos is surely porn row on New York's 42nd Street, just west of Times Square. Only Vandals and Huns can walk that way and not contemplate the decline of Western civilization. Seven of the fourteen 42nd Street theaters are owned by the Brandt Organization, a family-owned firm headed by Robert Brandt. The Brandts owned the theaters back when their fare was less offensive. Mr. Brandt argues that he must either show the XXX-rated stuff or close the theaters. Of course, no one ever says, "I show this junk because I'm a sleaze-ball."

The largest movie theater chain is the General Cinema Corporation, owned by Richard Allen Smith and his sister, Nancy Marks. Their father founded a chain of drive-ins in 1937. When he died, in 1961, his children inherited the business and still hold a quarter of the stock. Richard is chairman of the board and has modernized the enterprise, building multiplex shopping-center theaters. Ticket sales give the company a great cash flow, only part of which has been reinvested in theater operations. The rest has been invested in bottling companies, especially Pepsi-Cola. Smith and Marks have also developed their own brand of pop, Sunkist orange drink (a royalty is paid to the Sunkist Growers Association for the name). All this generates more cash and enables the company to expand again. Such methods are all very sound, very businesslike, and guarantee that no new theaters will be shaped like a Chinese pagoda.

Another surviving giant that began with drive-ins is Sumner Redstone's company, the Northeast Theater Corporation. Redstone opened his first drive-in in 1933 and had almost 5,000 of them going in the late '50s. Since then the number has declined to about 3,000 as he too abandons drive-ins for multiscreen indoor operations placed in shopping malls. (The drive-in origins of these large chains has a simple historic explanation. When the studios lost control of the theaters in 1952, the independent operators were naturally the people best placed to take advantage of the change. However, the filmmakers had so dominated the indoor theater business that the only independent operators of note owned drive-ins. The studios had never bothered to go into that end of the business.)

It's in the South, notably Texas, that drive-ins are still thriving and drawing new money. The biggest operator in Texas is Gordon McClendon, a radio man who is credited with having invented the Top-40 format. He builds large multiscreen drive-ins. The largest, near Houston, is "The I-45," a drive-in with six screens and room for 3,000 cars. Instead of using one of those old lousy drive-in speakers, you can tune in the sound on your car radio.

## *STAR WARS*

**Auctioneer's price:** $93,500,000.
**Owner:** George Lucas.

The story is often told of a Rockefeller for our age of supermedia: Young George Lucas (born 1944) made a small film in the late 1960s called *THX 1138* for $750,000. It had no commercial success, but got some critical attention and a major studio, Universal, financed Lucas to make a slightly larger film named *American Graffiti*, which became a great success at the box office and with the critics.

Despite this popularity the executives at Universal turned down Lucas's proposal for his next film—a story set a long time ago in a galaxy far, far away. The tale was no more profound than a comic book, but Universal didn't mind that. The picture would cost $10,000,000, but Universal could afford that. What they didn't like was Lucas's desire to treat his idea like a book and keep the rights to the film. The distributor could share in the profits, but the film would be Lucas's property. Decisions about sequels would remain in Lucas's hands. Universal saw no reason to stand for that and, in the name of sound business, passed up the opportunity to be in on the most successful film series in entertainment history.

In those days Twentieth Century-Fox leadership was directed by Alan Ladd, Jr., and he was more insightful. Despite the risk, Ladd agreed to finance and distribute *Star Wars*. Lucas wrote and directed the film and with the money he made from that movie he financed the sequel, *The Empire Strikes Back*, through his own company, Lucasfilm Ltd. Of course this arrangement made him still richer and more powerful. Through 1983 the first two films in the *Star Wars* series sold just under a billion dollars' worth of tickets worldwide and Lucas got about 10 percent of that for himself. He can expect to make millions more per year in royalties for a long time to come. (Lucasfilm nets about $15 million each year.) Those two films also led to the sale of $1,500,000,000 worth of T-shirts, toys, posters, etc., and the licensing arrangement gives Lucas a piece of that pie too.

The third film in the series, *The Return of the Jedi*, again financed by Lucasfilm Ltd., was another money-maker *extraordinaire*. It cost $35 million to make and in the first week in theaters it sold $45 million worth of tickets. Apparently Lucas has made himself a magic cow that can be endlessly milked for gold. Although *The Return of the Jedi* was billed as the last of a trilogy, a follow-up trilogy is already planned. And after that? Another trilogy, or maybe a tetralogy, or a couple of duets followed by an aria? Any producer worth his caviar ought to be able to keep this project going longer than the James Bond series. Just think of the great one they'll release in the year 2001.

As proprietor of Lucasfilm, Lucas stands under a steady shower of money, but he no longer writes or directs the *Star Wars* pictures. Instead he functions like an old-time studio head. While not yet in the Louis B. Mayer class, he is heading that way, for he is a novelty—an entertainer who spends lavishly and actually understands what he is doing.

*The Empire Strikes Back* was directed by Irvin Kershner; Richard Marquand did *Return of the Jedi*. They were paid handsomely for their services but did not seek and certainly could not get the proprietary rights, which Lucas maintained from the beginning of the project; however, Lucas made so much more money than anyone expected that he has paid hefty bonuses to his production crews. In the world of film entertainment such liberality usually comes only after every third finding of hen's teeth.

Note—Lucas is no longer sole proprietor of his company. His divorce settlement with Margaret Lucas gave her half of Lucasfilm Ltd.

## THE BEST CASINO IN LAS VEGAS

**Auctioneer's price:** $42,500,000.
**Owner:** Benny Binion.

There is only one casino in Las Vegas where the players can set their own limit; that is Binion's Horseshoe Casino in downtown Las Vegas, away from the famous "strip." There is no nightclub, no lounge act, no swimming pool—just gambling. If you want to bet a million dollars on the roulette wheel, you can. But there is a catch—you set your limit with your first bet. If you bet one million on red and the wheel comes up black, you cannot then bet two million in an attempt to recover your losses. One million is your limit.

Other casinos set their own limit. It's a ploy for tourists. Joe Sucker from Tidy Suburb, U.S.A., wanders into an ordinary Vegas casino and, although he's never played roulette before in his life, he has figured out a system. If he loses, he doubles his bet and keeps on doubling until he wins. That way he recovers his losses and makes a small profit. At first it works wonderfully, but then Joe hits a bad-luck streak. He's not worried, however, since he knows he cannot lose in the long run. He keeps on doubling—sure, he was going to spend the money on braces for the kids, on enough gasoline to get back home, on his hotel bill, but he's not worried. Suddenly, though, when he doubles his bet, the croupier shakes his head. He can't bet that much money; it's over the house limit. In an instant Joe has learned the reason casinos put a limit on betting. It has nothing to do with concern for Joe Sucker's welfare.

Binion's isn't against taking money that was supposed to pay for braces, but it isn't so eager to milk the suckers that it chases out the high rollers. Its solution to the doubling method has been the personal-limit rule. In the democracy of Binion's, oilonaires and diamond thieves can throw their lives away, too, just like the rest of us.

Not surprisingly, Binion's is owned by the Binion family. It was founded by Benny Binion and is now run by his two sons, Jack and Teddy, though Benny still likes to keep his hand in. He began as a Texas gambler, that is to say, he began illegally. After World War II he came to Vegas, where the law enforcement officers didn't object to his vocation. Those who followed him to Vegas have been more innovative, as far as attracting tourists is concerned, but Binion has succeeded admirably in his own ambition, attracting serious gamblers.

## DUNGEONS & DRAGONS

**Auctioneer's price:** $40,000,000.
**Owner:** Gary Gygax.

While there is nothing absolutely new under the sun, some things are less old than others. In the 1970s an almost new type of game appeared, a kind of cross between cowboys and Indians and Parcheesi, only there were no cowboys, no Indians, and no Parcheesi boards. As in cowboys and Indians, the players all assume fantasy identities; in this case the roles are fighting men, elves, dwarves, magic users, clerics, halflings, and thieves. Also like a game of cowboys, lots of people can play—up to eighteen. But cowboy games break down when one kid yells, "Bang, bang, you're dead," and the other kid replies, "You missed me." The new game uses dice, as in Parcheesi, to settle the nature of unfolding events.

Dungeons & Dragons is the name of the game. During the late '70s it swept through the college campuses with a speed normally reserved for medieval plagues and now it is well established among game players in pre- and post-college years. Its

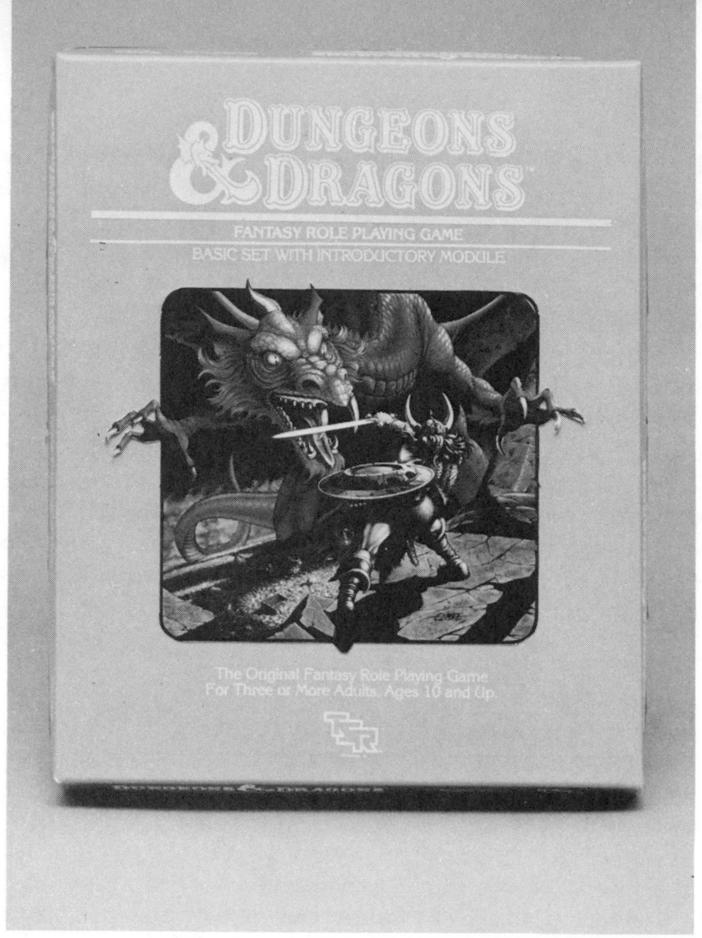


Photo: Dungeons & Dragons. DUNGEONS & DRAGONS is a registered trademark owned by TSR, Inc.

inventor is Gary Gygax, an insurance underwriter whose hobby was creating games to be played with toy soldiers. He tried to sell the game to Avalon Hill, a company that specializes in war games. They rejected it on the grounds that the game was too complicated. Since Avalon Hill sells some of the most intricate games ever devised, their complaint suggests that Gygax's game is insanely detailed.

It is, but fortunately for him many people love the detail. In 1974 Gygax lost his insurance job and founded a company called TSR Hobbies to try to market Dungeons & Dragons. TSR stands for Tactical Studies Rules. Heaven knows why those three words were chosen when any other three would have meant as much, though they wouldn't have sounded as gamesmanlike. By 1975 Gygax was working full time on the game. He sold it to fellow hobbyists and then, once the game began to reach campuses, Gygax was able to forget about his underwriting résumé.

Literal-minded stick-in-the-muds immediately began to fret that the popularity of the game meant that the current crop of students was in love with violence. We seldom hear such nonsense about chess, even though it simulates war, because everyone can see that the fascination of chess lies in the game itself. The same holds true for Dungeons & Dragons; the players get caught up in an alternate world, one where defeat and death may strain the spirit but do not harm the body. A more sophisticated criticism of the game is that its fascination lies more in the rules than the play. A chess player can concentrate for fifty or more minutes while working out the implications of a few well-known rules. A Dungeons & Dragons player, however, can spend a lot of time researching the rules. Thus, despite the fantastic nature of its characteristics, it is a game that calls less for imagination than for lawyerly instincts.

This quality has served Gygax well. He provides many game accessories—maps, illustrations and models of the characters, guides to the herbal ingredients of the magic potions, and material for the referees (known as Dungeon Masters). Keeping his followers supplied with details has been the secret of Gygax's success. His customers want more than just the rule book and some dice. They keep coming back, money in hand, for more details.

Rumors say that Gygax and his partner, Brian Blume, are not up to managing a multimillion-dollar corporation. True or not, the popularity of the Dungeons & Dragons game seems strong enough to survive whatever problems management might impose on itself.

## WALL-SIZE TELEVISION SCREENS

**Auctioneer's price:** $15,900,000.
**Owner:** Henry Kloss.

In the case of Henry Kloss the proverb about building mousetraps and beating paths has not worked out exactly right. He builds better stereo speakers, and anyone in the past thirty years who has looked for value in speakers has seen his products. During the 1950s he was an original partner at Acoustics Research, the company that first made hi-fi speakers available to the nonrich. In the '60s he had another company, KLH, whose speakers were popular with college students because they combined unusual quality with a good price. (The K in KLH stands for Kloss.) In 1968 he formed Advent, a company that once again produced better speakers at lower costs. So why hasn't the world beaten interstate highways to his door?

Kloss is an inventor, not a businessman. Thanks to Edison we tend to think of inventors as being master entrepreneurs, like John D. Rockefeller, but most inventors are more like poets. Their mode of expression is the widget rather than terza rima. Kloss makes things, wondrous things. Kloss sold his half of Acoustics Research for $50,000. A decade later the company was bought for $9,000,000. He sold KLH to the Singer corporation for stock worth $1,200,000, but the stock's price immediately tumbled and when Kloss sold his shares he got only $400,000. Advent fared worse and Kloss was forced out of its leadership.

The failure of Advent came because Kloss had grown tired of reinventing the speaker. He wanted to build a television with a screen large enough to fill a wall. He left KLH because its new owners would not let him work on a television and he formed Advent with the specific intention of bringing out a wall-size TV, just as soon as the thing was invented. The wonderful Advent speaker was designed and sold simply to provide an income while he worked on the television.

The trouble is that giant-screen TV is a bad idea. The sets work in bars, but not in the home. Kloss himself is not a TV fan and failed to appreciate the qualities that make television popular. He accepted the cliché that television is a visual medium and then added an American twist by assuming that a bigger picture would make TV a better visual medium. If he had only taken a week off to watch television he would have seen how rare it is for the screen to offer an image worth enlarging. From time to time there is an Alan Root documentary, but for the most part every image on television is like a thousand others we've seen before. Television is not a medium for images; it is for banality.

We all know you have to be careful about the phrases you

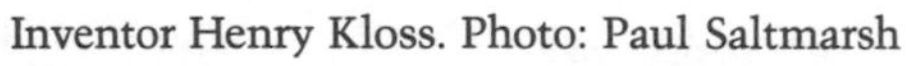

Inventor Henry Kloss. Photo: Paul Saltmarsh

carve in granite. "Pass the salt, please" can survive endless repetition in everyday life, but should not be placed over a door in the Supreme Court. Television is as banal and useful as "pass the salt" and enlargement of the picture does not ennoble it. It merely underscores the hollowness of the thing. So when people come to see a demonstration of giant-screen TV, they feel oddly disappointed. Somehow the favorite news anchor doesn't look better when blown up to Mount Rushmore proportions. The brawl in the underground parking lot is less exciting when you can see exactly how little happens and how much it is like last week's parking lot brawl. Even the grandmother raving hysterically in some unknown tongue about the massacre of her family looks tediously like all the other hysterical grandmothers shown on world news.

Kloss, however, invents; he doesn't watch. He has formed another company, called Kloss Video, and holds 55 percent of its stock. Technically, his television is a typical Kloss wonder. It throws a 6½-foot-wide color image that can be shown on any white wall. His rivals, mostly Japanese firms, cannot come up with anything to match it. But the world still has not beaten a path to Chez Kloss because, for all his genius, Henry Kloss is one more man trying to make big bucks from a form of entertainment he doesn't understand.

## BARNUM & BAILEY

**Auctioneer's price:** $15,200,000.
**Owner:** Feld family.

The recent history of the Ringling Brothers and Barnum and Bailey Circus pitted people who think about entertainment against those who think about pages in ledgers. The entertainers won. America's most famous circus was formed in 1880 when James Bailey joined forces with P.T. Barnum. By that time Barnum was almost seventy years old and a national legend, not for a circus, but for a museum of marvels. It was Barnum who came up with the famous slogan for the new circus, "The Greatest Show on Earth." He expanded the thing from one to two and then three rings, and ever since the circus's emphasis has been on providing the greatest, biggest, most colossal, unprecedented, super-duper, *ne plus ultra* spectacle anyone has ever encountered.

This tradition was kept up by the Ringling brothers when they bought the circus. The growing list of names in the circus's title pretty neatly summarizes its history. Showmen formed the company and then passed it on to other showmen. But during the 1970s the heirs of the Ringling brothers sold the circus to the Mattel Corporation. For the first time the purchase of the famous circus had nothing to do with a desire to entertain. It was part of a corporate strategy to diversify and reduce Mattel's dependence on the uncertainty of the toy market. One might ask if it is wise for people to enter trades they know nothing about because they are puzzled by the business they are in, but plenty of troubled corporations try that route.

While Mattel owned the circus, it left the management up to Irvin and Kenneth Feld, a father-and-son team. Meanwhile Mattel's diversification strategy was spreading confusion throughout the corporation. Mattel bought and soon sold a pet-supply company. It tried making movies and quit. It went into the children's book business and quickly realized that was a mistake. The corporation never did know what the Felds were up to and in 1982 Mattel quit trying to figure it out. Mattel sold them the company.

The circus's assets included 500 animals and 98 railroad cars. The Felds also got from Mattel several other shows that specialize in entertainment overkill ("Ice Follies" and "Holiday on Ice," Walt Disney's "World on Ice," and a Las Vegas show called "Beyond Belief"). The auctioneer's price above is just for the circus portion of their holdings.

## SEXUAL PARAPHERNALIA STORE

**Auctioneer's price:** $8,700,000.
**Owner:** Duane Colglazier.

When the topic turns to pornography, there is a marked temptation to try to be profound. Obviously an immense change has taken place in America and throughout the industrial world. The conquest of many venereal diseases and the development of reliable contraceptive methods have shaken a lot of fear from the subject of sex and brought about a revolution in the everyday lives of the middle class. What was once secret has become public. So now the Food and Drug Administration classifies vibrators as grade-two medical devices and inspects their manufacture, to be sure that the electrical apparatus is secure and not liable to cause shocks.

But a visit to one of the Pleasure Chest shops around the country will quickly drive away any thoughts that this huge social change offers much opportunity for profound insight. We are still at the stage when simple description is about all the mind can handle.

The Pleasure Chest corporation was founded in 1971 by an ex-stockbroker, Duane Colglazier. The first store was on the edge of New York's Greenwich Village. Colglazier initially planned to sell just water beds, but he soon added sideline items designed to increase pleasure while making love (presumably on a water bed). The sidelines proved so popular Colglazier got out of the water-bed business and expanded his line of what newspapers usually call "sexual aids." The Pleasure Chest catalog calls them "Amorous and Prurient Paraphernalia."

From there on the story is much like that of any other successful business venture. Colglazier worked hard, used his profits to increase his lines, to open more stores, and to develop a large mail-order operation. The company faced problems—many of the items customers wanted were simply not to be found. Colglazier solved these problems—his company went into manufacturing—and grew some more.

The second store the company opened was on Manhattan's fashionable East Side. Its Second Avenue location is in a well-known restaurant district where many executives like to eat. The floor of the shop is carpeted, the lighting is about what you'd expect in a small jewelry store, and the displays are simple. There is none of the neon and skid-row atmosphere that is found at most of its competitors. The place looks so respectable that passers-by are unlikely to be offended and unlikely to guess that anal plugs and cat-o'-nine-tails are sold within. This kind of confidently middle-class, confidently understated approach is surely behind much of the company's success. The police and post office don't bother Colglazier.

But when you get right down to it, no matter how similar the business methods, selling sex isn't the same as selling soybeans and not every shrewd and hardworking businessman has the stomach for Mr. Colglazier's line of work. Sex carries a lot of emotional baggage ranging from love to hate, joy to pain, and from self-confidence to self-loathing. A lot of the stuff sold at the Pleasure Chest falls into the evil end of all of these spectrums. When you read something in the company catalog that says

> Ride 'em cowboy and a hearty hi-ho Silver! Our Slave Bit is constructed from finest harness leather with a sturdy rubber mouth bit. . . .

hatred, pain, and self-loathing leap from the page. It may be legal, it may even be respectable, but it is not right.

## CIRCUS WITH A BIG TOP

**Auctioneer's price:** $4,900,000.
**Owner:** Dores R. Miller.

In 1803 an Englishman named John Davis published an account of four years spent walking through the brand-new United States. At one point he recounted, "The place I had reached was Asheepo [South Carolina], a hamlet consisting of three or more log-houses; and the inhabitants of every sex and age had collected round a huge elephant. Fortune had therefore brought me into unexpected company, and I could not but admire the docility of the elephant, who in solemn majesty received the gifts of the children with his trunk." Davis had happened upon a traveling menagerie. Its Welsh owner earned a slender living by showing his elephant and a pet monkey in America's backwoods.

A trace of that era has survived. Traveling circuses still exist, still visit rural America, and still have animals. At present, the one with the biggest menagerie is Carson & Barnes. Neither a Carson nor a Barnes has anything to do with the company. D.R. Miller, with his father and brother, bought the circus name in 1936 and D.R. has been with it ever since. He is now the sole owner.

Carson & Barnes performs twice a day every day from mid-March to early November, almost always spending only one day in a city before driving on to the next town, erecting a tent large enough to cover a football field, and performing two more shows. Twenty-five elephants move with the circus. Add horses, lions, tigers, llamas, zebras, donkeys, ponies, a hippo, a rhinoceros, a giraffe, and a few more species and the Carson & Barnes traveling menagerie comes to about 200 members. Most of the circus's business is still carried out in small-town America. Paris, Texas; Wilcox, Arizona; Parsons, Kansas; Newton, Iowa; Little Falls, Minnesota—those are the sort of places it visits.

The two other large tented circuses that still travel about America are Circus Vargas (owner: Clifford Vargas), which performs in the West, and the Clyde Beatty-Cole Brothers Circus (owner: Jerry Collins), which handles the eastern part of America. Between the three of them, most of America can still find a large tented circus somewhere nearby any summer.

Other traveling circuses that still perform under canvas include: Big Apple Circus; Fisher Brothers Circus; Franzen Brothers Circus; Great American Circus; Hanneford Family Circus; Happytime Circus; Circus Holiday; Hoxie Brother Circus; Big Strong Circus; Jungle Wonders Circus; Robert Brothers Circus; Ron Morris Circus; Sills Brothers Circus; and Williams Brothers Circus.

# CARSON & BARNES CIRCUS

## RUBIK'S CUBE

**Auctioneer's price:** $18,000.
**Owner:** Erno Rubik.

The first lesson in the story of Erno Rubik and his cube is not very uplifting: fads move quickly, but the law is a slowpoke and anyone trying to cash in on a sudden craze is apt to worry more about problems of distribution than of ownership. A second lesson is happier: even if you are robbed blind, you can still get rich.

Erno Rubik is a mathematician living in Budapest. He invented his cube in 1974 as a teaching aid and then thought there might be a market for it as a puzzle. He got a Hungarian patent for his idea and negotiated a deal with the state trading company, Konsumex, to sell the cube. Konsumex sold two million of the things—that's one cube for every five Hungarians.

News of the puzzle's appeal spread, and the Ideal Toy Corporation made an agreement with Rubik to sell the cube worldwide and pay him a royalty of 5 percent of the cube's profits. This decision was rather decent of the toy makers since the cube was unpatented outside of Hungary. They could have simply stolen the idea.

The cube was introduced to the world market in 1980 and took a firm grip on global passions during the summer of 1981. Actually there were two Rubik's Cube crazes that summer. One was the mad dash to buy cubes, the other was the race to make them. Not everybody was as foursquare as Ideal and the world was soon awash with Rubik's pirates. Un-Rubik cubes were made in Taiwan, Hong Kong, South Korea, and even Hungary.

Ideal got many court injunctions against the pirate manufacturers and importers, but it was like trying to kill flies with a cannon. Their court petitions grew more and more pathetic. Finally, when Ideal applied for the granting of a common-law patent, they listed ninety-six pirate companies they wanted stopped. The court took it under advisement and, in effect, said come back next year for a decision. By then the fad had eased.

Yet it is hard to weep for either Rubik or the Ideal Toy Corporation. Rubik became the first self-made millionaire in a

Communist country and cube sales helped turn Ideal's ledger around. In fiscal 1980 the company lost $15.5 million, but in fiscal '81, the peak year for Rubik's fad, it made a profit of $11 million.

And the pirates? Why, they got rich too. So did the sharks. Seeing Ideal's sudden wealth, the CBS corporation swam over and devoured the company whole, paying $58 million for the snack. By the time the courts ruled that the pirates were pirates, they had gone on to raid more attractive targets.

# 3

# CHIC THINGS

## GUCCI

**Auctioneer's price:** $450,000,000.
**Owner:** Aldo Gucci.

The essence of the chic style is revealed to anyone who enters a Gucci shop in Beverly Hills, Palm Beach, Bal Harbour, Chicago, or Manhattan. There, displayed before your eyes, is a society's solution to the problem of conspicuous consumption during an age of mass marketing. At the turn of the century it was only the Morgans, the Vanderbilts, the Phippses, and Rockefellers who showered themselves with the unnecessities of life, but today who doesn't do that? If you want to consume conspicuously these days, you must pay more for the same things everybody else is buying and then put the label on the outside of the item so everybody will see you can pay through the nose and keep on smiling.

Guccio Gucci founded a saddle shop in Florence, Italy. Traditionally Florence has been a center for leather works and the city's many tourists are still encouraged to buy leather coin purses, bookmarks, or boxes with the Italian name "Firenze" stamped in gold on the souvenir geegaw. Gucci made large, more serious leather items, including sturdy luggage. After Mussolini's invasion of Ethiopia the League of Nations imposed economic sanctions on Italy and it became difficult to get leather. In desperation Guccio began making canvas luggage trimmed with leather. Sturdy luggage is best for rail and boat travel, but airplanes charge a penalty for heavy weight and the Gucci invention persists.

In 1952 Guccio's oldest son, Aldo, opened a shop on Manhattan's Fifth Avenue. His father thought the idea was mad, but the shop did well and established the Gucci name in America. The next year Guccio died and Aldo, who prefers to be called "Dottore," took over direction of the whole company. Under his leadership the firm has gone from leather to contemporary chic. The company is still privately held by the Gucci family. Also in the business are Aldo's three sons—Georgio, Paolo, and Roberto—and a daughter, Patricia, who just entered her twenties. (Il Dottore is almost 80.)

Perhaps the most surprising feature of chic values is their transferability. In the old days it was widely agreed that Packard made a fine car and if you rode in one you got looks of admiration, but nobody thought if Packard made a good car, surely it would be equally admirable to own a Packard pen and pencil set as well. Today's society thinks differently. If you go into Gucci's shop, along with the leather shoes, boots, and luggage, you find Gucci jewelry, Gucci watches, Gucci toiletries, and Gucci clothing. Prominently displayed on most of these items is the name Gucci, or the initials GG (for Guccio Gucci), or the store's colors, two green stripes separated by a red stripe, a design reminiscent of the green, white, and red of the Italian flag. A leather sign in the store proclaims "Quality is remembered long after the price is forgotten." With these ostentatious brand markings there is no need to worry. You can say, "I've forgotten the price, but as you see"—pointing to the GG pattern spread over the entire product—"it cost plenty."

## ESTÉE LAUDER PERFUMES

**Auctioneer's price:** $405,000,000.
**Owner:** Estée Lauder.

Perfume is like the poor. We have it with us always. But it wasn't until American marketing that perfume and the poor got together. Most of America's cosmetics fortunes were made by selling at discount prices in dime stores and supermarkets. This kind of development threatened to kick the chic right out of perfume, but then came the Lauder family. In 1946 Estée Lauder and her husband, Joseph, founded a company that focused on selling through prestige department stores at prestige prices. Today the firm accounts for about half of all the perfume sales in department stores. This success might seem incredible when you remember how many different perfume stalls there are on the ground floor of the best department stores, but Estée Lauder has invented its own discount method. It includes attractive "gifts," such as special cosmetic cases, with a purchase. This tactic reduces the firm's profits but increases volume. Its "Youth Dew" is America's most popular department-store perfume and is one of the three best-selling fragrances in the country. Besides Estée Lauder's own brand, the company also makes scented cosmetics under other names: Clinique, Prescriptives, European Body Spa, and (for men) Aramis.

The company is a family-owned project. Estée, believed to be in her late seventies, is still chairman of the board. Joseph was active until his death in 1983. Estée's son, Leonard, is the chief executive officer and a younger son, Ronald, was active in the company until he left to work for Ronald Reagan. He is still on the board and is expected to return to the company. The family is credited with having a special gift for understanding fragrances in the same way that other families produce generations of great chefs; however, Estée Lauder fragrances are developed at an outside corporation called International Flavors and Fragrances. Final approval of a scent is up to the Lauder house and it adds diluting oils, but the chemistry of perfume is left to others.

The existence of contract fragrance developers has made possible the extraordinary spectacle of perfumes carrying the names of clothes designers. Coco Chanel made the change effectively, but is it actually possible that Yves Saint Laurent, Christian Dior, Calvin Klein, Oleg Cassini, Ralph Lauren, Halston, and Geoffrey Beene all have the know-how to mix rose oil and the thousands of other oils and spices available to the perfumer? Of course not. The fragrance is developed by an outside firm, usually the industry giant, International Flavors and Fragrances. The designer's name is licensed to a large company, which pays a royalty for its use. The name serves much the same purpose as putting Strawberry Shortcake (q.v.) on a child's toy, giving cachet to what would otherwise be an ordinary-looking product. A lot of dress designers have licensed their names to conglomerates that make perfume. Among them are:

| Designer Name | Perfume-Making Conglomerate |
|---|---|
| Calvin Klein | Minnetonka |
| Christian Dior | Moet Hennessy |
| Geoffrey Beene | American Cyanamid |
| Halston | Essmark |
| Oleg Cassini | Beecham Group |
| Ralph Lauren | Warner Communications |
| Yves Saint Laurent | Squibb |

Nobody knew more about the world of chic than Marcel Proust, who, in a moment of bold prophecy, wrote, "The day may come when dressmakers will move in society." But perhaps even he would be surprised by the extent to which their names have become the talismans that define society.

## AMERICA'S MOST ELEGANT JEWELER

**Auctioneer's price:** $263,000,000.
**Owner:** Ronald Winston.

The heart of the world's gem-quality diamond trade is on New York City's West 47th Street, between Fifth and Sixth Avenues. Con men, fences, and wheeler-dealers move perpetually through the crowd (during working hours there is always a crowd) because the astounding fact is this: almost one-half of the world's polished diamonds flow through this street.

But the really elegant diamond merchants are around the corner and a few blocks north, up Fifth Avenue. There you find the super diamond sellers whose New York offices are duplicated on Beverly Hills's Rodeo Drive and in the European capitals. The most prestigious of those is Harry Winston's, at the southwest corner of 56th Street and Fifth Avenue. Harry Winston died in 1978 and the present owner is his son, Ronald. He went to Harvard, studied chemistry, and even worked as a chemist for a while, but he is now firmly in charge of the family business.

Ronald seems a bit less exclusive than Harry. In the old days the shop's wrought-iron gate was kept locked, and a sign out front stated that admittance was by appointment only. The average sale back then came to $250,000. Today the front gate is actually open and one even sees advertisements for Harry Winston jewels. It is the regal jewels displayed in its salons that have made Harry Winston's reputation; however, most of the firm's revenue comes from selling smaller stuff. It is in fact the largest diamond distributor in America and the one-carat stone bought at J.C. Penney's was probably cut and set in the Winston cutting room.

A few score thousand dollars is all the average shopper need bring to Harry Winston's now. Despite these few nods to democracy, the place is still the greatest of the sellers. It was Winston who sold the world's largest uncut diamond, the Star of Sierra Leone (969.8 carats). Other great diamonds Harry Winston has sold include the Hope Diamond (world's largest blue diamond, 44.5 carats), the Star of the East (90 carats), and the Idol's Eye (75 carats). Surely, if revolution were to break out in England and the queen put to flight, when it came time to pawn the Tower jewels, to Harry Winston Inc. Her Majesty would go.

After Harry Winston the world's greatest jeweler is Cartier. Their New York establishment sold the 69.42 carat Burton-Taylor diamond. Cartier bought it at auction for $1,050,000 and promptly resold it to Richard Burton for his wife, Elizabeth Taylor. The diamond is worn as a ring or, considering its size, perhaps as a glove. At the time of the Burton-Taylor sale (1969), Cartier's New York store was separate from the original Paris firm. In 1972 the Paris Cartier was bought by Robert Hocq, a French businessman. He was killed in an auto accident in 1979, but before his death he had also bought the other Cartier firms. His heir was his daughter, Nathalie Hocq, who became president of the Cartier group at the age of 28. In America Cartier has stores in New York, Beverly Hills, Palm Beach, Bal Harbour, Costa Mesa, and Houston.

After Winston and Cartier, there is always that diamond mine on New York's West 47th Street. As city blocks go, the diamond block is a long one—600 feet—but even so the amount of bustle is startling. Ten thousand people work here and both sides of the street boast one storefront after another hustling diamonds. Squeezed into the block are hundreds of firms to buy, sell, appraise, and cut diamonds. The street-level operations, even the biggest and gaudiest of them, are small-carat affairs compared to the "by appointment only" firms on the upper stories. Those are the places where a fleeing Third World politician can enter, plop down a sackful of gems, and be handed one million dollars in cash on the spot. It's in those upstairs offices also that the world's greatest gems are cut. More important diamonds are cut in New York than anyplace else. (The number-two location is Antwerp, Belgium, with Bombay, India, rising fast.)

Not even the IRS can say which of these diamond firms is number one, but one of the biggest is owned by Alexander Hasenfeld, president and founder of Hasenfeld-Stein, Inc. Of course it is an upstairs firm, and don't look for this company in the Yellow Pages; the people Hasenfeld-Stein deals with all have the number on their rotary directory. The firm trades mostly in investment diamonds—unset stones bought to be resold rather than displayed. Of course if you are looking for an engagement ring that will pound a spike of envy through the liver of your ex-spouse, or if you have never thought it fair that only royalty wears boulder-size jewelry, you can buy a quality stone from Hasenfeld-Stein and have it set.

Hasenfeld's expertise is in buying rough stones at shrewd prices. His skill is best illustrated by the fact that he founded his firm only in 1947. At that time he was a newcomer to America, a refugee who arrived here after being liberated from the Nazi death camp at Auschwitz. The diamond trade was already well established in this country, but Hasenfeld bought the right stones and quickly moved to the front of the line.

## JORDACHE

**Auctioneer's price:** $255,000,000.
**Owners:** Nakash brothers.

Jordache Enterprises has the ad policy financiers ought to know better. Chairman of the board Joe Nakash explains, "If you need more ad money, you spend it. If we don't have it, I go back to the bank." The result of this eagerness to advertise has been a growth rate so phenomenal that it would be astounding even if Jordache made computers. That their fortune comes from selling pairs of pants seems well to the left of incredible.

When 1977 began there was no such thing as Jordache designer jeans. Four years later the company had a quarter of a billion dollars in sales. It also had spawned several subsidiaries. The Jordache Licensing Development Group, Ltd., does 100 million dollars' worth of business annually, licensing companies around the world to use the Jordache name. Another subsidiary, Allesio Jeans, aims for the customers who want designer jeans but, for some reason, not Jordache.

And all of it is privately owned by three guys living in the Queens borough of New York City. Three Israeli brothers—Joe, Ralph, and Avi Nakash—own 100 percent of the stock in Jordache Enterprises and all its subsidiaries. The three travel together to their Seventh Avenue office in Manhattan's garment district, discussing their plans and perhaps occasionally giggling over their money.

Often companies that have grown so dramatically are quick to sell stock to the public because the value of the founders' own investment rises far beyond the corporation's earnings. The Nakash brothers, however, like controlling the whole enterprise and are in no hurry to go public.

Jordache subsidiaries and license holders in the New York garment district include: Jordache Belt Co.; Jordache Blazer; Jordache Blouse; Jordache by Turnberry; Jordache Dresses; Jordache Fur-Like Fashions; Jordache Furs; Jordache Handbag; Jordache Hosiery; Jordache Hosiery for Women; Jordache Intimates; Jordache Junior Suits; Jordache Leathers; Jordache Little Miss; Jordache Men's Sportswear & Outwear; Jordache Neckware; Jordache Outerwear; Jordache Sweaters; Jordache Swimwear & Robes; Jordache Time Corporation.

Amazing as the Jordache success seems, almost the same tale can be told about the four Guez brothers. They immigrated to America from Tunisia, via France. In 1977 they too started a designer-jeans company, called Sasson, and advertised their way to absurdly large sums of wealth. The Guez brothers, however, are thought to be more interested in selling stock to the public.

Calvin Klein jeans are manufactured by Puritan Fashions, a garment company that dates back to the presidency of Teddy Roosevelt. In 1977, the year Jordache was founded, Puritan began to license Calvin Klein jeans and today Calvin Klein products account for almost 95 percent of Puritan sales. Not surprisingly, Klein and his business partner, Barry Schwartz, decided in 1983 to buy the company. It was a case of a whale taking control of a guppy.

## IMPORTER OF LUXURY SWISS WATCHES

**Auctioneer's price:** $110,000,000.
**Owner:** Gedalio ("Gerry") Grindberg.

In 1968 the Swiss watch industry placed a gun to its temple and squeezed the trigger. Scientists at the Swiss Watch Federation's research center in Neuchâtel brought forth the prototype of the electronic quartz watch. On that afternoon they rendered obsolete centuries of work on tiny gears, mainsprings, and balances. The quartz watch works on a principle discovered in 1880 by Pierre Curie. He showed that electricity makes a quartz crystal vibrate with unusual precision. In today's watches a battery vibrates the crystal exactly 32,768 times per second and is reliable enough to lose no more than a second or two in a month. No mechanical watch has ever been able to achieve that kind of accuracy.

The Swiss were in the best position to make immediate use of this miniaturized technology. They had the companies, the distribution network, and the reputation. Unfortunately for them, they were also smug and complacent. It was the Japanese companies with no reputation and no pride that seized the opportunity and broke into the established market. Since 1975 a quarter of the Swiss watch companies have gone out of business.

In the United States Gerry Grindberg watched these developments with trepidation. Grindberg is a Cuban refugee who formed the North American Watch Corporation in 1961, soon after he fled Castro. His company is the exclusive importer of Switzerland's luxurious Piaget watch. (Piaget itself was founded in 1874 by Georges Piaget and is still privately owned by his descendants.) Since 1967 North American Watch has also been the exclusive importer of Corum watches, a brand most famous for its watches made from gold coins. (President Reagan wore one of those for a while.) North American also owns two Swiss companies, Concord and Movado. Except for Movado, all of these watches are super-expensive, often costing many thousands of dollars. In the '60s and early '70s there was a small reliable market for costly watches and Grindberg's business prospered. He sold some stock to the public, but has held on to

54 percent of the voting power. Then came the quartz watch.

Grindberg and his investment were saved by the intricacies of the human heart. In 1970 a naive observer, confident that the future can be predicted through rational analysis, would have said that if you could buy a $20 watch that was as accurate as a $3,000 watch, sales of expensive watches would decline to zero. It turned out, however, that the makers of cheap watches were the ones to suffer. Ours is the great age of expensive watches. The Piaget Polo, a solid 20-karat-gold watch with a quartz mechanism costs nearly $14,000 and is so popular it is advertised on television as an ideal Christmas gift. The electronics revolution put an end to ticking, but not to vanity.

## THE BUSIEST EXOTIC TOUR COMPANY

**Auctioneer's price:** $56,300,000.
**Owner:** Lars-Eric Lindblad.

A Gray Line tour bus parked outside the White House does not provoke much of a sense of wonder or admiration. The bolder tourist knows it is possible to visit the capital city on one's own schedule at one's own pace. But how about traveling by ship up the Yangtze River, or around the Antarctic, or hiking up eastern Zaire's Virunga Mountains in search of gorilla? Unless you are an explorer, you probably don't want to go to these places under your own steam. Yet the commercial jet has made even the most distant places easily accessible. London to Nairobi is now a nonstop overnight hop. In Hemingway's days it took weeks by boat, then a disembarkation in the steam pit of Mombasa town, and finally a long narrow-gauge railway ride inland to the cool African plateau.

Sensing the revolution the 707 jet plane was to bring, Lars-Eric Lindblad founded Lindblad Tours in 1958. He had worked for Cook's, the British travel agency that had invented the guided tour a century before, in response to the earlier travel revolution created by the luxury train. Lindblad has long been considered the top of the luxury tour business and has grown dramatically in the last twenty-five years. On the average, two Lindblad tours begin every day.

The family seems certain to keep up the business. Lars's son, Sven, has been getting extensive training in the travel field. He worked at a Kenya hotel for a while and now directs a Lindblad subsidiary company called Special Expeditions. It gives fewer but even more exotic tours than the parent company. Travelers can voyage among spawning whales or enjoy a spectacular two weeks in Tanzania during the height of the wildebeest migration on the Serengeti plains.

A different approach to exotic travel is taken by the Club Mediterranee and its two American subsidiaries, Club Med Inc. and Club Mediterranee of Colorado. Club Med is a French company that favors the *villages de vacances* system popular in France. These vacation villages are a sort of resort motel, featuring lots of people and some recreation. The French dislike regimentation, so vacationers in these villages can do or not do what they choose. Most of the French vacation villages are decidedly un-exotic, but from the beginning Club Med has favored unusual sites. It began in 1950 by establishing a village on the island of Majorca. By now it has grown to nearly 100 villages in 24 countries. Club Med itself does not own the villages, but it often has a minority share in them and manages them all. This method of financing permits the headquarters company in Paris to retain control without having to put up much money. The founder/owner is Gilbert Trigano. His son, Serge, heads the U.S. operations. In America, Club Med has gained a reputation for swinging singles vacations. This development alarms the company, for in France the vacation village system is very much family-oriented.

## LE PLUS CHIC BUILDING

**Auctioneer's price:** $55,000,000.
**Owner:** Donald John Trump.

Buildings seem too substantial to be chic. The presence of a building alters the physical landscape, while the presence of a chic thing affects the psychological setting. The difference is that if you ignore a building, you bang into a wall, while if you ignore what is chic the chic ignores you back. In deference to this distinction, we usually speak of "fashionable addresses" rather than fashionable buildings. Oh, maybe you could have a chic little boutique, but it took Donald J. Trump to achieve the chic skyscraper.

In New York City the most fashionable commercial address has long been Fifth Avenue, especially the ten blocks north of 50th Street. In 1975, however, the city's financial crisis led to a cutback in police services. The town pretty nearly quit investigating burglaries and it did quit the struggle to keep Fifth Avenue fashionable. Three-card monte hustlers began setting up their games in front of fancy jewelers and were not ordered to move along. Peddlers began displaying their merchandise on the sidewalk. Tourists were presented with the strange spectacle of $10,000 tiepins on display in the shop windows and cheap socks being hawked in the street. Previously travelers had had to go to Calcutta to see such a gross disparity in the distribution of wealth.

After some years had passed the chic set abandoned hope of ever having the street returned to them, yet all was not lost. Donald Trump put up a building that brings the fashionable addresses indoors. His Trump Tower, at Fifth Avenue and 56th Street, has a six-story atrium full of expensive shops and a private security service ready and willing to chase off anyone who tries to hustle a three-card monte game. If you drive your car into the wall, you will probably come to a halt, but the building does seek to be as insubstantial as anything 68 stories high can be. First, its facade is reflective glass. It is, let us pray, the last great tower of glass that will ever be built in Manhattan. More contemporary design is revealed around the corner, at the new AT&T building. Its stone wall shines with such physical beauty and substantial presence that the Trump Tower seems to wilt like a stepsister beside Cinderella.

It is inside that chic appears in an incarnation so powerful that a stylish address is transformed into a chic building. The doorman is dressed like one of the guards at Buckingham Palace. His red coat and bearskin hat (pith helmet in summer) is the most ostentatious idea since Richard Nixon put the White House guards into costumes reminiscent of the chorus in *The Student Prince*. Once inside you recognize the place as Fantasyland for the designer-label set. A pianist plays in a large, nearly empty entrance hall. The musicians used are members of the Peter Duchin Orchestra. And walls, magical peach-colored walls made from Breccia Perniche Italian marble, dominate the space and guard against any outside intrusion from reality. Water, at the far end of the atrium, is artfully splashing down the wall. Its six-story fall is over one-third of Niagara's height. Escalators take you up to the jewelers and ivory sculptures or down to the gourmet food and costly perfumes. Chic may appeal to a certain hollowness of soul, but there is nothing hollow about the pocketbooks of these tenants. The rents for the larger shops come to as much as $1,000,000 a year.

Above the atrium are offices, and above them, condominium apartments, each selling for over $1,000,000. The top-level triplex costs $10,000,000. In Texas ten million in cash buys you twenty-five square miles of grazing land. In Idaho it gets you a couple of large counties. In New York it buys three floors and a great view of the AT&T building. Not many people, except maybe Donald Trump himself, have that much money to waste.

Trump's father, Fred, built a lot of middle-class housing in Brooklyn, Staten Island, and Queens, decidedly un-chic addresses. He developed a lot of political contacts with the state's old-line Democrats. When Donald went to work he was expected to follow the practice of his father, but instead he used his family's political connections to plunge into midtown Manhattan.

The Trump Tower was built on land owned by the Equitable Life Assurance Society, which agreed to sell the land only if it had a strong voice in managing the project. Half of the company that was formed to build the tower is owned by Donald Trump and half by Equitable. The tower cost $185,000,000 to build. Enough of the condominiums have been sold for the company to have recovered its original investment and then some. It still owns the atrium and office space, property projected to earn rentals of $28,000,000 a year. (Note that word "projected." The rentals are not that high yet. Trump's pastor is the Reverend Dr. Norman Vincent Peale and this rental projection comes from positive thinking.) The auctioneer's price above is for the atrium and office space.

There are no other skyscrapers to compare with the Trump Tower. However, in Houston, to hear the locals talk, God has appeared in the form of a chic urban market called the Galleria. Designed by St. Louis architect Gyo Obata, this super-center (250 shops) has a massive interior mall covered by a skylight 150 yards long and 40 feet wide. A Galleria 2 and Galleria 3 have been added. The owner/developer is Gerald Hines. In 1967, when he announced the project, Hines was an ordinary-seeming salesman of air conditioners and automobiles, but somehow he raised the $40,000,000 his project needed.

## OIL OF OLAY

**Auctioneer's price:** $46,100,000.
**Owner:** Smith Richardson family.

At first glance the Olay Company appears to be part of some anonymously owned mega-giant, but first glances are what tell you the earth is flat. Olay is a subsidiary of the Vicks Toiletry Products Division in the enormous Richardson-Vicks corporation. This huge corporation is actually a family enterprise. The chairman of the board is Smith Richardson, Jr. On the board of directors is his son, Stuart Richardson, his brother, Randolph

Richardson, his first cousin Lunsford Richardson, Jr., and his uncle, Huger King. Their stock plus that of the family-controlled Smith Richardson Foundation comes to about a quarter of all the shares in the firm, quite enough to assure continuing control.

The Smith Richardson family, which has major branches in both Connecticut and North Carolina, has made a fortune from selling various forms of goo to be rubbed on the skin. Their success with Oil of Olay is typical. In 1970, before it came under Richardson direction, worldwide sales of the Olay group were under $13 million. Today, thanks to extensive marketing, its sales have risen to over $100 million.

Just what is Oil of Olay?—a mixture of water, fatty acids, and oils to be rubbed into the face in quest of beauty. Of course, it takes a lot of advertising to sell skin goo and all of the Olay company products—Oil of Olay, Olay Vitalizing Cream, Night of Olay cream—are promoted vigorously. It's this high cost of selling that has kept the auctioneer's price for the Olay Company lower than might have been expected.

Rubbing goo has been the basis of the Richardson family wealth ever since 1905, the year Lunsford Richardson began selling Vicks VapoRub, which he had developed for children's croup or colds. His company hit the big time at the end of World War I when a worldwide influenza pandemic struck. Between April and November of 1918, over 21 million people are believed to have died from the flu. The epidemic drove sales of the soothing ointment to the million dollar mark by 1918. When the plague had passed, its survivors looked at the miracle goo and said to themselves, "Hey, this stuff works." The Richardson fortune was made.

Along with VapoRub and the Olay product line, other skin goos offered by Richardson-Vicks include: Topex, Clearasil cream, Clearasil lotion, Clearasil soap, Clearasil cleanser, and Bacimycin ointment.

## GODIVA CHOCOLATIER

**Auctioneer's price:** $35,600,000.
**Owner:** J.T. Dorrance family.

Consumption for status becomes literal when we turn to Godiva Chocolatier. Here one actually eats the status symbol. How about a pound of chocolate-covered candies for $200? As a souvenir of your pleasurable snacking you can keep the hand-lacquered Russian box the candies came in. And it certainly gives the ho-ho to your less blessed friends who think feasting on lobster and champagne is the ultimate in lavish eating.

Godiva arrived in the United States in 1966. It came from Belgium, where the chocolate-candy-making process is the reverse of the American method. Here we traditionally take the inner core and wrap it in chocolate. This gives us a variety of tastes that range from Snickers bars to chocolate cherries to Reese's Pieces. In every instance the shape of the candy depends on the shape of the core. Chocolate-covered peanuts don't get mistaken for chocolate-dipped cherries.

The European method is to first shape the chocolate shell and then fill the centers. This approach limits the things that can go into the center, but permits a more artistic control over the candy's appearance. The candies can be sculpted to look like Michelangelo's statue of David or just about any other design.

When it comes to candies in a box, however, this technical distinction hardly matters. Soft-centered candy made either way looks pretty much alike. The taste depends on the recipes for the chocolate and the soft center. Godiva's recipe is fine, but the company is hardly alone in being able to make a splendid-tasting chocolate. When a pound of candies that would usually cost $5 sells for $17.50, the sweet smell of the chic put-down is surely in the air. Mae West once ended a scene by ordering the maid to "peel me a grape." If ever an item seemed targeted at the part of the audience that thought the request was reasonable, triply priced candy is it.

Godiva is a candy that advertises in *Architectural Digest*, in *The Smithsonian*, and in *Gourmet* magazine. For a while it even sold candies designed by Bill Blass. Do not look for it by the checkout counter at your drug store. It was first introduced in this country at Wanamaker's department store in Philadelphia, and department stores are still the primary outlet. There are some Godiva shops as well. Of course sales of the candy increase every year.

Strangely, Godiva is wholly owned by the Campbell Soup Company, 60 percent of which is still owned by the John Thompson Dorrance family. The original Dorrance had the decidedly un-chic idea of putting soups into cans and feeding the masses with something cheap and nutritious. It is hardly the idea behind Godiva's success, but times change. One sign of change is the increasing separation between management and ownership. Campbell Soup is now headed by J.T. Dorrance, Jr., grandson of the founder, but when he retires the Dorrance family will no longer lead the company, although their stockholding will continue. Another change has been diversification, the gradual expansion into lines quite unlike the original business. Godiva is one example. Another is Pepperidge Farm bread, a tasty bread priced well above the ordinary brands used for a soup-and-sandwich luncheon.

## THE BIGGEST DISCOUNT FURRIER

**Auctioneer's price:** $25,000,000.
**Owner:** Fred Schwartz.

You can't keep a good symbol down. In the bad old days when wives were seen as no more than mirrors reflecting their husbands' achievements, mink coats were the ultimate symbol in wifely success, marrying well. Today much of a woman's identity comes from her own accomplishments, but the symbols of that identity have not changed. As women are taking a firmer grip on their own lives, fur coats are becoming more visible. Once they were evening attire, to be worn only on those grand occasions when husbands showed off their wives, but today it is common to see coats worth thousands of dollars worn on ordinary afternoons by shoppers in Houston's Galleria, or along New York's Fifth Avenue, or even on the sunbaked sidewalks of North Rodeo Drive in Beverly Hills.

The businessman who has been most successful at taking advantage of this change has been Fred Schwartz, a.k.a. Fred the Furrier, owner of the Harfred Company. He saw that the improvement in women's status was going to bring a commensurate improvement in the sale of women's status symbols, and he began to move. While others were writing books about how the social change would bring a greening of our consciousness, Fred was gearing up to let the old consciousness be the greening of his wallet. In the mid-1970s television viewers were surprised to see ads for fur coats, costing thousands, aiming directly at women in the audience. Husbands are never mentioned, except sometimes indirectly, as in post-Christmas ads showing a woman weeping while Fred says, "Didn't get the fur coat you wanted? [Your cad of a male let you down!] Come in and buy one yourself."

Fred opened his first store in New York City, a reasonable location since the city accounts for about one-quarter of the nation's retail fur sales. More surprising was his location: Alexander's department store, a decidedly un-chic address. Alexander's strikes many customers as what Woolworth's would be if it were a department store; however, it is directly across the street from the more fashionable Bloomingdale's department store. The chic customers at Bloomingdale's can dash across the street for their discount fur. That's another of Fred's successes, lower cost. Fur coats persist as old-fashioned items of conspicuous consumption. They do not come with visible brand markings or alligator logos, so discount carries no disgrace.

## STEUBEN GLASS

**Auctioneer's price:** $9,400,000.
**Owner:** Houghton family.

In 1933 A.A. Houghton, Jr., became president of the Steuben Glass division at the Corning Glass Works. It seemed to him that they were overstocked in ornate crystal, so he took a lead pipe and smashed $100,000 worth of inventory. Even for a brash young man of 27, that sort of behavior requires an unusually strong sense of job security. But then if Houghton didn't have such a sense, who would?

The history of the Corning Glass Works reads like a history of royal France. After a while all those kings named Louis merge into one great and eternal Louis. So it is at Corning, where the fifth generation of the Houghton family is in charge. The company was founded in 1851 by Amory Houghton. It was A. Amory Houghton who smashed up the crystal. His cousin, Amory Houghton, was Corning's president at the time. In 1983, after nineteen years as chief executive, another Amory Houghton retired as Corning's chairman of the board and passed the mantle of leadership to his younger brother, James. (At least all the brothers aren't named Amory.)

Poring through old stacks of *Who's Who in America* doesn't help much in sorting out the Amorys. Oh, sure, there are different dates, but the content of each biography is astonishing in its regularity:

> *Amory,* born in Corning, N.Y. Education: St. Paul's prep school, Harvard College. Employment: Corning Glass Works. Married. Children—Amory.

Under one or another Amory's leadership, great things went on. The first electric light bulb was made, Pyrex was invented, and then came fiberglass, sunglasses that darken in the light, and fibers for laser communications.

When we talk about the Houghton family, we are talking tradition. They seem to step from the pages of a William Dean Howells novel as unabashed Yankees who believe in trade and have continued to believe in it for generation upon generation. There has not come that usual softening wherein one group of

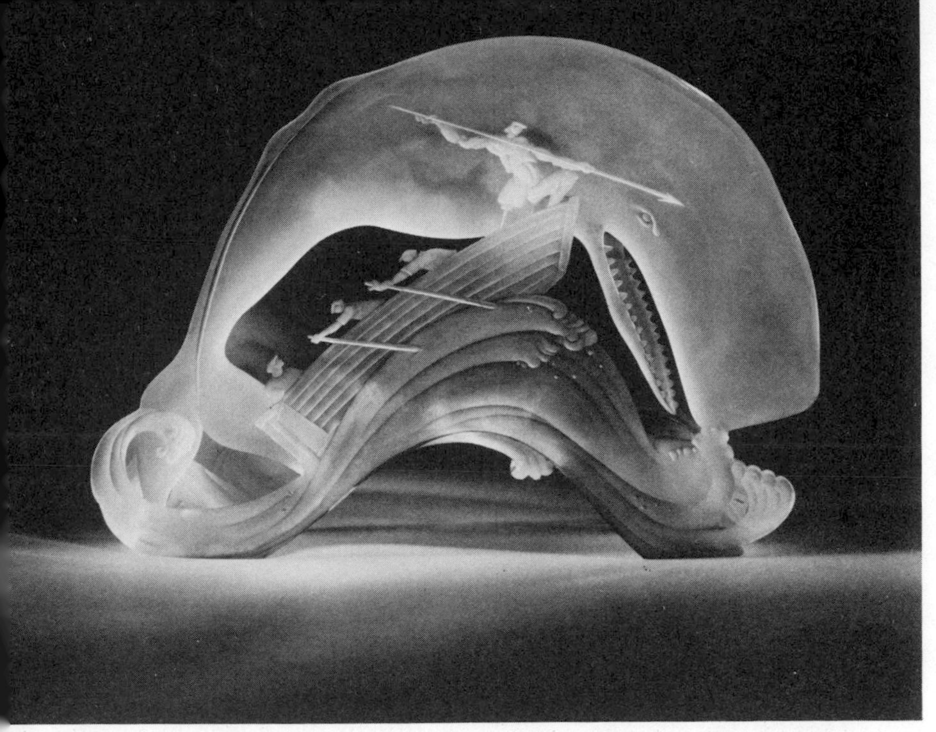

Moby Dick. Photo: Steuben Glass

Amorys decides to keep the money but assign the work to an overseer. A hundred and thirty-three years after the company's founding, Houghtons are still in control and still hold 30 percent of the stock.

Steuben Glass sells crystal. Some of it is practical—wine goblets and vases—but most of it is decorative. A small crystal scupture by David Pollard and Sidney Waugh, titled "Moby Dick," depicts harpooners in a dinghy beside an arching whale. Price: $18,200. This is the sort of knickknack Steuben Glass specializes in. It comes with no designer labels or logos etched in. Steuben shops have an atmosphere like a museum. There is a lot more browsing than buying. (The main store is in New York, on Fifth Avenue; display counters are found in a few department stores around the nation.) Such are the old-fashioned values of the Houghtons that the prestige of Steuben Glass is supposed to go to the company that sells the works rather than to the anonymous customers who buy them. Corning's annual sales are well over a billion dollars and Steuben contributes very little to that, but the family is proud to show off the grace and beauty of glass.

Attitudes like these are radically unlike the opinions of newer comers to the world of chic. A modern designer does not destroy $100,000 worth of merchandise on the grounds that it is junk. Yet A. Amory was able to keep his job and now, fifty years later, is the patriarch of the family. He is thought to be the richest Houghton of them all.

Another family enterprise whose cachet rests on quality rather than designer labels is L.L. Bean in Freeport, Maine. Leon Leonwood Bean started the store in 1912. His grandson now directs the operation, which specializes in sturdy outdoor wear at a fair price. Most customers know the company as a mail-order business; however, there is an actual store, which is open twenty-four hours a day, all year round. Even though it advertises in *The New Yorker,* Bean likes to deny that it is stylish. The denial is in keeping with their no-nonsense reputation; however, so chic has the Bean family's merchandise become that the temptation to flash their name seems nigh irresistible. For example, the world's most perfect piece of military technology, the Swiss army knife, can be bought in just about any hardware store, but L.L. Bean offers a chic model with their name clearly marked on the side.

## A PRESIDENTIAL YACHT

**Auctioneer's price:** $850,000.
**Owner:** Richard W. Arendsee.

It used to be that presidents had the use of several yachts. The last ship to achieve prominence was the *Sequoia*, a yacht available to every president from Calvin Coolidge to Jimmy Carter. For most of that time presidential yachts were about as controversial as the flag and the deepest fretting they provoked concerned their ability to withstand any tempests that might torment the Potomac River. During the latter days of the Watergate scandal, however, when the public was so angry with Richard Nixon that it would have begrudged him an extra ply in his toilet paper, the *Sequoia* suddenly became one more symbol of gross presidential privilege. As a way of demonstrating that he was not one to glory in the comforts of his office, Jimmy Carter sold the *Sequoia* shortly after his inauguration.

In 1981 the yacht was bought by Richard Arendsee, one of those confident Californians who had a fortune well in hand before he was beyond his thirties. He is president of Four Winds Enterprises, a moving company that ships household goods around the world. It does a lot of business with the State Department and earned merits for its efficiency in helping move American goods out of Iran when the revolution broke there. Getting rich from moving vans is hardly the most glamorous route to wealth, but riches is riches.

Arendsee's initial plan was to lease the yacht to a trust, thereby recouping his $1,100,000 investment, paying for the ship's upkeep, and maybe even getting back a little interest.

The former *Honey-Fitz*. Photo: Courtesy of Joseph Keating

Arendsee calculated that he needed a syndicate of fifty members, but the purchase has not gone as well as he hoped. Word got back to Arendsee that Ronald Reagan would not use the *Sequoia*. It is one thing for the president to eat off plates donated by rich friends, but riding on the *Sequoia* is much more public. It gives the other side too easy a debating point if, after a hard day of cutting benefits to the poor and middle-class, the president relaxes on his yacht. The presidential thanks-but-no-thanks reduced interest in becoming a dues-paying member of the Presidential Yacht Trust. Arendsee now hopes to find maybe ten members for the syndicate. Meanwhile docking and maintenance expenses continue.

Adding to Arendsee's woes is the fact that the *Sequoia* is not the most famous of the presidential yachts. The best-known one was the *Honey-Fitz*, used by President John Kennedy and his family. During JFK's brief presidency the newspapers carried many pictures of the president, Jackie, Caroline, and other members of the Kennedy clan relaxing aboard the yacht. When Lyndon Johnson became president he kept the old name, saying he would no more think of renaming the *Honey-Fitz* than he would the Washington Monument. Nixon called the yacht the *Patricia*, but the ship's association with the Kennedy years was too strong and he had it sold. Only then did the *Sequoia* become the primary presidential yacht.

In 1970, when Nixon sold it off, the *Honey-Fitz* was bought by Joseph Keating, owner of a combination restaurant/theater in Greenwich, Connecticut, called the Showboat Inn. The *Honey-Fitz*, now renamed *The Presidents*, is used primarily for private family sailing, but is also available for charter. The ship is decorated with photos of the Kennedy family enjoying the yacht, recalling a time when scenes of the president relaxing in costly splendor seemed a natural part of America's bounty.

# 4
# SPORTING ITEMS

## THE BEST-SELLING RUNNING SHOES

**Auctioneer's price:** $419,000,000.
**Owner:** Philip H. Knight.

In 1964 an accountant named Phil Knight and his college running coach, Bill Bowerman, started a track shoe company and sold 1,300 pairs of shoes, all of them imported from Japan. In 1983 the company, by then called Nike, sold 46,000,000 pairs; it was the best-selling brand of athletic shoes in the country.

The boldness of that initial investment is hard to imagine today when so many brands and styles of running sneakers are available, but in the 1960s the athletic shoe market was dominated by one German firm, Adidas, and the mass market was controlled by U.S. Keds. Shoe design was so standard that when you boasted to the kid next door you'd just gotten new sneakers the only reply was, "Did you get the low ones or the high ones?"

Knight and Bowerman went after Adidas. Bowerman had several thoughts about shoe improvement—essentially making shoes lighter and more springy—and he persuaded the Japanese supplier to use some of his ideas. The improvements did bring customers. The new shoe's light nylon material was snug without feeling tight. In styling, the nylon Nike was pretty much like any other low-cut tennis shoe, but on the foot it felt radically more comfortable. Of course other shoe manufacturers were able to switch from canvas to nylon as easily as Nike and the established companies expected to keep their marketing lead.

Then, quite unexpectedly, the sales of all running equipment expanded like gas released into a vacuum. The growing jogging market gave Phil Knight the opportunity to show his business smarts. He began giving his shoes away. At the trials for the 1972 Olympic team Knight gave his shoes free to any runner who would take them. This kind of promotion is still Nike's chief form of advertising. The athletes have wised up, however, and are paid to wear Nike products.

The greatest victim of Knight's promotions was Keds. Their strength had been familiarity, too airy a quality to survive a revolution. Joggers wanted "real" running shoes, not that canvas kid stuff. As Keds' prestige faded, people who wanted sneakers for leisure also bought the newer styles. Nike's low prices and photos of athletes in Nike shoes sent Keds to the guillotine.

Like many a revolutionary, Nike has found that it must work thrice as hard to hold even a third of the loyalty once given the old king. When you get right down to it, shoes are pretty much shoes, so in 1980 Nike established a new promotional project, called the Sport Research Laboratory, at Exeter, New Hampshire. Nike has been the leader in creating a new field, one that might be called advertising science.

Advertising science uses real equipment, relies on classical theories and experimental controls, and makes precise measurements, but the point of the work is to impress consumers. The "research" permits shoes to be as trendy as the fins on a '57 Cadillac while letting customers believe they are shopping rationally.

Advertising science neither seeks nor is likely to find new knowledge. Its characteristics are:

- *Masses of data that illustrate old principles.* Thus a Nike research article, "Biomechanics Research and Running Shoe Selection," by Tom Clarke, Ph.D., is full of charts, diagrams, and highfalutin words to report that "A thicker midsole/wedge combination in any given material will

Photo: All-Sport Photographic, Ltd.

provide more cushioning." Surely Aristotle, or at least Aristotle's cobbler, knew that.

- *New polysyllables to name old phenomena.* Newton's laws of motion imply that anything, including a leg, will have a tendency to buckle slightly every time it strikes the ground. We know the theory is correct because people with weak ankles and athletes whose footing cannot always be guaranteed need tight ankle support, hence the old-style sneaker known as "the high ones." Advertising science pretends such knowledge is brand-new. Nike coined a word for the phenomenon—*pronation*—and produced "laboratory evidence" (slow-motion movies) that confirmed the continued relevance of Newton's laws.
- *Fast results.* It can take decades for a major discovery at Bell Labs to find its way into the average home phone, but only two and one-half years after opening its "laboratory" Nike boasted that, thanks to research, "every performance shoe in our line has either been replaced or dramatically improved in the last two years."

While advertising science does not bother with many hypotheses, it brings in more money than Einstein ever saw. Phil Knight is chairman of the board at Nike, Inc., and continues to own nearly half the stock. A rule of thumb says you can't become a billionaire before age 70 unless you're worth more than $250,000,000 by the time you are 50. Knight has four more years to his fiftieth birthday and has already passed the benchmark.

And you thought running was just another fad.

## THE MOST FREQUENTLY SUED FOOTBALL TEAM

**Auctioneer's price:** $53,000,000.
**Owner:** Allen Davis.

Most of organized sport is low on prestige, constitutionally unstable, and profitable only to those who scramble hard and don't mind gouging eyes. But some sports, and professional football is tops among them, are fat, conservative, and opposed to all boat rocking. Yet even in the most conservative institutions there is always at least one member who is continually alert to his own opportunities and is unwilling to stifle them in the name of the general calm. If you want to find one of these upstarts, the easiest way might be to wait by the courthouse steps until a party to a lawsuit comes along.

Using the courthouse method, it wouldn't be long before you noticed Al Davis, owner of the Los Angeles, or maybe Oakland, Raiders. He and his club have been sued by the city of Oakland, sued by the National Football League, and sued by his senior partner. Davis has fought back by countersuing the league. Most maddening to the organizational regulars is the way Davis wins in court and his team wins on the field. In January 1984, after years of courtroom triumphs over league rivals, Davis's team won the Super Bowl.

Most owners see the National Football League as fat cat heaven. The money from television comes in automatically. The players' union is as tame as a tabby, not at all like the radical state found over in baseball. But Al Davis is different; he wants more and he knows how to get it.

Another of Davis's distinguishing qualities is that he understands the game of football. He started at age 21 as assistant coach at Adelphi. A few years later he entered pro ball briefly as a scout for the Baltimore Colts. Then he was a line coach at The Citadel, followed by a similar position at the University of Southern California. Shortly after he turned 30 he switched permanently to pro ball. He was assistant coach for the San Diego Chargers and was then hired as general manager and head coach for the Oakland Raiders. While he was working on the college level Davis had a reputation for sharp play, bending rules as far as the referees would let him. The Chargers' head coach, Sid Gilman, had a similar reputation and Davis was thought to be learning a trick or two for his repertoire. So when Oakland hired Davis to take charge of their program, they were not hiring just another aggressive coach.

For most coaches, reaching the level of head coach and general manager is the pinnacle of their ambition, but Davis kept rising. In 1966 he was commissioner of the American Football League (AFL). He held that post for only two months, but it was a historic period since during that time the AFL agreed to a merger with the National Football League.

Most striking was Davis's rise in the Oakland ownership. The Raiders were part of the new AFL and when Davis arrived the team was losing games and money. The ownership was changed. Davis got 10 percent while another 40 percent went to Wayne Valley, a San Francisco real estate developer. Another developer, named Ed McGah, also joined the partnership. Valley was the major owner and had the respect of other club owners, but he was outfoxed. Suddenly he learned that McGah and Davis had signed a contract making Davis "managing general partner" in charge of the club. Valley then made the mistake of his football life by taking the issue to court. Davis pushes on the rules, but when it comes time for a judgment he wins. Valley suffered a worse loss than he had supposed possible and was forced out of the ownership. McGah and Davis took control, with Davis as senior partner and chief executive officer of the Raiders.

The owners of other clubs were taken aback by Davis's coup, but they thought that now Davis had climbed to the top of his ambition. After all, what else could he conquer? Then Davis announced unilaterally that he was moving his club to Los Angeles. Previously the owners had all thought league approval was necessary before any one of them could do something so dramatic, but Davis is not the sort who goes hat in hand to ask, "Is it okay, guys?"

This time Davis took on two enemies. The city of Oakland tried to prevent the departure by seizing the team. The National Football League sought to block the move by forcing the team into receivership. The tangled struggle moved to the courts and still has not been fully resolved, but Davis has been winning and the team is now in Los Angeles. In the process Davis won an antitrust suit against the league and he, in partnership with the Los Angeles stadium company, was awarded $49 million in damages and penalties.

To league loyalists the monetary loss is less alarming than the power the antitrust decision gives owners. Each one is now free to pursue his individual opportunities as he sees fit. This kind of laissez-faire approach to business may be loved on the editorial pages of the *Wall Street Journal*, but it rocks a lot of boats. It also guarantees that Davis's ambition is not done. Contented members of society never love freedom the way malcontents do. Freedom brings novelty and the opportunity for change. What do satisfied people want with such things? Davis is a malcontent who has found himself a lot of freedom by going to court so often and winning all the time. What comfortable aspect of football is his jaundiced eye examining now?

## THE MOST POPULAR BASEBALL TEAM

**Auctioneer's price:** $45,000,000.
**Owner:** Peter O'Malley.

Without doubt the most popular ball club is the Los Angeles Dodgers. Their 1982 attendance was 3,608,881, a major league record. 1983 was nearly as big: 3,510,313. Dodger attendance is number one every year. The team is also popular on the road, consistently found among the top three teams in away-game attendance. In baseball, unlike football, gate receipts are still a team's principal source of income, so building fans' interest has long been important to investors.

Historically, Dodger owners have pioneered many ways to increase the money squeezed from a baseball team.

***Item:*** Larry McPhail: the man who introduced night games to the major leagues, takes charge of the Brooklyn Dodgers and puts the team under lights. Attendance rises.

***Item:*** Larry MacPhail then makes the Dodgers the first team ever to have all its games—home and away—broadcast by radio. Attendance rises.

***Item:*** New Dodger owner Branch Rickey seeks to increase the team's popularity by making it a winner. He breaks baseball's whites-only rule and signs Jackie Robinson. Often described as a noble and generous deed, the signing also helps establish Brooklyn as a winning dynasty. Attendance rises.

***Item:*** Yet another Dodger owner, Walter O'Malley, is making a profit in Brooklyn. He sees a chance to make even more millions on the West Coast and in 1958 moves the Dodgers to Los Angeles. Megabucks prove more common than dandelions out there and the team becomes the most valuable one in baseball.

Thus the pursuit of profits has kept the Dodgers intimately involved in most of the great major league developments. Night games, regular broadcasts, black stars, and nationwide distribution of the teams have made big league ball accessible to the whole country. It's enough to make a fellow suspect that keeping an eye on one's financial interests really does promote the social good.

The present Dodgers owner is Walter's son and heir, Peter O'Malley. He has all the charisma of a celery stick, but Peter is a good baseball man. The Dodgers have been in the O'Malley family since 1951 and they have always been contenders, often champions.

A few years ago there were many teams with long traditions of family ownership. Now there are only Los Angeles and three others:

- Jean Yawkey, president of the Boston Red Sox, is the widow of Tom Yawkey, Bosox owner from 1933 until his death in 1976.

- Dan Galbreath of the Pittsburgh Pirates took over the team from his father, John. This family is the richest of the baseball owners and, after Lamar Hunt, probably the richest in American sports. The John W. Galbreath Company (based in Columbus, Ohio) is consistently listed as one of America's ten largest construction firms.
- Calvin Griffith inherited the Minnesota Twins from Clark Griffith, one of the founders of the American League. Griffith may be the owner of baseball's least popular team. This title fluctuates from year to year, but the Twins seldom have many attendees.

## THE RACING FORM

**Auctioneer's price:** $35,000,000.
**Owner:** Walter Annenberg.

Anybody who doesn't think public advantages fall to the male side of the species should look to the heirs of Moses Annenberg. Six of them are living—five daughters and one son—and all received equal parts of their father's fortune, but only the son is known to the public. Even within the family it's the man, Walter, who casts all the votes on how the family's wholly owned company, Triangle Publications, will operate.

Recently many of the family holdings have been sold for cash. The newspapers that made Moses Annenberg rich—the *Philadelphia News* and the *Philadelphia Inquirer*—were sold ($55,000,000). A series of radio, television, and cable broadcast companies were also sold ($137,000,000). Even split six ways that works out to a lot of millions per heir and the surviving bits of Triangle Publications still have an auctioneer's total price of about $400,000,000.

So the publisher of *The Daily Racing Form* is hardly some poor racetrack tout. There are plenty of racing fans who understand that in order to throw their money away wisely they must study the field, learn the past performance records of the horses, check out the breeding, and evaluate the jockeys and the trainers. In order to help these people lose money the old-fashioned way, the *Racing Form* gives them plenty of information. Daily circulation is 93,172 copies and there are four regional editions (Chicago, Los Angeles, New York, and Toronto).

Most people do not think of the *Racing Form* as exactly presidential-level reading material, nor are Walter Annenberg's other publications much more profound. (The others are *Seventeen* and *TV Guide* [q.v.].) One of the original sources of Moses Annenberg's income was a racing wire service that reported the results at tracks around the country. Anybody who was interested could sign up for the service, but a lot of people who did were suspected of being bookies. Of course, many cynics suspect that businessmen who provide services to organized criminals are themselves a bit shady. As a result, the original Annenberg money has always seemed tainted.

Yet Annenberg's money piles to the sky and his companionship has been eagerly sought by presidents. Richard Nixon made him ambassador to the Court of St. James and Ronald Reagan made his wife, Leonore, chief of protocol at the State Department. Annenberg's palace, called Sunnylands, in Rancho Mirage, California, is an especially popular stopping place for bigwigs. In the last days of Watergate, President Nixon went out there to contemplate his ruin. After his election Reagan visited the Annenberg estate to rest and escape the gaze of the crowd. Prince Charles has stayed there. Frank Sinatra got married there. When the Shah fled Iran for the last time, a jar of Iranian soil in his pocket, Annenberg offered him a job as permanent guest in Rancho Mirage.

Annenberg is not shy about making contributions to laudable institutions. When his old prep school (Peddie School in Hightstown, New Jersey) announced a $3.5 million fund-raising drive, he got them off to a good start by giving the first million. The Metropolitan Museum of Art in New York City needed money; he had two million for them. Public broadcasting had a plan in mind and got a $150,000,000 grubstake from Annenberg.

The contradictions of his history make Annenberg a hard man to classify. Much of his father's money came from racetrack sources. Walter continues to publish the *Daily Racing Form*, but is not part of the bookie world. His loyalty to his friends may be admirable, but his friendships with controversial figures such as Sinatra, Richard Nixon, and the Shah of Iran make many people wonder. Yet ultimately observers keep coming to the same conclusion: Annenberg is rich but honorable. He does not blab the secrets that come his way. He does not get caught up in the sins of his companions. Wealthy, conservative, tight-lipped—sounds like just the sort of fellow likely to be courted by presidents and other people who know secrets and have a perpetual need for money.

The other important sports newspaper in America is *The Sporting News*, weekly circulation over 400,000 copies. For most of its history this weekly paper was primarily interested in baseball and even today, baseball season or no, every issue still carries news of each major league team. The Sporting News Company also publishes a number of annual directories for baseball, basketball, football, and hockey, enabling fans to get all the statistics they are likely to want about the players, the teams, and the championship tourneys.

The *Sporting News* was founded and perpetuated by the Spink family of St. Louis, but is now part of the Times-Mirror chain, publisher of the *Los Angeles Times*, and one of America's largest media businesses with eight daily newspapers, seven television stations, and seven magazines. Its chairman is Otis Chandler and the Chandler family owns 30 percent of the corporation's stock.

## A SKI RESORT

**Auctioneer's price:** $28,000,000.
**Owner:** Dave McCoy.

It is easy to advise people to get in on the ground floor of something that is going to be big, but it is not so easy to do. Certainly Dave McCoy had no reason to think he was getting in on something when he came to California's High Sierra in 1928. More likely he thought he was getting away from everything. Los Angeles was the nearest city of size and it was 300 miles away. (Today people say it's "only" six hours away by car.) The mountains offered some climbing opportunities, but because of a peculiarity of topography this part of the Sierra gets more snow than the rest of the mountains and is snowed under for most of the year. Of course the snow makes for great skiing, but back then skiing was chiefly a European sport. So in 1937, when McCoy began a skiing business on Mammoth Mountain, he would have needed access to a time machine to suppose he was getting in early on a burgeoning sport.

Today Mammoth Mountain regularly sees 20,000 visitors on a single day. It boasts the longest season for a major resort, stretching from November to July, and it gets about 1.5 million visitors annually. A chairlift was installed in the mid-1950s. Now over twenty lifts are needed and each of them pulls in about a million dollars' worth of ticket sales per year. Lots of hotels, restaurants, and supply shops have opened up, but McCoy is the man with the lifts. He can handle 25,000 people in an hour.

Mammoth Mountain is 11,053 feet high and offers a great variety of slopes for beginning, intermediate, and expert skiers. Its downhill race course drops almost 3,000 feet. Over half of the ski area is above timberline, making it easy for the better skiers to strike out on routes of their own. The weather is nearly perfect. The mountain averages 600 inches of snow per year and during the long season 80 percent of the days are sunny. Los Angeles skiers regularly drive by the many resorts that ring their city and spend the weekend at Mammoth Mountain Ski Area.

The blossoming of Los Angeles, skiing, and money to burn have made McCoy a rich man in his old age.

Entrepreneurs on the East Coast said to themselves that if they couldn't get in on the ground floor of the ski boom, they could still squeeze in someplace. The East doesn't have mountains that poke far above the timberline, doesn't have sunshiny winters, and doesn't have 50 feet of snow, but it does have plenty of people who, with a little encouragement, can rise to the level of customers. Hamburg Mountain in New Jersey is about 90 miles from Philadelphia and 50 miles from New York, so its convenience was bound to catch the eye of somebody interested in turning skiing's popularity into ready cash. Snow cannot be counted on, but if the weather stays cold, ski trails can be covered with up to three feet of artificial snow in two weeks. Normally this capacity is enough to permit a ski season that lasts from Thanksgiving to the vernal equinox in March.

The Great American Recreation Corporation operates two adjacent ski resorts—Vernon Valley and Great Gorge—on Hamburg Mountain. The season is half the length of Mammoth Mountain's and attracts about a quarter of the business. The difference in the spirit of the two operations is shown by the owner of the eastern resorts, Gene Mulvihill. He is chairman of the board and holder of slightly more than 40 percent of the stock. Mulvihill is a deal cutter, mainly interested in ranching, real estate, and securities. There is nothing of the grizzled mountain man who began with one tow rope here; how could there be in New Jersey? But even here the cash register sings its recurring song.

## SECRETARIAT

**Auctioneer's price:** $12,900,000.
**Owners:** Penny Tweedy and syndicate.

The story of Secretariat's spermatozoa can be viewed in two ways. From one angle, it literally saved the farm of owner Penny Tweedy. From the other, it deprived sports fans of the pleasure of watching a great athlete perform. The 1973 Belmont Stakes, which Secretariat won by thirty-one lengths, was so great a victory that even people who detest horse racing were moved. TV news still shows that bit of film at least once a year, but never again was anybody able to watch Secretariat run. He was worth far more as a stud animal than as a racer. Baseball fans yell when players earn a fortune while continuing to play, but racing fans are so accustomed to seeing the best horses retire just as they approach their prime that the disappearance of Secretariat was greeted only by shrugs and a few smutty jokes.

Secretariat was a business saver for Helen "Penny" Chenery Tweedy. Her father, Christopher Chenery, died early in 1973 and the inheritance tax was so steep Mrs. Tweedy thought she was going to have to sell the stable. She avoided that fate by forming stud syndicates worth a total of over $11,000,000 on her two greatest horses—Secretariat and Riva Ridge (winner of the 1972 Kentucky Derby). Thanks to their stud value, the taxes were paid and the farm was saved.

The Chenery farm (i.e., Mrs. Tweedy) retained five free shares in Secretariat. Claiborn Farm, Inc. (where Secretariat was bred), got four shares, and one free share went to Secretariat's trainer, Lucien Laurien. Twenty-seven other shares were sold at $200,000 apiece. The list of original buyers contains the top names in international racing.

**Brand-name millionaires:** Mrs. Allaire duPont; Paul Mellon; Bertram R. Firestone; Alfred Gwynne Vanderbilt; Ogden Phipps. (Phipps, descended from Andrew Carnegie's partner, Henry Phipps, was the owner of Secretariat's sire, Bold Ruler. Before Secretariat was born Phipps flipped a coin with Chenery to determine if the foal would go to the owner of the sire or the mare. Phipps lost. . . . Mrs. duPont was the owner of Kelso, racing's greatest winner. He was a gelding and so never quit running.)

**Heirs to huge fortunes:** Richard and Diana Stokes (wife is the heir to the Band-Aid billions); William M. McKnight (3-M); Mr. and Mrs. Paul Hexter (Hertz); George Strawbridge (Campbell soup); Dan Lasater (Ponderosa Steak Houses).

**Horse breeders:** Dr. William Lockridge; Walter Salmon, Jr.; E.V. Benjamin, Jr.; Milton Dance; William Farish III; Warner L. Jones; J.B. Faulconer and Hilary Boone; Richard Brooks; Howard and Charles Gilman; F. Eugene Dixon.

**International set:** Buyers from Japan (Zenya Yoshida; Tadao Tamashima), Canada (E.P. Taylor, Jean-Louis Levesque), Ireland (Captain Timothy Rodgers), Switzerland (Walter Haefner), and Britain (Jonathan Irving).

It might seem odd that eleven years after being set out to stud Secretariat's price has doubled (he was initially valued at $6,080,000), but while he has grown older stud prices have gone mad. The 1977 Triple Crown winner, Seattle Slew, was syndicated for $12 million. Affirmed, the 1978 Triple Crown winner, went for over $14 million. The 1979 Kentucky Derby winner, Spectacular Bid, brought $22 million. In 1983 Devil's Bag was syndicated for $36 million before he entered a single important race. A crash in the price of horseflesh has been predicted for years, but inflation among the wealthy is growing and no effort is being made to reverse it. There is no real evidence that the collapse is at hand. Secretariat is one of the two or three greatest Thoroughbreds that ever lived, and if he were just going into stud present rates suggest that his auctioneer's price would surpass $40 million.

## BASKETBALL TEAM OF BRIGHT STARS

**Auctioneer's price:** $12,400,000.
**Owner:** Harold Katz.

There are a few athletes whose ability and style transcend their sport. Not many trigger the worldwide admiration that Muhammad Ali inspired, but news of exceptional talent does spread. You don't have to be a baseball fan to know about Reggie Jackson or a golfer to know of Arnold Palmer. These larger-than-their-sport athletes draw new attention to their field and expand its prestige. All sports benefit from these heroes, but some need them more than others. The team sport most sensitive to the presence of legends is probably basketball.

The potential for great enthusiasm over basketball seems always present. Almost every American plays the game while growing up and understands the sport and its challenges, yet pro basketball is never as popular as this backyard play suggests. Interest does spread when a super-player emerges. Wilt Chamberlain's name was well known far beyond basketball circles and during their dynasty days the reputation of the Boston Celtics also extended deep into the world of non-fans.

Today's basketball team with the legendary names is the Philadelphia Seventy Sixers. The name of its star forward, Julius "Dr. J" Erving, is well known to many people who never follow basketball. The source of Dr. J's charisma is the sense he exudes of being in control. His original nickname, "The Doctor," spread when people said in anticipation of the evening's game, "The Doctor will be in and he's going to operate." His sense of command, more than statistics, is what brought Dr. J to people's notice. Fans speak of him as a dancer. They say he can leap from the foul line and dunk the ball. They speak of his perfectly proportioned basketball player's body. With qualities like that, even in the twilight of his career, he can move the non-fan by his play.

The other established legend on the team is Moses Malone, the 76ers center who is in his prime right now. He came to Philadelphia from Houston and, not coincidentally, after years of only coming close, the 76ers promptly snared a championship.

Malone originally came to the attention of the general public in 1974 when he became the first person signed straight out of high school to a professional basketball contract. From the outcry that followed one would have thought America was a society that, above all material things, loved education for its own sake. Television commentators shook their heads ruefully. What's this country coming to, they asked with straight faces, when its young men would rather sign a $3,000,000 contract than pursue a college degree?

The team's owner, Harold Katz, is another college-avoiding millionaire. He is a long-time basketball fan and claims to have played against Wilt Chamberlain when he was a high school student. Katz bought the 76ers in 1981, ten years after he started Nutri/System, a national chain of franchised weight loss centers. Customers sign up to lose a specific amount of weight and then come to the centers to obtain measured meals containing a specified number of calories. The food is taken home to be prepared and eaten.

Katz grew up in a rough neighborhood of South Philadelphia and for a while worked in his father's grocery store. Then he struck out on his own and was a millionaire by age 35. That sort of accomplishment generally brings congratulations, but lately he has lost a bit of the glow on his halo. The dispute is not with customers, but franchise holders. Some franchisees filed suit, claiming that Katz is exploiting them. Some stockholders also filed suit, claiming he used his inside information to dump some stock before it was generally known that Nutri/System had hit hard times. Of course being sued is a long way from being guilty. As Jack Kennedy said, "Where there's smoke, there is often a smoke-making machine."

## AMERICA'S OLDEST HOCKEY TEAM

**Auctioneer's price:** $11,000,000.
**Owner:** Jacobs family.

Despite the Canadian domination of the playing side of hockey, the United States was first to make money on the sport. The world's first professional hockey team was the Portage Lakers, who played in Houghton, Michigan, in 1903. Houghton is on a finger of land stretching into Lake Superior toward Canada. Its players were Canadians and Canada soon responded by forming professional teams of its own. Thus, from the start, pro hockey encountered the tensions that still hold it. The great players and fans are in Canada. The money is in the U.S.

The first American teams were short-lived affairs. During the days when Woodrow Wilson was president, professional hockey appeared briefly in the American Northwest. The Portland [Oregon] Rosebuds and the Seattle Metropolitans are well remembered by hockey historians, but not by anybody else. The year 1924 saw the formation of an American hockey team that is still alive today; they were the Boston Bruins, created when Canada's National Hockey League expanded to the U.S. Two other teams are almost as old: in 1925 came the Detroit Red Wings (originally called the Cougars) and Chicago Black Hawks.

The original Bruins' franchise cost only $15,000, but the owner, Charles Francis Adams, spent $300,000 buying the players of the defunct Pacific Hockey Association. That sale showed one of the subtleties of property. The Pacific league sold what it did not own. Its contracts had no restrictive clauses and the players could have negotiated with whomever they wished. Or Adams could have approached the players individually and signed them up as free agents. But the issue never arose. When nobody seems inclined to challenge a claim, a person effectively owns whatever he says he owns. The results of Adams's purchase were as tidy and conclusive as if the old league had actually had the right to sell its players.

The Adams family held onto the Bruins for three generations before selling out (in 1973) to a TV station. Even after the sale the team president was still an Adams. In 1975, however, the station sold the Bruins to SportSystem, a private corporation wholly owned by the Lou Jacobs family in Buffalo, New York. SportSystem's wealth is based on obtaining food concessions at stadiums and although that line of trade may sound trivial, SportSystem is one of the largest food companies in America.

The founder of the family fortune was Lou Jacobs, a man whose reputation has undergone many changes. At the time of his death in 1968 *The Sporting News* recommended that he be honored with a special plaque in baseball's Hall of Fame. He had helped finance many teams during times of economic troubles. After his death, however, news began to spread that Jacobs had gangland contacts going back many decades. *Sports Illustrated* ran a cover story about him titled "The Godfather of Sports." Along with financing baseball teams he was said to have loaned money to organized crime bosses. He was also said to have secretly financed a Las Vegas casino and to have skimmed money from its coffers. He died before those charges were brought, but several of his alleged partners were convicted of the charge.

That scandal, which was publicized by a Congressional investigative committee, gave the Jacobs family business quite a bad reputation. The name of the family's holding company was changed from Emprise to Delaware North Companies (SportSystem is owned by Delaware North, which in turn is wholly owned by the Jacobses.) The sons and their lawyers insist that they shouldn't be tarred with the sins of their father's old company and that Delaware North should not be blamed for what Emprise did. Apparently the other owners of teams in the National Hockey League agreed, since they had the power to block the sale of the Bruins and chose to be silent.

## SPORTS STATISTICS DATA BANK

**Auctioneer's price:** $4,000,000.
**Owner:** Seymour Siwoff.

The computer tapes, ledgers, cabinets, and scrapbooks of the Elias Sports Bureau contain the data that intrigues more Americans than any other set of figures. This small company in midtown Manhattan maintains the official records for baseball's National League, the National Football League, and the National Basketball Association. It also compiles statistics for sporting awards such as the Seagram's Seven Crowns of Sport and it makes the calculations that rank baseball's free agents. Even if it lost all that business this afternoon, the Elias bureau would still be worth a lot of money because of its data bank. Its records include:

Accounts of every major league baseball game played since 1916.

Official scorecards of all games in all three of the leagues it serves as official statistician.

Files on baseball, football, basketball, hockey, golf, tennis, and horse racing.

Computer programs for rating and ranking players according to the most reliable statistical standards in the business.

Naturally, much of America would like a peek at that data. A lot of it is published annually in the official record books of the various sports, but people want more. They call every day to settle bets. (No soap.) Representatives of computer magazines and data networks call almost as often; they want to plug into the bureau's data banks. They too are turned away.

The bureau's owner, Seymour Siwoff, has one thing to sell—accurate, complete information. Thanks to small computers, analyzing sports statistics has become a cottage industry, but Siwoff is the man with the full data. Others have to rely on newspaper box scores for the current figures and encyclopedias for the older stuff, a weakness that shows up in their work.

Possession of the data bank imposes a strong conservative ethic. Instead of trying to find clever new ways to analyze the figures, the staff at Elias devotes its energy to making sure its numbers are correct. Siwoff began as an accountant and has an accountant's suspicion of statistical tables. Accountants know too well how easy it is to turn a set of numbers into a coherent fantasy world. "Figures never lie," says Siwoff, "but figurists . . ." and his voice breaks off in a prudent chuckle. Although the Elias bureau does some fancy calculating of its own, its standards in every sport are the old statistics—batting averages in baseball, yards gained in football, and points scored in basketball.

Siwoff has owned the bureau since 1952 when he bought it from the estate of the Elias brothers. He has been associated with the firm even longer; he began working there as a part-time employee while he was a student at St. John's University. Most of his own employees are also young part-timers.

## LEISURE-TIME SPORTS PALACE

**Auctioneer's price:** $3,150,000.
**Owners:** Hunt brothers.

As a class, billionaires do not seek the limelight, but their money and ambition sometimes thrust notoriety on them. Thus the Hunt brothers—Nelson Bunker, William Herbert, and Lamar—gained national prominence when they tried to corner the silver market. For one brief spooky moment it looked as though the Hunts were going to force the commodities exchange into bankruptcy, but the Federal Reserve Board came to the rescue. Many a small investor was ruined in that game, but there is a saying in finance, "Owe the bank a thousand dollars and the bank owns you; owe the bank a million dollars and you own the bank." In the Hunts' case they were over a billion dollars in debt, so they owned the bank regulators too. If they had been allowed to fail, chaos would have spread through many veins of the economy, so they were not allowed to fail. Even today the Hunt family is worth over $4,000,000,000.

Typical of the unexpected little places that would have toppled with the Hunts' ruin is the Bronco Bowl leisure palace in Dallas. Lamar, Bunker, and William built the place in 1961. It is a conglomerate offering a golf driving range, baseball batting cages, and a 72-lane bowling alley. There is also a large theater, an arcade game room, a pro shop, and a beauty salon. The latter, of course, is for the wives to use while their husbands are playing. The Hunts are not leaders in social experimentation.

This kind of investment is most typical of Lamar. All three brothers like to invest in real estate, but Lamar likes sports. He founded the American Football League and World Championship Tennis, Inc. He owns the Kansas City (football) Chiefs and the Dallas Tornadoes soccer team. Lamar himself is no athlete and it often surprises people to see a no-nonsense businessman devoting so much time to sports. The surprise comes from a naive assumption that sports is fun and games. It isn't. It provides contacts that can be turned to commercial advantage. Members of the worldwide sports establishment are not "sportsmen," in the British sense of gentlemen athletes; they are businessmen who use sports as an entryway into circles beyond their own immediate group.

Although large, the Hunts' bowling business is only about two-thirds the size of America's largest. There was a 116-lane giant outside of Philadelphia, but it closed in 1983. The largest bowling alley is now believed to be in the Showboat hotel and casino in Las Vegas, with 106 lanes. The chief stockholder (22 percent) is J.K. Housells, Jr., the company's vice-chairman of the board. In most parts of America it is quite unusual for the largest share owner to be active in management, but relegated to second position. Housells began his career working in the Las Vegas district attorney's office. That was in 1948 when Vegas was just being established as a paradise for middle-class gamblers. By 1952 Housells had seen which way the wind blew and gone into

Showboat Bowling Lanes. Photo: Frank Valeri

the hotel business, starting at the Hotel El Cortez. In 1958 he joined the Showboat and began carving out an unusual niche in Las Vegas's ecology. Instead of competing for the biggest cabaret stars or the sexiest nudes, the Showboat specializes in more familiar leisure-time pursuits: bowling and golf.

## MOST POPULAR MINOR LEAGUE TEAM

**Auctioneer's price:** $950,000.
**Owner:** A. Ray Smith.

As a general rule television has not been kind to minor league anything. When you can see Pete Rose and Reggie Jackson on television, why go down to the class-C league stadium to watch Clumsy Joe?

It turns out there is a reason to go on over to the stadium. People like to step out. The same urge that pulls people away from their TV sets and into the movie theaters works in sports. The show in the living room may be technically superior and cheaper, but it is less exciting. The desire to mix with crowds and see live action can send folks running to watch Clumsy at the bat, if the management can make the visit to the stadium enjoyable enough.

Nobody takes stadiums more seriously than Ray Smith, owner of the Louisville Redbirds, the most popular minor league team in baseball history. For decades the 1946 San Francisco Seals held the minor league attendance record, 670,563 fans (7,451 per game), and nobody was expected ever to top that. Yet in 1982 the Seals' old record was smashed by the Louisville Redbirds with 868,418 (13,569 per game) and in 1983 the team trounced its own record with a paid attendance of 1,052,438 (16,444 per game) or one and a half times the old Seals' record. The 1983 Redbirds drew more people than did three major league teams. When asked to explain his success Smith talks about the facilities at the stadium and the pleasure of going out to a game.

Minor league owners have little influence over the quality of their team. Baseball's farm system puts control in the hands of the major league owners. In the case of the Louisville Redbirds, the team is the St. Louis Cardinals' AAA club. (AAA means the club is just below major league rank.) The Cardinals pay for spring training, pay the manager and trainer, and pay most of the player salaries. In return they get to make most decisions about who is on the team. The Cardinals move players about in accordance with a grand design that gives the needs of

St. Louis first, second, and third priority. Under these circumstances the team owners can tend only to the non-baseball side of the business. A. Ray Smith has been exceptionally able in exploring the depths of this non-baseball side.

He has owned the team since 1960 and initially he appeared to be a typical minor league owner. In those days the franchise was based in Tulsa, where Smith had a construction company. He bought the team ($85,000) as an act of civic pride; he wanted to keep baseball in Tulsa. By 1977, however, the local stadium was unusable and when the team moved he moved with it. The team began wandering about the landscape, playing in New Orleans for a year, then Springfield, Illinois, and finally Louisville. The wilderness years taught Smith a lot, and he works hard to attract whole families, not just the devoted baseball fans, to the ball park. In order to make the stadium an attractive place for a family outing on a summer's eve he emphasizes clean bathrooms, well-lit concession areas, and popular promotions.

Another strength of Smith's is that he is a full-time owner. He sold his construction business long ago to concentrate on his baseball team. This approach contrasts sharply with that of the owners of the least popular team in Louisville's league, the Wichita Aeros. The Aeros are the top farm club for the Montreal Expos and in 1982, the year Louisville broke the Seals' attendance record, the Aeros featured the league's best hitter (Roy Johnson, batting .367), the top home run slugger (Ken Phelps, slamming 46), and the most famous manager (Felipe Alou, 17 years in the majors). Even so Wichita drew only 106,754 fans, one-eighth of Louisville's attendance. Not surprisingly, the Aeros's owners don't focus all their attention on the team. It is owned by the Glickman family, which runs a scrap-iron operation. One of the ball club's directors and owners, Dan Glickman, is the local congressman. Civic pride can give you a team, but attentive ownership is needed to assemble a crowd.

The minor leagues of football are college teams and they tend to be state-owned or privately endowed institutions. The team fight songs, however, can have individual owners. The copyrights on classics like "On Wisconsin," "Notre Dame Victory March," "The Buckeye Battle Cry," and "Ramblin' Wreck from Georgia Tech" are owned by Paul McCartney.

## GOLF COURSE DESIGN COMPANY

**Auctioneer's price:** $810,000.
**Owner:** Robert Trent Jones.

The price of a professional service company is always the hardest to determine because so much depends on the professionals in charge. No landscape architect is more solidly established or less readily replaced than Robert Trent Jones. He has designed or remodeled over 450 golf courses, some of them most unlikely. His 7,016-yard Mauna Kea golf course on the island of Hawaii, for example, is built atop a field of lava. Of course all of the Hawaiian islands are composed of lava, but the Mauna Kea field is, in geological terms, fresh. When Jones first surveyed the site, the land was black ash, unclaimed by vegetation or any but the most specialized forms of insect life. The lava was crushed into powder and Bermuda grass was planted above it. It works, sort of, but the porous soil quickly drains away any moisture and it takes one million gallons of water per day (!) to keep the grass green.

Jones has had as much impact on the way people envision and play golf as any player. The classic features of post–World War II golf courses are long narrow fairways, spacious greens protected by bunkers, a number of water traps, and different tees for players of different abilities. These things are so common now that we tend to assume it is the natural way for golf courses to be, but the style had an originator—Mr. Jones. It was also the style of an age of abundance. In our less bountiful times, smaller and less manicured courses are being designed because they cost less to build and maintain.

Jones is in his late seventies now, but he still works. His initial ambition was to be a golf player, but a stomach ulcer

Robert Trent Jones. Photo: Robert Trent Jones, Inc.

dissuaded him. In 1930 he began designing courses in Canada. In 1940 he went into business for himself. His firm is based in Montclair, New Jersey, and he has another office in San Francisco. His second son, Rees, has followed him into the business and is now a partner with his father.

America has about 11,000 golf courses, so it might seem we have about all we can use, but the rest of the world still is eager for plenty more. France has enjoyed a golfing boom and needs course designers. Japan is so golf-crazy it sometimes seems the islands are to be transformed entirely into fairways and putting greens. Saudi Arabia has the money, the space, and no sense of the ridiculous, so it too wants more golf courses. Around the world Jones's prestige is solid and still spreading.

There are plenty of other golf course design companies; most are smaller and run by unknowns, but a few have famous names. Golfing champion Jack Nicklaus has started his own company and he actually does the designing. His most admired work is the Singletree golf course near Vail, Colorado. It is more common for golf champions to do what Arnold Palmer did. He has a design company too, but the chief designer is an architect named Ed Seay.

## SPORTS CAMP FOR GROWN-UPS

**Auctioneer's price:** $89,800.
**Owners:** Cecil Randolph Hundley and Allan Goldin.

As mid-life crisis strikes, men begin to tally the things they haven't yet done and the things they will now never be able to do. One item that appears on many a man's list says, "Never going to hit a home run in the major leagues." Under the strain of such self-knowledge some men weep, others confess their sins to the *New York Times*, and a few run off with their neighbor's daughter; others simply refuse to believe it. These last are candidates for the All Star Baseball Camp, in Scottsdale, Arizona, where the watchword is "You could have."

The project began only in 1983 and already imitators abound. The original camp used former Chicago Cubs players to teach baseball techniques. That idea proved so popular that the next year the camp offered applicants a choice of training with former Cubs, former St. Louis Cardinals, or former San Francisco Giants. The men who turn up at these camps are all of that age where even Ty Cobb, Hank Aaron, and Willy Mays had to give it up. The trainees are lawyers and executives, stockbrokers and accountants—men who followed the roads more traveled by and have not quite forgiven themselves for their prudence.

At the Cubs camp they get to meet the likes of Hall of Famer Ernie Banks, endurance champion Billy Williams, and third baseman Ron Santo. They get to wear the Cubs uniform and hear some ballplayer they always admired pound them on the back and say, "All right." They bring their own glove and maybe snag a ball hit by Banks. After a week of that they leave Scottsdale and head back toward home. And if they are a bit less dissatisfied with themselves, it was $2,500 well spent.

The smart guys who came up with this program are Randy Hundley and Allan Goldin. Hundley caught for the Cubs during the late 1960s and early 70s on what was probably the best of the post–World War II Cubs teams. Goldin used to be president of Evelyn Wood's Reading Dynamics schools, famous for teaching techniques of rapid and intense skimming through books. Their claim is that you can absorb the 3,300,000 words of Proust in a weekend and know the book better than the fellow who took six months, so Goldin came to the baseball camp with a strong background in selling impossible dreams.

## THE FANCIEST RACING BIKE

**Auctioneer's price:** $35,000.
**Owner:** John Howard.

A bicycle called the "Pepsi Challenger" has been pedaled at over 124 miles per hour around an asphalt track by its owner, marathon bike champ, John Howard. It was designed by Doug Malewicki (who designed Evel Knievel's flying motorcycle) and Skip Hujsak. Money for the project came from Howard's winnings in bike races sponsored by Pepsi-Cola and Campagnolo-USA (a racing-bike company).

Under normal circumstances air resistance is thought to

make it impossible for a bicycle to exceed speeds of 62 miles per hour. Howard evades the problem by riding directly behind a racing car that serves as a windbreak. His bike has two drive chains and fourteen gear ratios. The handlebars are low, but not curled. His crash helmet comes complete with two-way radio because it is vital for Howard and the car driver to coordinate their movements precisely. Stopping is especially frightening and must be perfectly coordinated if the bike and car are to avoid a crash.

Howard's speed of 124.2 mph is a world record for asphalt surface racing, but in 1973 at the Bonneville Salt Flats Allan Abbot, riding a less elaborately designed bike, set the world record at 138 miles per hour. Howard had hoped to own the fastest bike; instead he has just the fanciest.

## THE CHAMPION RODEO BULL

**Auctioneer's price:** $12,000.
**Owner:** Christensen family.

The champion Brahma bull, as voted by the top twenty cowboys in the Professional Rodeo Cowboys Association, is called Oscar's Velvet. Originally he was named Oscar 2, but Black Velvet whiskey developed a publicity campaign that made it worthwhile for rodeo stock contractors to name their animals "Velvet." Every time a rodeo animal with Velvet at the end of its name appeared in a show, the owner was paid $25. When Oscar's Velvet won the prize as best bull of 1983, Black Velvet paid the contractor $10,000. If the bull had still been appearing as Oscar 2, the title would have paid nothing beyond prestige.

Oscar's Velvet is owned by the Christensen Brothers Rodeo company, one of rodeo's best-known stock contractors. Their saddle bronc, Warpaint, is still remembered by rodeo fans as one of the greatest bucking broncos of all time. The company was founded nearly fifty years ago by Bob and Hank Christensen. Bob, Jr., now runs the business. His father and uncle are still

Oscar II (a.k.a. Oscar's Velvet). Photo: Lorena J. Blodget

alive and still follow the business. The company owns several ranches, each managed by family members. The main operation is based in Roseburg, Oregon.

Oscar's Velvet was initially bought for $15,000, the highest price ever paid for a bucking bull. The auctioneer's price given above is slightly lower because he is now eight years old and rodeo stud fees are only now becoming an important consideration. The average price for a rodeo bull is only $3,500. Oscar's Velvet's father was a great bucking bull named Oscar. He was featured in the Academy Award–winning documentary *The Great American Cowboy,* which ended with the champion cowboy trying, and failing, to ride the great bull.

Oscar's son is considered to be in the same class. In his first five years on the rodeo circuit he was ridden only six times. During his championship season Oscar's Velvet bucked so hard that he injured a leg and had to spend two months recuperating. When he returned to the circuit he wore a leg brace. (Leg injuries are a recurring danger for these bucking bulls.)

Usually a ride atop Oscar's Velvet lasts no more than a few nanoseconds. The cowboy cannot tarry while trying to recover his wind, since the bull comes in for the kill if he sees the man on the ground. The rodeo clowns do what they can to distract the bull, but the cowboy had better run.

Apart from advertising schemes, the money to be made in owning a champion bull like this one comes from the reputation it gives a contractor's stock. A rodeo supplier with a tough line of animals is hired to stock many more rodeos than a supplier whose Brahmas and broncs are considered a bit tenderhearted. Brahma bulls make a long-lasting investment. The ride may seem endless to the suffering cowboy, but at best it lasts only eight seconds, not enough time for the bull to work up a sweat. If he can protect his legs, a bull can be a dozen years old and still muster eight seconds' worth of labor.

# 5

# INFORMATION

## A TELEVISION NETWORK

**Auctioneer's price:** $1,840,000,000.
**Owner:** John Werner Kluge.

The giants of ABC, CBS, and NBC make little old Metromedia look so tiny it seems pitiful, but dry your sentimental eyes. Metromedia's net profits are more than those of ABC and CBS combined. They are also larger than RCA's total profits and RCA owns, among other things, NBC. So despite the fact that most readers probably tune in their Metromedia station only to watch old M*A*S*H episodes, this network is soaring. It owns many profitable subsidiaries:

*Television stations:* KRIV (Houston); KTTV (Los Angeles); WCVB (Boston); WNEW (New York); WTCN (Minneapolis/St. Paul); WTTG (Washington, D.C.); WXIX (Cincinnati).

*AM radio stations:* KHOW (Denver); KJR (Seattle); KLAC (Los Angeles); KRLD (Dallas/Fort Worth); WCBM (Baltimore); WIP (Philadelphia); WNEW (New York).

*FM radio stations:* KMET (Los Angeles); WASH (Washington, D.C.); WMET (Chicago); WMMR (Philadelphia); WNEW (New York); WOMC (Detroit); WWBA (Tampa/St. Pete).

*Programming:* Metromedia Productions.

*Traveling shows:* Harlem Globetrotters; Ice Capades.

*Billboard advertising:* 45,000 signboards.

Metromedia was founded by John Kluge, a German-born American who seems to have taken a vow to become a media giant. After World War II he began buying and selling radio stations as if they were Monopoly properties. By 1959 Kluge, then age 45, was thoroughly experienced in the things that have made Metromedia into a money machine—selling little stations for bigger ones, diversifying investments, and borrowing money to grow still larger. Even though broadcasting is concerned with entertainment and information, Kluge's expertise has nothing to do with that. Money, markets, and technology are what he knows. Programs can be found in lots of places. It is the transmitter and license that makes broadcasters.

After more than a dozen years in radio Kluge bought the two television stations of the DuMont Broadcasting Corporation. At first this purchase seemed like one more move in his Monopoly game, and in a way it was, but now he had television stations and after that all the acquisitions and diversifications were done under the Metromedia umbrella. Today, as far as size is concerned, Metromedia's commercial broadcasting business cannot grow any larger. Federal regulation prohibits one corporation from owning more than seven television, seven AM, and seven FM stations. This network's slots are all filled. Progress these days means swapping for stations in bigger markets.

At the time of the DuMont purchase Kluge's business was privately held, but he began selling stock publicly in the early '60s. This method raised the capital to permit Metromedia's expansion and shot Kluge into the category of ridiculously rich. In the old days going public was the last step toward converting a large company into personal fortune. These are the *new* days. In 1983 Kluge, along with some other investors, announced that Metromedia would again become a privately held corporation.

By borrowing money, Kluge and his partners plan to buy out the other shareholders and then repay the loan through the company's profits. Perhaps later they can do it again: go public and make a fortune selling stock, then buy out the shareholders with the profits the company will make in the future. Essentially this kind of mechanism is a money pump and Kluge is senior partner at the well.

Most people don't make anything close to Kluge's money, but there are lots of people who grew rich from owning small broadcasting networks. Some of them are:

- *Gene Autry:* The former cowboy star owns 50.1 percent of Golden West Broadcasters, with two TV, five AM, and three FM stations. He also owns the California Angels baseball team.
- *Roy E. Disney:* Walt's nephew has his finger in many pies. He and his family are full owners of Shamrock Broadcasting, with four TV, two AM, and five FM stations.
- *John Earle Fetzer:* The former owner of the Detroit Tigers baseball team is one of America's wealthiest men. He owns 100 percent of three TV stations, 90 percent of a fourth one, and 50 percent of two AM and two FM stations.
- *Curt Gowdy:* A longtime announcer with the New York Yankees, the Boston Red Sox, and NBC's Game of the Week, he now owns Curt Gowdy Broadcasting, with three AM and two FM stations.
- *Merv Griffin:* Griffin's television career is as long as Johnny Carson's. One of his earliest investments was the purchase of two AM stations and one FM station; he still owns them.
- *Congressman Cecil Heftel:* Several representatives and senators own broadcast stations. The largest owner is the

congressman from Honolulu. He has been in Congress since 1976, but has retained his position as president and owner of Heftel Broadcasting, with two TV, one AM, and two FM stations.

- *Hipp family:* Francis, Herman, and Hayne Hipp of Greenville, South Carolina, are not famous but their family owns 30 percent of the Liberty Life Insurance Company. Liberty Life in turn has an enormous broadcasting subsidiary, the Cosmos Broadcasting Corporation, with six TV, two AM, and two FM stations. The Hipps offer a good example of how old money has been used to buy broadcasting rights and turn substantial wealth into a Himalayan pile of money.

- *Senator Nancy Kassebaum:* Alf Landon, the man Franklin Roosevelt buried in the 1936 election, outlived his opponent by three decades and established a small network of radio stations in Kansas. His daughter, now a U.S. senator, has radio stations in Wichita and Topeka.

- *Danny Kaye:* While it is common for stars to invest in broadcasting companies as limited partners, it is unusual for them to become principal owners. Kaye owns 80 percent of Kaye-Smith Radio, with two AM and three FM stations.

- *Richard Marriott:* John Willard Marriott turned a root beer stand into one of America's largest restaurant and hotel companies, the Marriott Corporation, a quarter of which is still owned by the Marriott family. J.W.'s son, Richard, has used some of his money to develop First Media Corporation, with three AM and seven FM stations.

- *E.T. Meredith III:* The Meredith family owns 44 percent of the giant Meredith Corporation, whose subsidiary, Meredith Broadcasting, owns five TV, three AM, and three FM stations. They also publish *Better Homes and Gardens* magazine.

- *Buck Owens:* Using his given name, Alvis Owens, Jr., the country and western superstar owns two AM and two FM stations.

- *Roy Hamilton Park:* This man is proof that the superrich and superpowerful can remain unfamiliar to the general public. He is the sole owner of a chain of nearly seventy newspapers and seven TV, seven AM, and seven FM stations. He lives in Ithaca, New York. His media empire is spread across the country.
- *William Ziff:* Ziff and family are the sole owners of the Ziff Corporation, an enormous publishing firm that specializes in middlebrow magazines for hobbyists, airplane passengers, and special-interest readers. Their best-known magazine is probably *Psychology Today.* Ziff also owns four TV stations. The man is loaded.

## *THE NEW YORK TIMES*

**Auctioneer's price:** $617,000,000.
**Owner:** Sulzberger family.

In 1896 Adolph Ochs paid $75,000 for 11 percent of the stock in *The New York Times* and became its new publisher. The fortunes of the paper were then at so low an ebb that Ochs was able to make an arrangement granting him 50 percent plus one share of the stock, if he ever made the paper profitable for three consecutive years. It took only four years for him to get that stock and become the paper's majority owner. Today, ownership and control is still in the hands of his descendants.

From the beginning Ochs knew the kind of paper he wanted to publish. He would make it a paper "of record," reporting events in an aloof tone that described and explained without shouting in the "Remember the Maine" tone favored by the yellow journalists of the day. Ochs also charged 3¢ when 1¢ was the price of the most popular papers. He was interested in getting "the right sort" of readers—the ones who attract well-heeled advertisers—and Ochs's formula still works. *The Daily News* is New York's most widely read paper, but the *Times* is the one with the Tiffany ads.

Ochs was anxious to ensure that his heirs would preserve the *Times* as he founded it and in his final years he had many sessions with his lawyer. In section 53 of his will Ochs urged his heirs "to perpetuate *The New York Times* as an institution charged with a high public duty," and he included a requirement that "no disposition of the controlling shares of the stock of The New York Times Company be made . . . except as a unit."

The controlling shares and titles are still in the family. Ochs's only child, Iphigene, married Arthur Hayes Sulzberger, who became publisher on Ochs's death. The present publisher, Arthur Ochs Sulzberger, is Ochs's grandson. (There was a brief period when the publisher was Orvil Dryfoos, Ochs's grandson-in-law.) Sulzberger control of the *Times* has been assured by dividing the paper's stock into two classes. Class A gets dividends, and can be bought as an investment, but does not bring power over the company. Class B is where the real voting power lies. Its shareholders elect 70 percent of the directors and have the sole vote on most company issues. The Sulzberger family owns a quarter of the Class A stock and three-quarters of the critical Class B stock.

As for the clause urging the *Times*'s owners to preserve the paper's public role, that ambition has been more than faithfully honored. When Ochs died in 1935 the *Times* was admired and listened to, but there were too many papers for it to be the institution it has become. Today the *New York Times* is a national newspaper. The pages of the national edition are transmitted by satellite from New York to plants in Illinois, California, Florida, and Texas. It has an authority unknown since Victorian times when the members of the gentlemen's club that ruled Britannia all read *The Times* of London.

The Vietnam War eroded American faith in many institutions, but the *New York Times* emerged from that upheaval with its public standing in good repute. At first the *Times*, like the public in general, tended to take official statements at face value and assumed that America's leaders were honorable men. The great shift in public opinion came after the Tet offensive of early 1968. From a military point of view, the battle was a disaster for North Vietnam. Its troops were soundly defeated everywhere, but official American statements had previously insisted that the war was already in the mopping-up phase. Tet exposed those reports as shams and President Johnson had to suffer the consequences of having everybody find out on his own that wars are not easily ended.

At this decisive moment it was the *New York Times*, rather than the president, that revealed plans to increase America's troop commitment to over 200,000. This report was just the start of what turned out to be years of exposés, all of them encouraging a clear distinction between official statements and the truth: the Pentagon Papers showed that the government's policy had, from the beginning, included plans to deceive the public; news of a massacre in the village of My Lai traveled from the *Times* to the army rather than in the opposite direction; secret bombings of Cambodia were reported in the *Times*, officially denied, and then proven true. By the end of Watergate, in 1974, America had lived through six years of seeing newspapers expose the highest members of the government as liars and connivers. This process transformed the *Times* into something new to history—a pillar of the Establishment that defined its duty as exposing the frauds of other Establishment leaders.

A decade after the Watergate climax this distinction between the government and sources of information about the government has become so familiar that many people suppose it to be a natural part of any free society. It is, however, unprecedented, remarkable, and disturbing. Of course, even more disturbing is the continued presence of lies that need exposing.

In the days when the *Times* was rising to preeminence, the most famous newspaper publisher was William Randolph Hearst. Hearst died in 1951, at age 88, and left his estate to a foundation, but his children managed to regain control of the corporation. In 1974 the foundation agreed to sell out to the family. The auctioneer's price for the Hearst Corporation is $1,300,000,000. Most of the stock is owned by Hearst's three surviving sons: William Randolph, Jr.; Randolph Apperson (this Hearst is the father of Patty, the most famous of the living Hearsts); and David Whitmire. These three brothers hold 60 percent of the stock. The rest is held by William Randolph Sr.'s grandchildren.

## A SMALL-TOWN NEWSPAPER EMPIRE

**Auctioneer's price:** $548,000,000.
**Owner:** Hoiles family.

A big-city newspaper's quest for mass circulation usually encourages editorials guaranteed not to startle any of the readership. It has been left to the small-town papers to take the bold or shrewd or cranky positions. The towns with reputations for imaginative editorial stands are places like York, Pennsylvania; Lewiston, Idaho; and Emporia, Kansas. Once a town starts growing to a size that permits a really large circulation, one of the established newspaper chains moves in and starts writing bland editorials. But what happens when a small-town newspaper publisher committed to eccentric opinions operates a chain of small-town papers?

The Santa Ana *Register* of Orange County, California, was bought in 1935 by Raymond Hoiles, a man whose editorial opinions stood well outside the national mainstream. Hoiles held that the rights of property owners are absolute and he was not afraid to reduce his axiom to the ridiculous. He argued that nobody should be taxed to support public schools and no private company should be held responsible for any of the public consequences of its acts, like polluting or doing slipshod work which promotes accidents. Of course, government services like Social Security, unemployment compensation, and regulating trade were also anathema. Radical or not, Hoiles had his opinions and in the manner of small-town newspaper publishers he gave them full voice. Then his paper began to grow.

Santa Ana is immediately south of Los Angeles, and as that city swelled, so did the suburbs. The *Register*'s readership expanded and now the paper has a circulation of almost 250,000. As his paper grew richer Hoiles started buying others. Today his chain of "Freedom Newspapers" consists of thirty-one dailies and five weeklies, plus a couple of radio shows. But it is in the nature of non-bland opinions to travel poorly. Instead of making it easier to spread Hoiles's libertarian notions, growth has threatened to silence them altogether.

For example, in 1980 Freedom Newspapers bought the

Greenville, Mississippi, *Delta Democrat-Times*. That paper (present circulation 16,000) was another famous small-town journal, published by Hodding Carter and nationally respected for its reports and editorials about Mississippi's civil rights struggles. In California attacks on public schools can stimulate discussion about property rights, but in Mississippi the context becomes entirely racial. Under desegregation, most of the public schools in the Greenville area have become predominantly black, so instead of being startling, an attack on public schools sounds like one more familiar racist cry.

Meanwhile, the growth of Santa Ana has brought problems for the original paper. The *Delta Democrat-Times* can flourish with a circulation of 16,000, but the Santa Ana *Register* has to fight to survive with 250,000. Greenville advertisers have nowhere else to go, but competition for Orange County advertisers is ferocious. The easiest way to attract big advertising money is to attract well-to-do readers first, and since 1979 the *Register* has aimed specifically at developing a readership of families with incomes over $35,000. It has prospered in this effort, but at the price of minimizing its viewpoint. The whole paper used to reek of libertarian crankiness, but those radical opinions are now fairly well restricted to the editorial page and, as the fight for reader respect grows, there is much doubt about how long they can survive even there.

The present publisher, David Threshie, is married to Raymond Hoiles's granddaughter, and all stock in the chain is privately held by members of the Hoiles and Threshie families. Presumably the paper is not about to become a liberal rag, but it could well become just one more conservative-to-moderate voice hemming and hawing its way through opinions as predictable as sunshine on the Fourth of July.

A lot of people worry that the news media are not always responsible, but the Freedom Newspapers chain makes one worry that there may be no future at all for the irresponsible media. The abandonment of crackpot ideas may sound like progress, but don't forget that every opinion now held to be self-evident truth began as the irresponsible musings of some kind of nut.

The obvious counterexample to this concern over the decline of the irresponsible press is the growth of Rupert Murdoch's worldwide empire of eighty magazines and newspapers. (Stock in Murdoch's company, called News Corporation, is traded on the Australian stock exchange. Half the stock is held by Murdoch family members.) The American subsidiary of his News Corporation includes five papers (*Boston Herald, Chicago Sun-Times, New York Post, San Antonio Express, San Antonio News*), three magazines (*New York, The Star, The Village Voice*), and a limited partnership in the new private organization of Metromedia. Murdoch is Australian and his father, Keith, was one of Australia's great journalists, most famous for breaking the news that the invasion of Gallipoli during World War I was a disaster. At the time many officers considered the story irresponsible because, while true, it ruined several careers and hurt public morale. This kind of irresponsibility, which ignores the wishes of established authority and the pressure of public opinion, is a major source of new attitudes and important information.

Rupert is irresponsible in another, cruder, way. His is the sort of irresponsibility that defends itself with no argument more profound than "Don't blame me." The editorials and alleged facts of his publications buttress attitudes the readers are assumed to hold already. Thus the leftish notions and data of the *Village Voice* appear beside the conservative clichés and reports of the *New York Post*. The only standards Rupert seems to worry about are those of his accountants. Everybody likes looking into a mirror, and the better Murdoch can reflect a publication's audience the more popular it is likely to be. Under these circumstances Murdoch can say he just gives his readers what they want; if you want to blame somebody, blame the readers. Murdoch is not responsible.

## TV GUIDE

**Auctioneer's price:** $322,000,000.
**Owner:** Walter Annenberg.

There are literate Americans who have never laid eyes on *TV Guide*, but unless you, reader, were born and bred in Alaska, you are not one of them.

The basic facts: weekly circulation fluctuates around 17,000,000, depending on the time of year (summer is the off season). The magazine has 108 local editions covering the 48

Initial *TV Guide* cover, April 3, 1953. Photo: Courtesy *TV Guide*

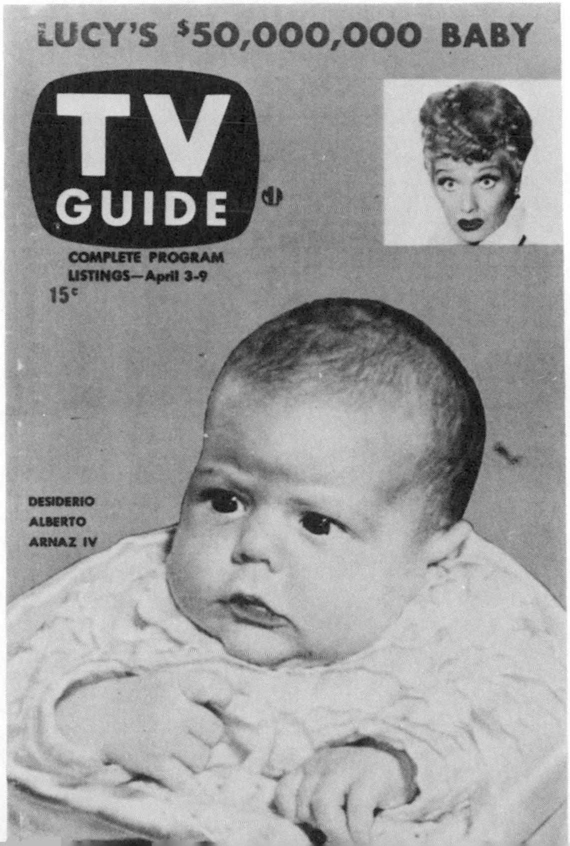

contiguous states and Hawaii. It began in April 1953 and its first cover featured Desi Arnaz, Jr. Annual advertising revenue is about $250,000,000. The most popular issue, in both advertising and circulation, is the annual fall preview of new shows. The most expensive ad is the second-cover gatefold, a special foldout ad that comes directly behind the front cover and costs $227,000. The entire project is owned privately by Walter Annenberg and his sisters (q.v.).

Editorially the magazine supports Annenberg's conservative views, but editorial point of view has nothing to do with *TV Guide*'s success. The magazine is a technological triumph. Computers, satellite transmission of data, and techniques of mass-market distribution make it possible to publish a standardized product that is filled with accurate local information. Anybody trying to compete with the magazine has a choice of

New cable listings cover, April 21, 1984. Photo: Courtesy *TV Guide*

fighting for just one of *TV Guide*'s 108 regional markets (in which case the competition is doomed from the outset) or betting the hundreds of millions of dollars necessary to obtain the start-up technology. Even then one can lose the whole investment, as Time-Life did with its short-lived *TV-Cable Week* project.

## MOST POPULAR SUNDAY SUPPLEMENT

**Auctioneer's price:** $142,000,000.
**Owner:** Newhouse family.

Despite all the changes in the technology of entertainment, Sunday morning is still what it was forty years ago—newspaper entertainment with colored funny pages, expanded sports sections, and a supplemental magazine focusing on gossip, easy steps to self-improvement, and humor. Only the largest papers can afford to publish their own weekly magazine; most prefer to take one ready-made. The most popular such magazine by far is *Parade,* carried in 134 newspapers, including many that publish a local supplement as well. Each week *Parade* publishes over 21 million copies and has about 35 million readers. That gives it an audience larger than most television shows.

The magazine is wholly owned by the Newhouse family. The patriarch, Samuel Irving Newhouse, began with a small newspaper, the Staten Island *Advance,* which he bought in 1922 for $98,000. By the time of his death in 1979 the family owned twenty-nine daily newspapers with a total circulation of 3,217,470 (110,947 per paper, on the average). They also own the Condé Nast line of magazines (*Vogue* being the most famous of the line), a group of television stations, and *Parade,* decidedly the single most popular Newhouse property. S.I.'s two sons, Donald and S.I., Jr., are in overall command of the business, but eleven other members, including uncles and cousins, have small fiefdoms within the family domain.

The Newhouse estate has fallen into frightful problems with the tax man. The Internal Revenue Service has estimated that S.I. left his heirs property worth $1.5 billion and is seeking to collect $914,279,782 of it in back taxes and fraud penalties. This kind of claim guarantees years of legal struggle. If they lose, the Newhouse heirs are probably going to have to sell many of their assets to pay the bill. At the moment the Newhouse family empire consists of:

***Newspapers***—Ann Arbor, Michigan, *News*; Bay City, Michigan, *Times*; Birmingham, Alabama, *News*; *Cleveland Plain Dealer*; Flint, Michigan, *Journal*; Grand Rapids, Michigan, *Press*; Harrisburg, Pennsylvania, *Evening News*; Huntsville, Alabama, *News Times*; Jackson, Michigan, *Citizen Patriot*; Jersey City, New Jersey, *Journal*; Kalamazoo, Michigan, *Gazette*; Mobile, Alabama, *Press Register*; Muskegon, Michigan, *Chronicle*; Newark, New Jersey, *Star-Ledger*; New Orleans *States Item*; New Orleans *Times-Picayune*; Pascagoula, Mississippi, *Press-Register*; Portland *Oregonian*; Saginaw, Michigan, *News*; Springfield, Massachusetts, *Union News Republican*; Staten Island, New York, *Advance*; Syracuse, New York, *Herald-American*; Syracuse, New York, *Herald-Journal*; Syracuse, New York, *Post-Standard*.

***Cable TV***—New Channels Corporation; Vision Cable Communications. Also own 80 percent of Metro Vision.

***Magazines*** (besides *Parade*)—*Bride's*; *Gentleman's Quarterly*; *Glamour*; *Gourmet*; *House & Garden*; *Mademoiselle*; *Self*; *Vanity Fair*; *Vogue*.

***Books***—Random House. (The Newhouse purchase of Random House brought it many book lines: Random House, Alfred A. Knopf, Ballantine Books, Vintage Books, Modern Library).

## *THE NATIONAL ENQUIRER*

**Auctioneer's price:** $112,000,000.
**Owner:** Generoso Paul Pope, Jr.

Many people cite this weekly tabloid with its unreliable gossip about celebrities, its pronouncements by dubious experts, and its gaudy layout as proof of the old cynicism that "nobody ever went broke underestimating the taste of the American public." Actually, the journal may prove just the opposite. Generoso Pope bought the paper in 1952 (price: $75,000) and for two decades his editorial approach aimed for a standard so low even its most faithful readers tended to deny any acquaintance with the journal. In those days the *Enquirer* favored headlines like "Starving Dogs Eat Baby Boy's Face." Just flipping through the tabloid with its pages of elephant-man-type photos and meat-cleaver prose could make you woozy.

Early in the 1970s the *Enquirer* changed its approach. The magazine had a following, but the crudeness of its taste (if *taste* is not too grand a word in this context) kept its audience relatively small. Then Pope's editorial style changed. It was aimed for the supermarkets and shopping center racks in the suburbs. Starving dogs were out; astrological predictions came in. Scientific proof of life after "death" was cited on a regular basis. Instead of mangled babies, its cover photos favored TV personalities who had found love.

The appeal of this format seems undeniable. The *Enquirer*'s circulation of over four and a half million copies per week is nearly double that of *People* magazine. The paper's vulgarity and its contempt for whomever it writes about still troubles many people, but the *Enquirer* no longer seems like a magazine for Gestapo men on the lam. Indeed, the magazine seems a fine metaphor for the post–World War II age. Tasteless, vile, degrading—it is all of those things, but when the beasts that previously dominated the stage are recalled, why, it doesn't seem half bad.

## *EBONY* MAGAZINE

**Auctioneer's price:** $97,800,000.
**Owner:** John Harold Johnson.

We are all used to the idea that many of America's richest people based their wealth on oil, but less attention has been paid to the fact that many great fortunes are based on publishing and broadcasting. In 1983 *Forbes* magazine published a list of 400 of America's greatest fortunes and found that as many were based on media empires as on oil (44 apiece). Even more striking, the great oil fortunes tended to be old money (about one-half were inherited) while only a quarter of the media wealth was inherited. Given that situation, it is not surprising that America's richest black is a publisher.

John Johnson, owner of the Johnson Publishing Company, publishes *Ebony* and *Jet*, magazines whose combined readership is twelve million, nearly half the black adults in the country. The company also has a children's magazine, *Ebony Jr!*, a book division, and several radio stations.

*Ebony* is the best known and most widely respected of the company's publications. It was founded in 1945 and aimed specifically at returning World War II black veterans who had acquired, en masse, a wider knowledge of the world. *Ebony*'s consistent message has been that blacks can make it, and its issues are full of stories about successful blacks.

Much of John Johnson's own success story is the typical black Horatio Alger tale: he was born in the South; his father died when he was only 6; his mother devoted her life to giving him a sense of values and confidence in his own worth. When he was 15 he and his mother moved to Chicago because there was no high school for black children in his Arkansas town. He did well, and the Urban League invited him to a dinner given for promising high school seniors. The point of the evening was to encourage self-confidence, a particularly difficult faith to sustain in the depression/Jim Crow years of the '30s. The speaker at that dinner was Harry Pace, president of a black life insurance company. Johnson introduced himself to Pace and got a job.

John Johnson's biography developed its unique pattern when

he began to find ways of getting powerful whites to take him seriously. His first venture was a magazine called *Negro Digest.* Johnson used his insurance company's mailing list to raise enough capital to get started; however, the magazine distribution business was controlled by whites who refused to believe a magazine for blacks could find a readership. Johnson got all of his friends to ask for the magazine at newsstands. When a few places agreed to give *Negro Digest* a try, Johnson's friends bought up the copies. The Chicago distributor concluded there was more interest in the magazine than he had imagined and agreed to carry it. Circulation quickly rose to 50,000. In 1943, when the magazine was a year old, Johnson persuaded Eleanor Roosevelt to write an article entitled "If I Were a Negro," and of course the piece got a great wave of publicity in the white press. *Negro Digest*'s circulation immediately trebled to 150,000.

*Ebony*'s success also turned on gaining white cooperation. The readership was there from the beginning, but advertisers stayed away. Johnson tried to persuade many companies to advertise in *Ebony* and finally succeeded with Zenith. Its president, Commander Eugene McDonald, had been on the North Pole expedition with Admiral Peary, and a black named Matthew Henson was a leading figure on that journey. When Johnson approached Commander McDonald, he brought along an issue of *Ebony* with a story about Henson and the Peary expedition. After McDonald looked up from the magazine's pages, he said, "I don't see why we shouldn't be advertising in this magazine," and the white-built advertising wall began to crumble.

Most of America's publishing fortunes were made by people who saw a market and served it. The men who got rich this way often pictured themselves as self-made geniuses; the cooperation of others—of distributors, authors, and advertisers—was taken for granted. Johnson too had to identify a readership and its wants, but he could never assume outside cooperation was inevitable, nor could he fall back on a strategy based on some stereotype of whites. In every case he suited his plan to the situation—appealing to a distributor's interest in sales, a liberal's eagerness to give advice to blacks, and a corporate executive's pride in a great noncommercial adventure.

## BANTAM BOOKS

**Auctioneer's price:** $83,000,000.
**Owner:** Mohn family.

They are not the richest, but the most prestigious publishing houses are those that try surfboarding the waves of contemporary taste. Most of their books have the life span of a subatomic particle that appears and vanishes in the same nanosecond, but some of the books find millions of readers and become milestones of the culture.

The biggest of the big league houses is a paperback publisher, Bantam Books, founded in 1945 by Ian Ballantine. The original capital was put up by a consortium of hardcover publishers who wanted to expand their market. It worked better than they could have hoped. Bantam now publishes about 500 titles per year, or two every working day. Although a small number of its books are published in hardcover or as "trade" paperbacks, most of the books, about 400, appear as mass-market volumes sold at newsstands and from magazine racks as well as in bookstores. Bantam prints tens of millions of books per year. The most successful single book it ever published was *The Exorcist*, by William Peter Blatty; over eleven million paperback copies have been printed. Bantam's most successful author is Western writer Louis L'Amour. Total paperback printing for him is 140 million copies. He has published almost ninety books, and eighty-five of them have surpassed the million-copy mark.

In 1980 Bantam was bought by a giant German corporation called Bertelsmann Publishing AG. At that time Bertelsmann already owned 51 percent of Bantam. The other 49 percent was owned by Italy's Agnelli family, owners of Fiat. Bertelsmann bought out the Agnelli holding and is now sole owner.

Bertelsmann Publishing is an enormous family business, equal in size and scope to Time-Life. Ninety percent of the stock is still owned by descendants of the company's founder, Carl Bertelsmann. The owning family now goes by the name Mohn as, in 1887, Carl's granddaughter married a Mohn. The current Mohn in charge is Reinhard. He was the family member who changed Bertelsmann, originally a German publisher of religious books, into a European empire of books, book clubs, magazines, records, and record clubs. For tax purposes most of the company's stock (72 percent) has been transferred to Reinhard's son, Johannes, but all voting power is still held by Reinhard.

Any German over 60 has to answer the primal question of European politics: where were you when the jackboots began to stamp? Reinhard was 12 when Hitler came to power in 1933, the perfect age to become cannon fodder when the Third Reich's expansion began to encounter opposition. Luckily for Mohn, he was sent to North Africa with General Rommel rather than to the Russian front. He was captured by the American army and spent the last two years as a prisoner of war in Kansas.

Of course Bertelsmann AG is too huge, and American literary tastes are too foreign, for the Mohn family to offer many shrewd insights into Bantam's policy. Corporations of the size and breadth of Bertelsmann function much like the Roman Empire. Caesar could not address himself to the problems and culture of a distant province, so a procurator was appointed to run the place and ship tax money back to Rome. Bantam does not have the power to tax, but it does have a steady river of cash flowing into its banks. Some of the money is needed to meet operating costs; the rest is shipped back to imperial headquarters.

The largest hardcover publisher of trade books is Random House, which is wholly owned by the Newhouse family (q.v.). There is a certain irony in the fact that Random House is a family business. It was founded by Bennett Cerf and kept private until 1959. Cerf feared that inheritance taxes would make it impossible for his firm to stay in the family, yet today it has been bought by another publishing family, one that had nothing to do with Random House's initial success and reputation.

One of the best-known children's books series is Golden Books published by Western Publishing. The Mattel toy company bought this publisher in 1979. At the time it seemed like a reasonable idea, since Western Publishing is aimed at the same young market that plays with toys, but Mattel's expansions have not fared well and in 1983 they sold the company. The new owner is Richard Bernstein, a New York real estate investor. His qualifications to direct the company are not at all clear, but he has taken several members of the firm's management as partners in the business. How odd that the ability of future generations to learn about the three little kittens who lost their mittens depends on the unknown skills of an investor in midtown Manhattan's office buildings.

## *THE NEW YORKER*

**Auctioneer's price:** $78,400,000.
**Owner:** Peter Fleischmann.

Next week's agenda for casual conversations among America's tastemakers and social observers is determined over the weekend as they read through *The New Yorker.* Its short stories are controversial and its articles sometimes offer more detail than insight, but there's not much doubt that no other magazine offers more prestige to a contributor.

The reputation of the *New Yorker* magazine is based squarely on the strength of its writing and on the sophistication of its taste. Along with famous staff writers such as James Thurber, John Updike, and Janet Flanner, the *New Yorker* has always managed to attract contributions from topflight writers. Nobel Prize–winning contributors to the magazine have been William Butler Yeats, Thomas Mann, Sinclair Lewis, Nelly Sachs, Samuel Beckett, Pablo Neruda, Heinrich Boll, Saul Bellow, Isaac Bashevis Singer, Czeslaw Milosz, and Gabriel Garcia Marquez.

The bulk of the magazine's founding capital was put up by Raoul Fleischmann, an heir to a middling fortune based on bread baking. (The much larger Fleischmann's yeast fortune belongs to another branch of the family.) Fleischmann's initial investment, in 1925, was $25,000, but it quickly ran to $400,000 because expenses had to be met while the magazine was in the red. Within a few years, however, the *New Yorker* began making a profit. Magazine staffers grumbled that Fleischmann gave himself large dividends instead of paying the writers better, but, of course, writers always feel they are treated poorly by their publishers. The tragedy is they are always correct.

Fleischmann does not seem ever to have thought of trying to use his position to further any intellectual ambitions of his own. The magazine's first editor, Harold Ross, shaped the original contents. Raoul's only son, Peter Fleischmann, is the magazine's current publisher, chairman of its board, and chief stockholder of the corporation. He owns or controls nearly 27 percent of the *New Yorker*'s stock, but he too is known for staying out of the editorial side.

## MOST POPULAR ON-LINE DATA SYSTEM

**Auctioneer's price:** $58,000,000.
**Owner:** Bancroft family.

*On-line* (adjective) = available via telephone.

*Data* (noun) = information.

When you do it, it's called phoning for information. When your computer does it, the term is "accessing on-line data." The smart money says on-line data is the coming medium of information.

The systems work by attaching a computer to a phone. Dial a number as you would with any ordinary phone call. In this case another computer will answer. After the connection is made the caller requests information from the answering computer. The information can be anything—news, stock prices, sports results, call-girl phone numbers, the latest senatorial vote, airline schedules—whatever seems important enough to generate money.

The most popular on-line operation, with over 60,000 subscribers, is the Dow Jones News/Retrieval service. It offers highlights from the latest *Wall Street Journal*, information on current stock prices, corporate financial data, economic forecasts, weather around the world, and sports. The service can also provide an automatic search throughout articles in the *Wall Street Journal*, *Barron's* magazine, and the Dow Jones News Service to find any reference to a particular name or number. This system is impressively modern, but the combination of very high cost and moderate demand makes old fogies wonder if on-line data will ever become more than an expensive service for the elite. The *New York Times* abandoned its on-line project after ten years and ten million lost dollars. Technology has been the key to increasing media power, but it is nearly irrelevant to media content, and content is still the primary concern of information consumers. Before on-line data gains mass appeal it is going to have to discover something interesting to say.

Dow Jones began its on-line service in 1974. It was a typical avant-garde development for the publishing empire whose daily publication, the *Wall Street Journal*, is the newspaper of record for American capitalism. In the nineteenth century the Dow ticker made it possible for investors nationwide to follow the prices at the New York stock market. The on-line data business is, in essence, an enlargement of the stock ticker operation.

Long ago there actually was a Mr. Charles Dow and a Mr. Edward Jones. They devised the system of stock averages that bears their name and they came up with the ticker, but their business was sold early in this century to a Boston financier, Clarence Barron. His name survives in the company's weekly magazine, *Barron's*. Nearly 60 percent of the Dow Jones stock is still in his family. The voting power of the family is expected to grow even stronger. Early in 1984 the corporation proposed a new class B type of stock with ten votes per share. At first this new stock will make no difference in the voting structure, but over the next few years most ordinary investors are expected to convert their B stock into the economically more valuable common stock, so the voting strength of the Barron family will grow even greater. A similar arrangement was worked out years ago at the *New York Times* (q.v.). Barron's heir was a daughter who married Hugh Bancroft. Their one surviving child, Jane Bancroft Cook, lives quietly, splitting her time between Sarasota, Florida, and Cohasset, Massachusetts. She puts little stress on her fortune, recently estimated at $600,000,000. The rest of the Dow money is spread among the grandchildren and great-grandchildren of Hugh Bancroft. The family heirs now number over thirty members.

## THE BIGGEST BIBLE PUBLISHER

**Auctioneer's price:** $49,500,000.
**Owner:** Sam Moore.

Most of the high school and college students who land summer jobs selling books door to door do not keep it up even for a single season, but each year a few of them turn out to be splendid salesmen. Sam Moore was such a one. He came to America from Lebanon to study business at the University of South Carolina and took a summer job selling Bibles door to door. The result, no pun intended, was a revelation: there is a living in Scripture. Today Moore is America's most successful Bible publisher.

From a commercial point of view, the Bible's great opportunity lies in its lack of a copyright; anyone can type it up and sell copies, which is just what Moore did. In 1962 he ran a small company that sold Bibles door to door, then he printed up his own deluxe edition of the King James Version and began reaping profits rather than just commissions. There are not many such surefire best sellers available to new publishing companies.

Once begun, however, publishers usually like to see a copyright on their books. Moore's breakthrough came in 1968 when he bought the American branch of Thomas Nelson & Sons, a British publisher with exclusive rights to the Revised Standard Version of the Bible. New translations and paraphrases can be protected by copyright, so the acquisition of a popular new text is valuable. In the late 1960s the Revised Standard was the most admired of the new biblical versions.

Even so, half of all Bibles sold in America still use the King James Version. Without copyright protection, Moore has succeeded by offering enormous variety. All together Moore's company offers over 500 forms of the Bible, including:

> ***Versions:*** King James with modern spelling and punctuation, King James with original spelling and punctuation, Revised Standard, American Standard, the Good News Bible, Catholic editions (available in English or Spanish), and the New King James.
>
> ***Bindings:*** cloth, leather, imitation leather, pigskin, vinyl, denim, paper.
>
> ***Other options:*** ribbon markers, rounded corners, gilt-edge paper, snap closing, zipper closing, illustrations, family record section, giant print, tiny print, words of Christ in red, wide margins for personal annotation.

By offering most of the permutations possible, Moore can offer a range of Bibles broad enough to satisfy just about anybody who can read. Some illiterates have money too. The New Testament is also available on cassette tapes.

## MOST POPULAR REGIONAL MAGAZINE

**Auctioneer's price:** $40,000,000.
**Owner:** Emory Cunningham.

Nearly 200 magazines serve cities, states, and regions. Most of them have small circulations and little influence beyond their own circle, but a few have become important enough to help shape the national impression of their region.

*Southern Living* has been especially successful in helping to change an image. It was founded in February, 1966, by Emory Cunningham. Cunningham was already publisher of *Progressive Farmer.* He was a southerner, born and still living in Alabama, and he had grown tired of the portrait of the South which had developed over the previous ten years. From Little Rock, Arkansas, to Selma, Alabama, the years since 1956 had brought news photos of white adults yelling hatred at black children, fat sheriffs setting dogs on demonstrators, and Klansmen parading around flaming crosses. Cunningham decided to provide a different portrait of his region.

He has blended the old southern notion of graceful living with the newer concept of a sun belt. Every issue has information about charming houses with lovely gardens and stylish decorations. Foods, entertainment, and recipes are also discussed. The thriving sun belt image is promoted in monthly portraits of different southern cities and in travel reports.

Each issue is also rich in color photos. It emits a sense of stylish taste that has long been one of the South's strongest points of pride. Cunningham introduced the magazine at just the right time, when tempers were starting to cool and southerners were eager to remind themselves that their region was more than a land of turmoil. The magazine quickly became a success. Its present circulation, 2 million, accounts for 18 percent of all regional magazine sales.

The publication is still privately owned by Emory Cunningham. He lives and works in Birmingham, Alabama. Besides *Southern Living* and *Progressive Farmer* he also publishes *Decorating & Crafts Ideas* magazine.

Much of *Southern Living*'s format has been modeled on *Sunset*, one of the oldest regional magazines. It has served the west since its founding in 1898 by the Southern Pacific Railroad. The original publishing idea was to promote travel and trade along the railroad line. The magazine was bought in 1928 by William Lane and is still owned by his sons. William, Jr. is the present publisher. Its circulation is 1,400,000, second only to *Southern Living* for regional magazines. It was *Sunset* that first hit on the formula of lush photos, city portraits, and home features. Today the formats of *Sunset* and *Southern Living* are so similar that the Lanes and Cunninghams regularly compliment one another on their fine products.

## ORIGINAL ECONOMETRIC SERVICE

**Auctioneer's price:** $10,000,000.
**Owner:** The Republic of France.

One maxim of the prophecy business says, "If you can't forecast it right, forecast it often." A second holds that "If you can't predict the future, predict the desire."

These two principles continue to guide most successful prophets. New techniques make it easier than ever to measure precisely where we stand, but we are not yet so good at figuring out where we are headed. So forecasters still give us a lot of revised predictions and we are still promised a lot more good news than we ever seem to get.

Technology keeps tempting sages to believe that, at last, they can predict the future and get it right the first time. Back in the 1960s, when economists were beginning to translate their theories into computer programs, they hoped to be able at last to make accurate predictions of future economic conditions. Instead, they have ended up making frequent predictions.

The pathway toward this disappointment was paved by the Wharton School of Economics at the University of Pennsylvania. In 1963 Lawrence Klein founded Wharton Econometric Forecasting and in 1980 his work won him the Nobel Prize for economics. By now the firm's clients include the U.S. government, America's top banks, leading corporations, and many foreign governments as well. It has offices in Philadelphia, Washington, New York, San Francisco, and Chicago. The econometrics industry could hardly be more respectable, yet revised economic forecasts are only slightly less common than revised weather forecasts. The computers manipulate enormous lists of numbers, but the watchword beneath their coat of arms is still "Time will tell."

The problems and disappointments of economic forecasting have not, however, reduced the demand for the services of companies who do it. In 1963 Wharton offered the first commercially available forecast, a prediction of how the American economy would do over the next three months. Today it includes forecasts of: the world economy as a whole; Communist economies; Arab economies; Latin American economies; Mexico's economy; the economies of countries along the Pacific rim, from New Zealand to South Korea; monthly trends in foreign exchange; international agriculture; American industry; U.S. regional economies; and the automobile industry. In short, just about everything that continues to baffle us is forecast by computers.

There is an ironic side to this mushrooming economic data. Wharton has not been able to steer its own way into a profit. Of course there are many profit-making economists, but Wharton is locked into a series of complex equations that, while often wrong, pay no attention to the customer's hopes. The computer ignores the prophet's need to find pleasing predictions. Inevitably, business suffers.

Wharton wisely began as a nonprofit enterprise, wholly owned by the University of Pennsylvania, but it was later sold to avowed profit seekers. Its most recent buyer was the Compagnie Internationale de Services en Informatique (CiSi). They bought the firm in early 1983 from Ziff-Davis, a publishing company that had lost $10,000,000 during the three years it owned this commercial seer.

CiSi is a subsidiary of the French Atomic Energy Commission. Like America's own Nuclear Regulatory Agency, France's commission is a governmental body. Its chairman is appointed by the president of France and the government's budget includes money for its operation. As one might expect, its work includes classified projects for French nuclear weapons and development of nuclear-generated electricity; 43 percent of France's electricity comes from nuclear reactors. During the 1960s the energy commission diversified and its subsidiaries now do many things we don't usually associate with atomic energy agencies. It makes microchips, X-ray scanners, conducts research into solar energy, and even makes paint for automobiles. The commission was also one of France's pioneer computer users and in 1970 CiSi was established as the data-processing subsidiary of the commission. CiSi continues to make calculations for nuclear projects, but now most of its work has nothing to do with atomic energy. Even so, CiSi is still owned by the French government and a part of CiSi's profits is returned to the French treasury every year.

## *SOLDIER OF FORTUNE* MAGAZINE

**Auctioneer's price:** $877,500.
**Owner:** Robert Brown.

Robert Brown's golden idea came at a time when he sure needed something. It was late 1974 and he was 42; his mail-order business was faltering; his savings totaled a mere $10,000 and winter was coming on. He decided to take all the savings and start a magazine, a special publication focusing on unusual fantasies. Fortunately for Brown, he knew so little about magazine publishing that he didn't realize how ludicrous the idea was. Standard advice to any company starting a new magazine is that it must be able to spend at least five million dollars and wait five years before realizing a profit.

Brown's gamble was bolder still, for the magazine was directed, not at the usual magazine reader who simply wants to know how to become richer, thinner, or more beautiful, but to those with a peculiar interest: the life of a mercenary soldier. His bet paid off. It seems there are lots of people who dream of mayhem's glory, and Brown's publication, *Soldier of Fortune* magazine, has acquired a circulation of almost 200,000.

Brown does not claim that all his readers are really mercenary soldiers, although he works hard to promote the idea that his magazine is a sort of trade publication for dogs of war. He subtitled it "The Journal for Professional Adventurers," and runs a famous three-page help-wanted section for would-be mercenaries. He also knows how to make flamboyant claims that titillate his followers, as when he offered a $10,000 reward for the capture of Idi Amin. Things like that persuade readers they are among the macho elite and they feel extra tough the next time one of them takes a potshot at some traffic sign.

Brown himself does have some mercenary experience. He was trained as a Green Beret and, after leaving the army, signed on for a stint of mercenary work in Rhodesia. Of course that background further enhances a reader's dream that he is part of the world of real men. In the magazine-distribution business, however, *Soldier of Fortune* is considered an unusually successful gun magazine. Many of its sales are in gun shops and, despite the notorious classifieds, the bulk of the advertising revenue comes from mail-order companies offering knives, guns, ammo, and survival gear. That's what Brown is really doing: selling gun ads.

## A LETTER-WRITING SERVICE

**Auctioneer's price:** $10,000.
**Owner:** Linda Wells.

There is good evidence to suggest that writing was invented for use with the prehistoric parcel post. Those first bits of mail were rather dull—most likely they were invoices—but civilization knows a good thing when it sees it, and the spread of writing seems to have been slowed only marginally by the small number of readers. Illiterates who had something to say would hire an educated person to do the writing. In Third World countries it is still common to find a freelance clerk near the post office who will compose a letter for anybody who wants to send a message, but does not know how to write.

Junk mail takes us straight back to the origins of writing. Its purpose is commercial, its content is unmemorable, and its author is specially learned in the craft. The only truly modern aspect is that the recipient has no desire to get such mail. Most people transfer junk letters from their post box to a trash can so quickly that the author has perhaps half a second in which to hook the reader. The few experts who can land that hook and reel in some fish are well paid for their talent.

The top writers earn so much to write a letter (as much as $25,000) that they obtain only a few commissions per year. The Henry Ford of the business is Linda Wells; her prices are low enough to generate a high-volume trade, and she turns out a letter a week. Her clients have all the brightest technology—computers and data banks filled with the names and addresses of likely customers. They also have volumes of marketing surveys filled with statistics on the most effective techniques of mass mailing, but Ms. Wells is the one able to give substance to all that power. Her clients appreciate her skill and she draws in over $300,000 a year, making her one of America's few writers who would be taking a financial step down by becoming a doctor.

When doctors retire they often sell their practice to a recent graduate of medical school, but there is no College of Junk Mailology. Newcomers learn by doing and they have to compete with those experts who are already established. It is easy to compare the effectiveness of different writers. Companies often send out two separate mailings and then check to see which one brings in the most business. The author of the better letter is given more work. Generally newcomers are advertising copywriters who have learned enough and made enough contacts to break off on their own.

So there is yet another antique aspect of Linda Wells's business. It is precapitalist, relying on an accumulation of know-how and experience rather than an accumulation of wealth and equipment. Her business thrives, but in certain fundamental ways it is nontransferable. The precapitalist solution to this problem was the practice of apprenticeship, but since the apprentice-master relationship had many of the characteristics of slavery it is no longer permissible. Thus, if Wells's letter-writing business were put up for auction, she would hardly have anything more to sell than furniture, a word processor, and some files. The super-modern phenomenon of computerized mailing lists that steer tons of unwelcome letters to homes all over America turns out to rest on an economic arrangement so old it was known in the pharaohs' day.

# 6

# HIGH TECHNOLOGY

## WANG LABORATORIES

**Auctioneer's price:** $1,690,000,000.
**Owner:** An Wang.

The power of electronics is enough to tempt even Job to pride except for one question that comes up time and again: What the heck good is it? There is something absurd about the fact that we use super-satellite communications and the world's most powerful computers just to keep track of the weather, but we have the equipment—what else is there to do with it? If you have a practical answer to that question, you can become oh, so rich.

One use of electronics that has recently begun to spread is the performance of traditional clerical tasks. The pivotal spot in the automatic office is the "workstation," what used to be called the desk or office. There the station master does all the familiar clerical tasks:

***Word processing.*** Despite the fancy term, this work is very similar to typing. The critical difference is the ease with which corrections and editing changes are made. Typographic errors can be corrected immediately with the touch of a key. Words, sentences, or any other block of text can be deleted, moved, or repeated at will. Once a text is ready, it can be stored and printed as needed.

***Business systems management.*** In olden days this work was called filing and bookkeeping. Electronic filing uses predefined forms, but instead of being printed on paper the form appears on a screen and is filled in from a keyboard. Bookkeeping, reduced to its essence, is quite similar to filling out forms. The old style used a ledger rather than a form, but each entry line calls for the same information. As in ancient days, electronic forms and ledger entries must be completed by people, but computers can be programmed to sort through the files to produce inventories, bills, paychecks, dunning letters, tax statements, and the thousand other recurring documents companies use their files and books to produce.

***Telecommunications.*** Charles Dickens called this job "correspondence." Memos, letters, and reports can be transmitted over phone lines from one workstation to another.

Electronic equipment designed for these tasks rely on microprocessors, the so-called computer on a chip. Reliable statistics on the spread of machines to offices are hard to come by, but the world's bigget office automator is confidently believed to be Wang Laboratories of Lowell, Massachusetts.

The company was founded in 1951 by An Wang, a physicist from Shanghai, China. He moved to America immediately following World War II and took up U.S. citizenship a decade later. As a graduate student at Harvard he invented the magnetic-core memory. Until the mid-1970s most computers used these core memories, but new machines have silicon chip memories. Wang's company became a public corporation in 1967. Wang, his wife, and a family trust still control a bit over 40 percent of the stock. Wang's son, Frederick, is Executive Vice President of the firm and is thought to be in line to assume leadership when his father retires.

Computers were initially perceived simply as calculating machines and the main users were scientists and engineers. Wang was one of the first to realize that the advances in miniaturization offered new ways for businesses to use computers. From the perspective of the mid-1980s this insight seems none too startling, but as recently as 1970, despite decades of speculation about the role of computers, the widespread use of computers in home and office was not predicted even by best-selling authors who wrote about the future's glories. Most people still assumed that progress for computers lay in getting smarter. Instead computers have become more mundane. They now do many of the repetitive tasks that once only a bored human could do.

Wang is sometimes portrayed as a lucky man who got in on the ground floor of the new technology. That view overlooks the fact that lots of bright young men contributed something important to the development of computers. What really separates Wang from the other technocrats of his generation has been a continuing ability to see what the new machinery can be used for.

An electronic giant that took microprocessors down a different road is Hewlett-Packard. The company's founders, William Hewlett and David Packard, are half a generation older than Wang, just enough to keep them thinking that technical gadgets are for technical operators. A good example of their style is the way they sold calculators. Hand-held calculators began to appear in the early 1970s. The first models sold for about $100 and were the simple types that now cost $10. In 1972 Hewlett-Packard introduced the "electronic slide rule," a calculator able to do the mathematical chores needed by engineers. This approach enabled Hewlett-Packard to avoid the price wars that plagued the industry, but it also kept the electronic slide rules from becoming popular consumer items. With the invention of the microprocessor Hewlett-Packard continued to think in terms of technical uses. The company has been particularly energetic at bringing computer technology to medical procedures. The two founders, both in their seventies, are still active on the board of directors and are still the leading shareholders. Packard owns 18 percent, Hewlett 14 percent. For most of their lives the two men have been well-to-do, but recent booms in high-tech stock have made the both of them billionaires.

## A DATA-PROCESSING COMPANY

**Auctioneer's price:** $1,000,000,000.
**Owner:** H. Ross Perot.

Texas's most famous non-oil millionaire, Ross Perot, is something of a stuffy can-do fellow, a type that seldom holds the public's attention for long, but Perot pops into the public eye time after time. In April, 1970, he lost $450,000,000 in a single day when the price of his company's stock collapsed by $90 per share. It was history's greatest one-day loss, on paper, and during the whole collapse of that period he lost a billion dollars. Since then the stock has risen and slipped a few times. On some days Perot is a billionaire again; some days he's not.

Also during the early '70s, Perot caught the public eye when he denounced North Vietnam for its treatment of American prisoners of war. Later he was active in raising funds for the Vietnam War Memorial in Washington. In 1979, during the early stages of the Iranian Revolution, he financed a jailbreak for a couple of employees being held prisoner in Tehran. (His company had provided the Shah with extensive data-processing services.) These sorts of actions have made Perot a hero to some, while others have scorned him as a conservative cowboy aching to be called "Kemo Sabe." Both images fail to reveal his actual accomplishment.

Perot was an IBM salesman whose job was to sell computer hardware and programs. He had the imagination to see that there could be a business that sold only the results of these machines rather than the equipment itself. He founded the Electronic Data Systems Corporation (and still owns 50 percent of the stock). Instead of trying to explain to people what computers do, Perot's pitch was: look, these machines can handle all your records, but because they are so complicated, let experts run the machines and you enjoy the results. The pitch worked so well that even governments have turned their responsibilities over to Perot.

Electronic Data Systems provides information processing to 750 banks and over 3,000 credit unions; it handles Medicaid finances in fourteen states and keeps track of Medicare in thirteen states. Food stamp programs, city and state welfare programs, U.S. Department of Agriculture storage of surplus food, Immigration and Naturalization Service Identification cards, Social Security modernization, and many Blue Cross and Blue Shield systems are handled by this Texas company.

The largest single data-processing contract ever agreed to, worth $656,000,000 was given to Electronic Data Systems to organize an army project, code named VIABLE. Viewers of M*A*S*H can easily understand the system's duties by recalling the chores of Radar O'Reilly. VIABLE handles personnel files, searches for stocks of needed supplies, and keeps up with the operation of a particular base. More glamorous duties, like triggering World War III, are assigned to other systems.

The most unusual aspect of the VIABLE contract was the way it transferred power and responsibility from the army to Electronic Data Systems. Normally the Department of Defense likes to control everything, but in this case they tried something new.

- When the army asks for bids on a contract it usually issues a list of specifications for the goods and services it wants. In this case, however, it simply described the army's computer problems and asked for proposed solutions. Thus, the operation and specifications for VIABLE came from Electronic Data Systems rather than the military.

- Huge contracts like the VIABLE one always require support from numerous subcontractors. As a rule, the army awards the subcontracts, however, Electronic Data Systems has negotiated its own subcontract arrangements.

- The one power the military throws to the winds is cost control. Cost overruns are so much a part of the defense business that only a fool takes seriously the initial price

> agreed to in a contract; however, in VIABLE, cost control is one of the few powers retained by the army. Electronic Data Systems cannot increase its bill.

The system is in partial operation now and is supposed to be completed in 1985. (Another unusual feature of the project's history is that it has been consistently ahead of schedule.) The VIABLE network will link forty-seven army bases in the U.S. and Panama to ten super-computers. Each computer can perform several million operations per second and each has a memory of twelve million characters of data. The computers have access to a data bank capable of holding 8.4 billion characters, about 1.6 billion words.

From a practical point of view, the system means that instead of taking five days for Radar to locate the carton of tongue depressors Hawkeye so desperately needs, the computer can locate the stuff in five minutes. (But *nota bene*, "locating" a tongue depressor is not the same thing as obtaining one.)

Prophets of the American future say the country is moving from manufacturing to service and usually this change is taken to imply that, for the next generation, opportunity is going to mean no more than the chance to manage a fast-food outlet alongside Interstate 75. Perot's business shows that service can be more interesting and more lucrative. When even the Pentagon starts turning its work over to an outside service, something startling is in the air.

## MOST-WIDELY-SOLD HOUSEHOLD COMPUTERS

**Auctioneer's price:** $672,000,000.
**Owner:** Irving Gould.

The miniaturization of computers has brought their cost down to the price of a television set. Naturally a lot of entrepreneurs figured that the future lay in selling computers to ordinary families, but they never found a compelling reason for people to buy one. Not until Commodore International came along, that is.

Commodore's first small computer was the PET, introduced in 1978. At the time, no household use for the thing was evident. Programs available for the machines were few and unreliable. Games played on it were dull. The first customers were "hobbyists," people who bought the computer just to learn how to use it. This same motive was behind the sales of other household computers, but Commodore was the one to realize that this use was the ultimate purpose of the machine.

Other companies ran television ads showing actual uses for the machine. A boy learned enough French to greet his grandparents. An adult balanced his checkbook. No doubt some people were impressed, but the word-of-mouth was poor. It is easier and quicker to balance your checkbook with a calculator. (Nobody uses his head anymore.) French taught via computer is even less helpful than French taught by record sets. Word processing is nice, but most people don't write very much and fewer still revise what they write. Filing programs adapted for storing recipes and keeping track of shopping coupons are too cumbersome to ever become popular. Games are fun for a while, but the novelty wears off. The fad of attaching the computer to a phone and communicating with strangers via "electronic bulletin boards" probably has a half-life identical to that of the CB radio fad. So what good are these machines?

In 1982, Commodore introduced the Commodore 64 computer and launched a series of ads stressing the one thing household computers are great at. They acquaint you with computers.

> If you don't buy a computer, you will never become familiar with their operation and if you never become familiar with their operation, you will never be able to get a computer.

Commodore added a few ordinary advertising touches to its appeal. It took a cup of guilt from the folks at "ring around the collar" and tossed in the educational concern of encyclopedia salesmen, but the boldness and strength of the claim was the unbroken circle that you need it because you need it.

During 1983, a price war ripped out the heart of much of the household computer industry, yet Commodore soared. It became the most successful of the household computers and continued to make good profits straight through the war.

Meanwhile, inside Commodore, intrigue was afoot. The company was founded by Jack Tramiel, a Pole who came to America after his liberation from the concentration camp at Auschwitz. Later he went to Canada and started a firm that assembled Czechoslovakian typewriters. Even in Canada, that is the sort of business which seems guaranteed to keep your company small, but on a trip to Japan, Tramiel saw a desktop electronic calculator. He realized in a flash that mechanical office machines were doomed and he began converting to the manufacture of electronic devices. Tramiel's handling of the computer business gave him the reputation of being super-shrewd, but he made one great mistake. Somebody else became the dominant shareholder.

In 1965, a financial scandal made it impossible for Commodore to get money from banks. Tramiel saved the company by selling a controlling interest to Irving Gould, a Canadian investor. Gould became the company's chairman and still owns 18 percent of the stock, but his interests are wide. He is also chairman of a Canadian company called Superpack Corporation Limited and chairman of Interpool, an American subsidiary of a giant Dutch company called Thyssin-Bornemisza. For most of his years with Commodore, Gould's other interests and Commodore's weak balance sheet assured Tramiel that he would face no challenge from Gould in the running of his company. In 1983, Commodore's sudden prosperity changed the picture and, in early 1984, Tramiel suddenly retired. A friend of Gould from Thyssin-Bornemisza became the new president. Everyone at Commodore was as stony and sober faced as the politburo members when Khrushchev suddenly retired. The story that leaked to *Fortune* magazine was that Tramiel got into an argument and threatened to resign if he didn't have his way. Instead of surrendering, Gould accepted the resignation. It is not enough to be the founder and presiding guru of a bustling company. If you want power, be the owner.

The first small computer to snare the public's eye was the Apple, introduced in 1978. It never was cheap enough to become a household appliance. Its niche was with small businesses and professionals. The initial investors in Apple have taken most of their money out of the business. The founding investors were Arthur Markkula ($90,000) and Arthur Rock ($57,400). The technical end of the business was led by Stephen Jobs who, as a teenager, had built his own microcomputer. Rock no longer has a significant share of Apple. Markkula still holds 10 percent. Jobs has 13 percent.

America's boom in super-cheap computers was led by Timex, a company famous for offering cheap watches in the pre-quartz days. During the early part of 1983, their super-cheap, miniature computer was quite popular, but as price wars cut the costs of other computers, sales of the small Timex item dropped and, in 1984, Timex pulled out of that business. Timex is wholly owned by Fred Olsen, a Norwegian shipping magnate with a taste for modern technology. (He also controls 70 percent of the stock in Nimslo cameras, a 3-D camera invented by two men in Atlanta, Georgia, Jerry Nims and Allen Lo.) The Timex computer was called "Timex/Sinclair" because it was an American version of a British product invented by Sir Clive Sinclair. Sir Clive appears to be a genius. He also invented the pocket calculator and the digital watch, but in both cases the bulk of the market went to other makers, chiefly Asian, leaving Sinclair to contemplate exactly what the loss of Britain's empire means to the English merchants it once enriched.

## COMPUTER MONITORS

**Auctioneer's price:** $599,000,000.
**Owner:** Kyupin Philip Hwang.

Although many home computers are plugged into an old Sony, the best computer video screens are not television sets. The ordinary household TV is not sharp enough to give crisp letters for reading text and will damage the screen if they are allowed to sit for long periods showing exactly the same image. Thus, the spread of computers has offered new opportunities in the video screen business, an industry that shook out most of the marginal manufacturers twenty-five years ago.

The biggest beneficiary of this development has been Philip Hwang, a Korean-born technician who now lives in Sunnyvale, California, also known as Silicon Valley. Hwang founded his company in 1976 and, like everybody else in electronics, began manufacturing his product in a garage. These days the screens are assembled in Korea, a modern twist to the traditional story of immigrant success. Instead of just coming to America, getting a job and sending money back home, Hwang came, got money, and then sent jobs back home. His company, TeleVideo, is now America's leading supplier of video display terminals. Hwang still owns a bit over two-thirds of the company stock.

In the high-tech world, this week's breakthrough is next week's nostalgic laugh. Liquid crystal monitors, similar to the displays on digital watches, are coming up fast and Hwang may have to step lively to preserve his millions.

## DISK DRIVES

**Auctioneer's price:** $345,000,000.
**Owner:** Sirjang Lal "Jugi" Tandon.

Most of the programs and data used by small computers are stored on disks that look like 45 rpm records except that they always stay in their jackets and the disks have no groove. Their information is preserved magnetically, as on a cassette tape. The disks can be very densely packed, containing as much as 250,000 characters on one side of a 5¾-inch disk.

A disk drive is the machine that extracts information from the disk. It works like a record player in the way it spins the disk and resembles a tape deck in the way it uses a magnetic recording head to read or change the disk. It is unlike anything else in the way it jumps from one spot on the disk to another.

Suppose a writer is editing an article stored on one part of the disk and he decides to insert something stored elsewhere on the disk. The drive has to be able to locate that other article. Perhaps the extra material begins at the 126,431st character on the disk. To work properly the drive has to find precisely that spot. The 126,432nd character won't do.

The maestro of this technology is Jugi Tandon, an immigrant from the Punjab region of northwest India. The domination of the high-tech field by immigrant-owners may come as a surprise to many readers, but our newest comers have always been the ones to move into the newest slots, the ones more established Americans are hesitant to fill precisely because they are already established.

Tandon came to America in 1960 and got an engineering degree at Howard University in Washington, D.C. He developed a disk drive for Memorex. In 1975, he started his own company which made recording heads for disk drives. By 1978, The Tandon Corporation was the leading supplier of recording heads. At the time Radio Shack was thinking of introducing a small computer and began looking for contractors to build the disk drives. All of the companies they contacted reported that they could only supply enough machines if Tandon could provide enough recording heads. So Radio Shack turned to Jugi Tandon and asked him to produce the drives. Tandon Corporation now holds 60 percent of the market share. It provides the drives used in Radio Shack, IBM, and Kaypro computers and Tandon lives in terror lest one of them, especially IBM, takes its business elsewhere.

The company went public in 1981. Tandon sold most of his stock for scores of millions, but held on to 11 percent. His family is also the sole owner of Tandon India. That company, run by Jugi's older brother in Bombay, makes the recording heads for the drives.

## BIGGEST COMPUTER STORE CHAIN

**Auctioneer's price:** $196,000,000.
**Owner:** William Millard.

The largest retail computer chain in America is ComputerLand, founded in 1976 when the idea of a computer store seemed pretty novel. They carried Apple computers and grew with the success of that product. When IBM came out with a personal computer, ComputerLand gave Apple the heave-ho and grew even richer with the popularity of IBM. Then, when Apple introduced its Macintosh model, ComputerLand carried that too.

In an earlier day, the rise of a new consumer technology offered plenty of opportunities for independent retail businesses and proved to many ordinary Americans that individual initiative held the road to wealth and progress. Today the power of marketing favors the more feudal arrangement of retail chains. ComputerLand has over 500 stores and its buyers can make deals no little guy with one shop and a good location can hope to match. Retail sales of consumer computers became standardized almost before most consumers knew there was such a thing as a computer store.

The chain system of franchised operations is a marvelous way to gain riches and power through other people's money. ComputerLand is owned by William Millard, a California man who has been knocking around the computer world for a couple of decades. Millard was, of course, in no position to build over 500 stores on his own. Instead he found folks all over the country eager to give him money to join the system. In the old days a powerful earl had his vassals swear fealty. Today, Millard's franchisers pay up to $75,000 for a dealership. In both cases, the underlings agree to do as the lord instructs them and, in return, the lord agrees to protect his vassals. ComputerLand protection comes in the form of national advertising and good prices on the store's wares. In return, the dealers pay Millard's company 8 percent of the store's gross. This sharecropping fee removes much of the retail advantage from the dealers and the stores do not offer great savings to customers.

Yet customers come to them because they are well advertised and well located. Also, as part of a big chain, the stores can be relied on to be there a year from now. Thus shunned, the small entrepreneur does indeed fold, proving the wisdom of all those who shopped elsewhere.

This kind of circular self-generating and self-enhancing power has sent Millard's worth through the roof. His business is less than ten years old and already he is in the top third of the *Forbes* list of America's richest men.

## A GENE-SPLICING COMPANY

**Auctioneer's price:** $114,000,000.
**Owners:** Herbert Boyer and Robert Swanson.

The tale of this fortune is more suited for a TV miniseries than a reference work.

> ***Episode One:*** In 1953, Francis Crick and James Watson discover the structure of the DNA molecules found in every living cell. Their finding proves that DNA contains the genetic information that regulates an organism's chemical activity. A few years later the genetic code is deciphered.
>
> ***Episode Two:*** It is 1973, two molecular biologists—Dr. Stanley Cohen and Dr. Herbert Boyer—succeed in removing the genetic information from one DNA molecule and inserting it into another, a process popularly called gene splicing. In effect, they have given one organism the power to make organic chemicals natural to some other life form. Boyer and Cohen's feat makes them sure candidates, and likely winners, for the Nobel Prize. There is so much talk about the commercial potential of the finding that Boyer and Cohen are under heavy pressure to patent their technique. They balk, protesting that they are interested in science, not commerce. They finally agree to apply for a patent, but insist it go to Stanford University, the place where the research was done.

***Episode Three:*** Late 1975, Herbert Boyer is approached by Robert Swanson, a young man of 28 who wants to go into business. Boyer is persuaded to join forces with Swanson and each man puts up $500 to form a new company called Genentech. There is only one problem: although their business will depend on a process devised by Boyer, Stanford is trying to get the patent. If they get it, Boyer can be forced to pay for the right to use his own process.

***Episode Four:*** The prospect of great wealth begins hacking at the social web supporting biological research. Boyer's hope for a Nobel Prize seems lost. (His science is no longer "pure" enough.) Universities are pressing for their right to any money that is made from research done in their laboratories. The University of California brings suit against Genentech after the company cloned some cells that were first bred at the university laboratories. Stanford continues to seek its patent on Boyer and Cohen's process. It urges Genentech to buy permission to use the splicing process before the court reaches a decision on the patent application. Genentech shakes its head. It doesn't want to pay Stanford anything and is hoping the application will be denied.

***Episode Five:*** Late 1980, Genentech offers its stock to the public. Boyer and Swanson become instant multimillionaires as hysterical speculators pay absurdly inflated prices for the new stock. A few weeks later Stanford wins its patent. Control over the splicing process is no longer entirely in Genentech's hands.

***Episode Six:*** It is 1984, thirty years after Watson and Crick made their discovery, ten years after the first gene splicing. Dr. Boyer drives his luxurious Porsche past a man on a bicycle. The camera swings in on the pedaling man's face. He is Dr. Stanley Cohen, Boyer's partner in the gene-splicing discovery; he is not in business, not rich, and not a Nobel Prize winner either.

The promise of gene splicing is great and Genentech was first out of the gate, but so far the industry's future is, as they say, still ahead of it. Some medicines created by gene splicing, such as interleukin-2, are expected to become as important as penicillin in combating infections. They aren't here yet, however. Genentech's most valuable development to date has been the production of growth hormone. In humans, this product is already helping children who otherwise would become midgets grow to a more normal height. Genentech has also produced cattle and pig growth hormone. Because agriculture has been much quicker than medicine to make use of new biological techniques, the development of animal hormones may well be the first area (outside the stock market) where gene splicing has a great social impact.

## A SOLAR POWER COMPANY

**Auctioneer's price:** $13,300,000.
**Owner:** Sanford Robert Ovshinsky.

The life of inventor Sanford Ovshinsky has been shaped by the ebbs and flows of public interest in "alternating energy forms." Ovshinsky is now past sixty and for most of his adult life he has been promoting ways to create energy without relying on oil.

Back in the 1950s, when this interest was getting an ever more powerful hold on Ovshinsky's imagination, nuclear energy was the most widely considered alternate energy. The federal government encouraged the discussion as part of its general thesis that no one should regret that the United States brought the world into the atomic age. From Hiroshima onward, enthusiasts of the arms race have insisted that the atom was our friend.

Friendly or not, atomic power plants cost a lot to build, and people like Ovshinsky could have nothing to do with such things. Even established utility companies doubted the cost-effectiveness of the idea and began building nuclear plants only when it was clear that if they didn't, the government would. Being a practical man, Ovshinsky did not linger over his limitations. In 1960, he founded the forerunner of a company today known as Energy Conversion Devices. A quarter of a century later he is still president; his wife, Iris, is on the board of directors and his family controls two-thirds of the voting stock. Energy "conversion" is distinguished from generation because it takes existing energy, such as sunlight or heat, and changes it into a more usable form, such as electricity.

During the 1960s, because fossil fuels were cheap and nuclear power was the official energy of the future, there was almost no interest in the sort of energy sources Ovshinsky was promoting. His prospects began to brighten only when there was a great public revulsion over pollution and an accompanying loss of faith in the integrity of official pronouncements. As the 1970s began, there was a widespread feeling that if someone like Ovshinsky could come up with a good way of converting sunlight into electricity, it would end pollution and take the official know-it-alls down a peg. Then the world learned about OPEC.

Suddenly everybody agreed on the need for alternate energy sources, but the need was so pressing that there was no time for Energy Conversion Devices to find the gizmo that would save us. Nuclear technology was already at hand, so it was embraced with unexpected fervor and for the rest of the '70s Ovshinsky was ignored again.

Now the tide is again flowing with Ovshinsky. Many of the nuclear power projects begun in the '70s have proven to be as financially devastating to American enterprise as the numerous overblown developmental schemes in the Third World. Many nuclear power stations now stand with the Aswan High Dam, Brasilia, and a thousand less publicized investments, as catastrophes of ambition that sucked up available capital and opportunity. After investors in the nuclear industry began losing money, Ovshinsky started being able to find corporate partners:

- Standard Oil of Ohio has formed two partnerships with Energy Conversion Devices. One is to do research into inexpensive cells for solar energy. A second is to market the cells in North America.
- Atlantic Richfield (Arco); a partnership to conduct research into nonsolar aspects of energy conversion.
- ANR Energy Conversion Company; a partnership to study the conversion of heat into electricity.

- Sharp Corporation of Japan; a partnership to market solar cells throughout the world, except in North America. Sharp already includes Ovshinsky's cells in many of its calculators.

If he ever comes up with something that works on a commercially acceptable scale, Ovshinsky's story seems likely to become a legend. Its moral—all legends have a moral—will tell of the importance of persistence. If he fails, the legend will have some other moral. Morals are always in plentiful supply; more rare is Ovshinsky's passion for an idea.

## MICROSOFT BASIC

**Auctioneer's price:** $6,650,000.
**Owner:** William H. Gates.

For all its glory, a computer is still an electric machine controlled by on/off switches. The first computer programs were actually written out as on/off signals. (A program is a device for the orderly tripping of computer switches.) Those programs looked like 0001101111001, meaning "off off off on on off on on on on off off on." Apart from a few idiot savants, not many people in the world could seriously hope to work with such programs, so along with the evolution of the computer there has been a steady evolution of computer programming away from machine efficiency and toward human comprehensibility.

The initial step was to get beyond the on/off switch and start using symbols like the number 2 and the + sign. That way a programmer could just write X=2+2 and forget about the 1s and 0s. Of course, the switches didn't go away. First the machine had to be programmed to convert "2" into a particular pattern of on/off signals, but after that first program was written, programmers could ignore on or off positions. The creation of easy-to-use programming codes has made it possible for hobbyists, grade-school kids, and small-business owners to use computers. The silicon chip wouldn't have started a brawl, let alone a revolution, if for, say, 89, users still had to type in 1011001.

This movement away from machine needs toward human ones fostered an illusion that the machines were becoming increasingly human. The illusion is further encouraged by the metaphors of computer programmers who like to call their programming codes "languages" and call the storage of on/off patterns "memory." This terminology has diverted a lot of popular attention toward the imagined cleverness of the machine, rather as though instead of praising Edison for the electric light we admired the cleverness of the bulb for shining whenever the light switch said, "On."

The most popular "language" for home computers was a system developed between 1963 and 1965 by Professors John Kemeny and Thomas Kurtz, two mathematicians at Dartmouth College, New Hampshire. It is called BASIC, an acronym for Beginner's All-purpose Symbolic Instruction Code. Although developed for students, Basic's easy-to-learn rules made it ideal for the microcomputer industry (an industry that was nowhere in sight when Basic was first written). Basic permits programmers to write instructions that almost sound like English.

Under other circumstances the great popularity of Basic would have meant an unexpected treasure store for Kemeny and Kurtz, like writing a novel that becomes a bestseller fifteen years later. But writing a computer language is not like writing a novel. By itself Basic does nothing, and nothing is how much Kemeny and Kurtz have received in royalties for developing Basic. (Kemeny did go on to become president of Dartmouth, so his ability was not entirely unappreciated.)

The money from Basic has gone to the people who sell programs that convert Basic into all the little 1s and 0s that trip a computer's switches. The leader in this business is the Microsoft Corporation, founded back in the dark ages of microcomputers (1975) by a twenty-year-old kid. Microsoft was the first company to introduce Basic to the small computer and over 500,000 copies of their system have been sold. What Microsoft actually sells is a licence to use its Basic system. Every computer has its peculiarities and idiosyncrasies, especially if looked at in terms of how its switches work, and Microsoft Basic has to be adapted to the quirks of each new machine. Microsoft clients include Apple, IBM, Radio Shack, Kaypro, and Texas Instruments. They have also persuaded the Japanese computer industry to incorporate Microsoft Basic into their programming standards and Microsoft Basic is now built into nearly all Japanese home computers.

The company was founded by Bill Gates, a Harvard dropout who spent his college days developing a way to adapt Basic to a new computer chip called the 8080. Computer whiz kids are as common as dandelions in spring, but Gates has an unusual marketing and organizational sense that has permitted Microsoft to grow rapidly in an especially competitive field. The fact that Gates retains ownership of all the company stock suggests that he has an old-fashioned kind of entrepreneurial drive, quite unlike the modern eagerness to found companies and then sell out while the bidding it at its highest. Such judgments must be a little tentative, of course. Gates is not yet thirty and it is too early to be forecasting life patterns on the basis of his early success.

The world knows a good thing when it is free, and many companies besides Microsoft also sell Basic systems. Some of the ones on the market are: Basic Model II; Basic–Version 1.4; Cromemco's Structured Basic; Data General Basic; Data General Business Basic; DOS Basic; Dynabasic D; Structured Basic; Super Basic; Commercial Basic; Compiled Integer Basic; S-Basic; Basic09; 6800 A/Basic. Recently Kemeny and Kurtz have come up with a system they call True Basic, finally getting around to locking the barn door some twenty years after the horse fled.

## MACHINES THAT LISTEN

**Auctioneer's price:** $2,640,000.
**Owner:** Scott family.

Soon technology will bring us wondrous moments like the following:

A thirsty man approaches a vending machine and inserts a

few quarters. "Gimme a Coke," he says. The machine just stands there. "Gimme a Coke," he repeats. More stillness from the machine. The man tries the old-fashioned technique of kicking the machine and then yells, "Gimme a Coke, damn it." The machine replies, "Please, don't swear at me, sir."

Voice communications with machines is about to burst upon us. In 1978, Texas Instruments introduced a toy called "Speak-n-Spell" that spoke words and letters. Now machines that listen are becoming available. Their most practical application is in commercial processes that tie up the hands. For example, a quality-control inspector can use both hands to examine an item on an assembly belt while speaking "Okay" or "Reject" into a microphone. The item is returned to the belt and automatically transported to either the reject pile or to an area for further processing.

Even more precious is the power it will give handicapped people who can control machines simply by talking to them. It offers quadriplegics a way of controlling light switches, televisions, and other common machines.

Several companies are already in this business. The one that ordinary folk are most likely to encounter is Scott Instruments of Denton, Texas. They make voice-controlled terminals that work with home computers like the Apple. The devices cost under one thousand dollars, so at least some hobbyists can afford them.

The company was founded in 1978 by E.V. Scott. At that time he was the sole owner. He was also a proud dad helping his son Brian, a psychologist specializing in speech perception. Brian is the technical brains behind Scott. As so many founders of high-technology companies do, Scott soon began selling stock to the public. Today, the Scotts still hold about a quarter of the shares.

Listening machines do present some problems. For example, many workers on tedious jobs spend a lot of the time talking to co-workers. They do their routine labor with their hands and pass the day chatting. They are not likely to welcome devices that force them to talk only with machines.

Another question concerns efficiency. There are situations in which voice control is the best and simplest way to operate a machine, but there may not be enough of them to permit commercial success. One company that concentrated on these practical applications was Threshold Technology of New Jersey. During most of the 1970s it struggled to make money but finally, in 1982, filed a Chapter 11 bankruptcy. The market was not there. Other companies are hoping to persuade people to use voice terminals in situations where a keyboard can serve just as well. Unfortunately for those ambitions, keyboard technology is cheap and easy while speech-recognition machines are at the cutting edge of computer science. It is going to be a long time before keyboards and voice terminals are close enough in price for prudent customers to ignore cost considerations.

Another problem is the etiquette of language. Technicians assume that because it is easier to talk than to type, people would rather talk to a machine. But, put bluntly, people often feel stupid when talking to a machine. Language is used to establish relationships. It is no accident that around the world people address their leaders humbly and profusely while the leaders reply in short condescending phrases. If the leader is really powerful and the speaker truly lowly, a wave of the hand, a nod, or a dismissive snap of the fingers may suffice.

When it comes to less exalted levels we still see language establishing a whole network of relationships. Children do not speak to parents in the same way they speak to other children; restaurant customers do not want to be called "Chum," by the waiter and ministers who say, "Call me Freddy," are not taken seriously.

Now what is the proper form of address between man and machine? Has the world grown so egalitarian that even vending machines and typewriters must be spoken to politely, even a little patiently? Soft-drink machines are a nuisance and an insult, but at least you get to punch them and in pressing a button you assert sharply and unambiguously that you are master, the machine is servant. The Scotts are betting that we are willing and ready to abandon that feudal relationship for a more democratic one.

## A SPACE-LAUNCH COMPANY

**Auctioneer's price:** $2,500,000.
**Owner:** David B. Hannah, Jr.

If calculation of the auctioneer's price for Space Services Inc. of Houston, Texas, had been limited to the usual consideration of assets, debts, and prospective income, the company would have had a negative value, meaning the auctioneer's price would have represented the minimum amount needed to pay somebody to take responsibility for the company. But something happens to people's judgment when they start talking about space. Visions of "The Future" dance in their heads and the word "impossible" loses force. Potential assets are auctioned for large sums.

The company's chief assets, both of which are intangibles valued at $0.00 on an accountant's balance sheet, are:

- *A successful launching.* On Sept. 9, 1982, at 10:17 a.m. (Central Daylight Time), the company launched an old Minuteman rocket, renamed Conestoga I, from Matagorda Island, Texas. It flew for ten minutes and landed 321 miles away, in the Gulf of Mexico.
- *A sympathetic press.* "One small step for capitalism," is the way most newspaper and magazine articles reported the successful launch. Business publications, especially, ought to have known better, but they are not eager to question the thesis that free enterprise is leading us into the future, so the claims of company chairman David Hannah have been reported uncritically.

Thus, an entrepreneur might be able to make use of the company's names and files, if he were willing to sink a great deal of extra capital into the venture.

At some time, however, the entrepreneur is going to have to ask what a space-launch company has to sell. It will not do to settle for the answer widely reprinted in the press. Hannah says oil companies can use satellites to do prospecting. Satellite photos of the earth can help geologists determine what lies underground. This service is already provided by the Landsat, an

Conestoga I on the launch pad. Photo: SSI Photo

earth-photographing satellite, and it has shown us many wonderful things about the earth. As a government operation Landsat is splendid, but it has not been profitable.

Communications satellites seem an obvious possibility, but Mr. Hannah does not raise that idea, perhaps because his little rockets cannot be expected to carry and orbit a modern satellite. Compared to the kinds of payloads NASA and the Soviet Union carry, Space Services Inc. seems pitiful. Capitalism can only triumph in this sort of competition if it begins with plenty of capital, but Mr. Hannah's company is woefully underfunded. For the first launching he persuaded fifty-seven investors to put up a total of $6,000,000. If he were opening a restaurant in Houston, that kind of backing would be aplenty. For a space program, however, it is mighty slender. With so little money, the principal concern of the company switches from rocketry to finding more investors.

It is a risky venture; all the press reports concede that much. Still they go on to quote Mr. Hannah's reminder that his investors are mostly oil men and that no business contains more risks than does oil. While it is true that drilling for oil involves risks, at least the drillers know what they're after, where they can sell it, and how much it will bring. But a successful launch of another small rocket, even the successful orbiting of a payload, still won't establish the profitability of the company. Somebody is going to have to find a commercially useful task for a rocket, one that can be repeated many times for many different customers.

There isn't anything in Mr. Hannah's background to demonstrate that he is the somebody who can do it. Shortly after he graduated from Rice University in Houston, he helped found a real-estate development firm called Ayrshire. It grew as Houston grew and over the years Hannah made a lot of contacts in the oil business. He became friends with George Bush, long before the vice-presidency. In those circles Hannah got to know a lot of wealthy people willing to invest in daring deeds. Yet the real estate business is nothing like astronautics and not every shrewd wildcatter is shrewd about everything else.

## THE LASER PATENT

**Auctioneer's price:** $895,000.
**Owner:** Gordon Gould.

It is hard to imagine a legal doctrine more certain to assure employment for lawyers than the romantic lie which justifies patent law. Invention often seems to emerge from a cultural setting rather than from an individual mind. Patent law, however, assumes that for every invention there is an identifiable inventor. Really major inventions often conclude with races to the patent office. The winner of the race becomes a millionaire; the losers start looking for lawyers.

The laser was one of the most promising inventions of the 1960s and continues to inspire legal maneuvering. The first working laser was built in 1960 by T.H. Maiman of Hughes Aircraft. With a budget of only $50,000, Maiman beat the teams at both Bell Labs and a second company, called TRG, that were spending millions to try and produce a narrowly focused and greatly amplified beam of light. But it was too late for Maiman to get the laser patent, which had just been assigned to Bell Labs. The inventors of the machine described in the Bell proposal were Charles H. Townes and Arthur Schawlow. The machine depicted in that first laser patent had not yet been made to work and a quarter of a century later it has still never functioned. But they did get the patent.

While Maiman was succeeding in the laboratory and Bell was triumphing in court, a third party named Gordon Gould was getting nowhere. As a graduate student Gould was the first person known to have used the word "laser" in writing. The name appears in a notebook he kept in 1957. The notebook also contains a design for a light amplifier of a type that is still in common use today. About a third of modern lasers use Gould's "pump" method of amplification and his notebook has been displayed in the Smithsonian Institution.

Gould was not naive about the importance of a patent and on Nov. 13, 1957, he did have his notebook notarized. In March, 1958, he left Columbia University to take a job at TRG. His new employer soon submitted a proposal to the Defense Department for a laser research grant. They got a million dollars to continue the studies, but Gould was banned from the project, having been denied security clearance.

If Gould had stayed with the project, TRG would have had a strong incentive to start patent proceedings on his design. As it was, Gould was left to muster whatever devices he could. Individuals seldom do well in combat against Bell Labs, the Defense Department, and a swelling industry whose members have no wish to pay royalties. Yet eventually Gould did begin to win some allies. He signed an agreement with REFAC Technology Development Corporation, giving them half the rights to his patent in return for their assistance in winning his case. REFAC hired a legal firm to plead the case. Instead of charging a fee, the lawyers got a quarter of any patent rights they secured. In October, 1977, Gould won his case and got a patent.

Nobody wished to pay any royalties, however, and the case grew even more complicated as REFAC began suing companies for patent violations. The companies defended themselves by insisting that Gould's claims were nonsense. They pointed out that as early as 1916 Einstein wrote about the possibility of amplifying light radiation. In 1954, Einstein's theory was given practical expression when Charles Townes built a machine (called a "maser") that amplified and focused microwaves. Gould worked only two doors down from Townes, so anything he thought of was probably already in the air.

But Gould's case has proven surprisingly resilient. In the air or not, Gould's notebook was where the technology first emerged on paper and patent mythology sets great store by who was first. Gould has been winning his cases. General Motors volunteered to be sued in order to smash Gould's claims. Years later, tired and beaten, General Motors settled its suit, agreeing to pay royalties.

But while Gould was winning his cases he was losing his grip on the patent. The enormous cost of pressing the suits has forced him to sell more and more of his one asset, the promise of future royalties. Today Gould is a minority holder in his own invention. He owns twenty percent of the patent. REFAC has forty percent, as does a second corporation, Pathlex.

# 7
# HOUSEHOLD NAMES

## du PONT

**Auctioneer's price:** $11,800,000,000.
**Owner:** Bronfman family.

Most people figure that the du Pont family still owns du Pont chemicals (officially known as E.I. du Pont de Nemours & Co.), but that is no longer the case. The family now consists of several hundred heirs of Pierre Samuel du Pont de Nemours, the man who defended Louis XVI when he was on trial for his life during the French Revolution. Pierre's second son, Éleuthère Irénée, founded a gunpowder company near Wilmington, Delaware, in 1802. He grew rich as a result of the War of 1812 and his sons led the company to national importance, largely on the base of a colossal fortune raised during the Civil War. At the start of this century a procedure for assuring continued family control of the corporation was worked out, but in 1967 the du Pont family retired from the firm's operation.

It looked as though du Pont would go the way of many an old family company—the descendants would sit on holdings which were large enough to bring wealth, but not power. Recently, however, the Bronfman family, through its Seagram's operation (q.v.) has gained over a fifth of the corporation's stock. They now own twice as much stock as the entire du Pont family and have several seats on the board. The Bronfman fortune was based on liquor sales during Prohibition. As Canadians working in Canada, they were able to make liquor legally, and they found many eager American customers who bought the stuff by the boatload. What the buyers did with it was anybody's guess. (Try asking Eliot Ness.)

Another famous brand name with a Bronfman presence is Scott Paper. Presumably there are Americans who touch neither nylon nor liquor, but even they must use toilet paper. One fifth of Scott Paper's stock is now owned by a Canadian company, Brascan Limited, which in turn is largely controlled by the Bronfmans.

All three of these businesses—distilling, paper making, and the whole array of du Pont's enormous operation—are based on chemistry, changing the intrinsic properties of a substance. For reasons which are a little hard to grasp, the chemical revolution that occurred a century ago has almost no hold on the historical imagination. Even the great oil companies are commonly described as offshoots and supports of the industrial revolution, rather than being recognized as revolutionary developments in their own right.

Around the time of the Civil War, the du Pont company in America and several firms in Germany discovered chemical processes for the manufacture of dyes and, a bit later, agricultural fertilizers, fibers, fuels, and medicines. The fruits of these discoveries account for a large part of the material difference between the everyday features of nineteenth and twentieth century life.

Another enormous foreign holding in American chemicals is that of Dr. Friedrich Karl Flick. He has over 28 percent of the voting power in W.R. Grace, a chemical producer that deals in everything from bird guano to cocoa butter. As a young man,

Flick worked for Grace in order to learn business management, then returned to his home in Germany. Apparently he retained a sentimental attachment to the firm, for he has been buying it up. His holding is much larger than that of the chairman of the board, Peter Grace.

Flick is one of the world's richest men, a multibillionaire worth two Gettys. His holding company, Friedrich Flick Industrieverwaltung KGaA, controls sixty-three other companies scattered across the western world. His father was a war criminal, convicted and imprisoned for plunder and spoilage, for using slave labor, and for helping to finance the S.S. Flick's defense claimed he had had no idea of the many crimes performed by the Nazis. His company used slave labor and Flick had visited a company factory after its conversion to a concentration camp, so the claim was even harder to believe. Flick's dogged insistence on ignorance led to a memorable exchange when he was on trial (source: *Trials of War Criminals before the Nuernberg Military Tribunals* Volume VI (U.S. Government Printing Office, Washington: 1952):

> QUESTION: Didn't you notice when you went into the building the extra barbed wire fence, machine gun towers, that had been constructed since your last visit?
>
> FLICK: No, it was dark and I didn't see anything of that.

The younger Flick has recently had troubles of his own. Like a cartoon mafioso, one of Flick's senior employees kept financial records of all the company's shady operations. The idea was to make sure Flick never tried to fire him. The books fell into the hands of the police and for much of 1982 and 1983 the German public was entertained by revelations of bribes and tax evasion. Even in peacetime, even in a democracy, you can buy a lot of mischief with a few billion at your disposal, and the Flick Affair, though little noticed in America, has shaken West Germany to its roots.

## FORD MOTORS

**Auctioneer's price:** $5,630,000,000.
**Owner:** Ford family.

Presumably, Henry Ford II is tired of hearing that he is not the man his grandfather was. "Who the heck is?" he might reply. Although the retort is just, the observation will not go away for Henry Ford II just isn't the man his namesource was.

The first Henry Ford was the kind of man Americans instinctively appreciate. He took newfangled technology, and through a respect for the mass market he made his company the largest automobile manufacturer in the world. Getting rich is good; getting rich by serving the working stiff is better; and getting rich by materially improving the lot of the common man is best of all. Ford's business permanently changed the way ordinary people experienced everyday life. They appreciated the change and the man who had made it possible.

There was a less welcome side to the great Henry, but it too struck a cord in the American soul. There was nothing personal in Ford's hatreds, and he hated many groups—Catholics, Jews, unionizers, bankers, Wall Street investors, and, believe it or not, capitalists. Yet he was always amazed when people took his hatreds personally. He wrote a book denouncing "The International Jew" and accepted a decoration from Adolf Hitler, but he was genuinely puzzled when his Jewish friends were hurt and withdrew from him. He knew he was too nice a guy for their anguish to come from anything other than misperception.

Henry Ford thought of himself as a deeply and unabashedly nice guy. This confidence gave him an ease and charm that dulled the edge of the many nasty and mean things he did and said. Millions of ordinary Joes think they are nice guys, but most really successful men have a moment early in their lives when they realize they are shoving some people or ideals aside. They may not care, may even relish the thought, but they understand that from another's point of view a sense of grievance can be felt. Henry Ford was different. He never doubted that he was a really nice guy.

Perhaps his innocence resulted from the lateness of his first step onto the ladder of success. He was 40 years old when he founded the Ford Motor Company. Plenty of men don't achieve business success until well after that age and in politics great success at age 40 qualifies a fellow for the title "boy wonder," but most successful people begin competing long before their fortieth year. Ford, however, was a mechanic in his youth and did not enter the world of ferocious business competition until middle age. Evidently by then he was so used to thinking of himself as a nice guy that no amount of contradictory evidence could change his mind.

As he grew more powerful Ford was alert enough to see that he did have enemies and rivals. He realized that because he was a force for good, his challengers must simply be evil. Mercy was not to be wasted on their kind. Ford became obsessed with security; his most trusted advisor was Harry Bennett; chief of internal security at Ford. Bennett's spy system among the workers reportedly turned one-quarter of the labor force into informers.

Ford's cheery-eyed malevolence kept him popular for a long time, but eventually people saw that behind the lack of pretension was a bigotry and self-deceit that permitted any kind of cruelty. When Ford pronounced the 1930s depression "wholesome" and "the best times we ever had," people quit listening to him. There was nothing personal in Ford's hatreds because he lacked the moral imagination to understand that other people can honestly come by other points of view.

Thus, on a moral level, there is ample room for Henry Ford's heirs to best their illustrious ancestor. Henry's only child, Edsel Ford, did in fact seem to be a better man, but he died before his father and never escaped the old brute's shadow.

At the end of the World War II control of the company was passed to Henry Ford II. He was 28. As it turned out young Henry was no moral exemplar and does not seem to have ever sought to be one. He was caught handing in a ghost-written senior thesis at Yale and left without a degree. His nephew, Benson Ford, Jr., claims that when Henry's brother, Benson Senior, died, Henry stepped in the dead man's sitting room and helped himself to pieces of expensive jewelry he found there. So it is as an automobile maker rather than as a moral leader that Ford has left himself to be judged. He did lead the Ford Motor Company for thirty-four years (1945–79).

When he took over the company the American automobile

industry dominated the world. When he retired, it didn't even dominate America. Obviously Henry Ford II isn't solely to blame for the change, but he was a prominent part of the general failure of his generation to maintain America's industrial inheritance.

As usual with bunglers, the second Henry was taken quite by surprise at his own incompetence. For most of his reign, Ford was enormously profitable and it seemed that nothing could do the company serious harm. In 1957, Ford Motors introduced the Edsel and over the next three years the company took a $300,000,000 bath on that dud. It hardly made a dent in the company's balance sheet. During the same period Ford introduced the hardtop convertible. It flopped. Again the accountants yawned. So what?

There was an unheeded warning in all this. The market was not always where Ford thought it was. Ford could compete for the stylish consumers with Thunderbirds and Mustangs. Its Lincoln Continental was considered the world's most elegant car, but the company had been founded on sales to ordinary citizens and for those regular folk Ford had no new ideas. There were no successors to the Model T's and Model A's as the car for Everyman.

Early in the 1960s it became apparent that there was a local market that Ford and the other American companies were not tapping. Europe's postwar recovery was now well advanced and the German Volkswagen was discovering a market of young affluents-to-be. These were people who grew up during America's postwar boom. They took material comfort for granted and fully expected to be rich themselves. It was just that right at that moment they were students, or young marrieds, or still not quite settled and could not afford both the best car and the best stereo, so they bought a Volkswagen instead. It was cheap to begin with and cheaper to maintain.

"Who cares?" wondered people at Ford. Those cars are cheap and when they can afford it the people will buy Fords, Mercurys, and eventually even Lincolns. The affluents-to-be thought exactly the same thing, but in the meanwhile they grew accustomed to the idea that a satisfactory car need not be American-made. Later the Japanese began exploiting the same market and then one October day in 1973 OPEC announced that the price of oil was being jumped from $3.01 a barrel to $5.12. Soon thereafter an increasing number of Americans began to suspect it was going to take longer than they thought before they became affluent. And just like that, the American car ceased to be Everyman's car. The market that the first Henry had discovered was abandoned by the second.

The Ford family, of course, has remained well beyond affluent. When the company was formed it had a number of shareholders. After 1917, Henry began buying out the other investors until he became sole owner. In 1936, for tax purposes, the Ford Foundation was created and given a large block of company stock. The Foundation began selling its shares to the public in 1955, and at that point absolute family control of the company was lost; however, the Ford family's stock, called Class B shares, controls 40 percent of the voting rights.

## SALOMON BROTHERS

**Auctioneer's price:** $2,250,000,000.
**Owner:** Harry Oppenheimer.

The floor of the New York Stock Exchange is larger, but the Salomon Brothers' headquarters, just off Wall Street, contains the world's largest privately owned trading room. The firm needs such a room because it trades over $5 billion worth of securities every day. It is also the world's largest bond-trading firm and America's largest private investment bank. It handles financing for Britain, Sweden, and other sovereign states. It was Salomon Brothers that advised Chrysler on the financial restructuring program that saved the company. The firm's senior economist, Henry Kaufman, is so respected that when, in autumn 1982, he said that matters looked promising, the stock market entered a boom the likes of which hadn't been seen since the 1960s.

A boom of that size could not have been caused by Kaufman, but his optimism removed the last remaining impediment. Salomon Brothers knew the importance of Kaufman's prediction. Ninety minutes before it released his report saying he expected interest rates to decline, Salomon began buying bond futures. Insiders estimate they bought $400,000,000 worth and made a one-day profit of $8,000,000.

Most Wall Street investment firms are partnerships, owned by the company's senior managers, but Salomon Brothers is owned by a South African gold miner. The firm did begin (in 1910) as a partnership, owned and operated by the Salomon brothers. As recently as 1978, the managing partner was still a Salomon and he was adamantly against any merger proposals. He retired, however, and a new breed took over.

Salomon had grown by obeying the old New England motto, "Save your jam for tomorrow; no jam today." On paper, the partners did very well. A new partner's initial investment of $20,000 was joined with the rest of the firm's capital and grew rapidly into millions, but the money was locked up in the firm. The millionaire members were forced to lead conservative lives. In 1910 that sort of policy was normal and not surprising, but seventy years later it was distinctly old-fashioned. By then the average partner was 42 years old. He had been born just at the outset of World War II, began his career during the Kennedy years, and was familiar, at least via television, with all the earthly pleasures his sober life denied. Then one weekend in August, 1981, all the partners were brought to a secret meeting north of New York City and given the news no Pilgrim forefather ever lived to hear, "Tomorrow has arrived. Jam for everybody!" An offer had been tendered to buy the firm. In return, the average partner was to get $7,800,000. Nobody got under a million dollars and senior members like Henry Kaufman got eleven million.

The buyer was a large metals company called Phibro, that is, in turn, controlled and largely owned by a Bermuda-based company, the Minerals and Resources Corporation. Whenever you read about a gigantic outfit based in Bermuda you can bet dollars against cough drops that the company is under the control of somebody who is not based in Bermuda. In this case the Minerals and Resources Corporation is owned and operated by a series of South African firms whose holdings grow more Byzantine at every level, but if you have the energy to trace it to the end, it leads to the richest man in South Africa, Harry Oppenheimer, and his son, Nicholas. Oppenheimer's diamond company (DeBeers) controls the flow of four-fifths of the world's newly mined diamonds. His gold company, Anglo-American, produces one quarter of all the noncommunist world's gold. Other Oppenheimer companies handle more copper than any U.S. firm, sell more oil than many of the Arab emirates, and buy more grain than South Dakota produces.

The South African government of small farmers and small businessmen is concerned chiefly with holding the rest of the world at bay rather than with controlling international commerce. Its laws have erected a series of walls between South Africa's races and then between South Africa as a whole and the rest of the world. Oppenheimer's Bermuda corporation provides one way of eluding that Fortress South Africa mentality and now that he has picked up Salomon Brothers he has an unprecedented unity of control over strategic minerals and investment operations. It gives him the sort of worldwide grasp that has previously been reserved for the great Japanese trading companies.

Oppenheimer's purchase price of Salomon was $550 million—a great bargain. The company is worth four times that, but after all those years of settling for dry toast, the Salomon partners were delighted to accept a quarter of a jar of jam.

This book does not list many people whose claim to wealth is based mainly on holding a powerful stock portfolio. Most investors are company outsiders and they remain outsiders even if they buy a substantial amount of a company's stock. A corporation's founder can hold only 10 percent of the stock and still be considered the owner because he is still the largest shareholder, occupies a senior executive chair, and has the political muscle to keep control in the family. An outsider who buys 10 percent of the stock usually has to put up a great struggle to become an insider. His stock purchase may simply spark anxiety on the part of management who redoubles its effort to keep the outsider out. Yet a few investors are important enough to mention:

***Fayez Sarofim*** is an Egyptian-born money manager whose firm, Sarofim & Co., is located in Houston. Sarofim's family lost much of its Nile valley farmland when it was seized during Nasser's land reform program. He began his American business in 1959, using start-up money provided by his father. Most of his clients are large pension funds, including those of Rice University, Ford Motors, and the State of Oregon. With control over so many millions of dollars Sarofim has been able to buy substantial portions of many companies including Pennzoil (10 percent), Teledyne (10 percent), American General Insurance (8 percent), and Diasonics high tech (6 percent). Sarofim does not try to control the companies he invests in, so his purchases are generally greeted with smiles rather than panic.

***Carl H. Lindner II*** does like to have a say in the companies he invests in. Lindner has been most effective at using the money pump of being private, going public, and then going private again. In 1961, the American Financial Corporation (AFC) was a small savings and loan company in Cincinnati. Lindner sold the stock publicly and reaped one fortune. In 1981 he took it private again, through borrowed money, and brought himself an even larger fortune. The AFC's voting stock is now wholly owned by the Lindner family. AFC is mainly in the insurance business, writing about one billion dollars worth of policies each year. It is the sole owner of Great American Insurance Company, Stonewall Insurance Co., Moore Group, Transport Underwriters Association, and Transport Management Company. Lindner likes to use the company money to develop large stock holdings in other companies. He is the biggest investor in Gulf + Western and in Penn Central.

***Saul Steinberg*** also uses money from his privately held insurance companies to invest in a large stock portfolio. Insurance companies are a fine source of investment money because so much of their income is in cash and because they are not obligated to produce any commodity with the money. Steinberg's operation is called Reliance Group Holdings.

## LEVIS

**Auctioneer's price:** $1,560,000,000.
**Owner:** Haas family.

Jeans have been around a lot longer than cowboys. Shakespeare knew about them, maybe even wore them. The same is true for Chaucer. Originally the cloth was called "fustian," after the cotton-weaving town in Egypt that made the cloth. By Shakespeare's day, however, the word "jean" was well established. The name came from Genoa, the Italian city that imported the Egyptian cloth and then reexported it to England. The American contribution to this long history was the addition of the letter -s to "jean" and the decision to dye them blue. (If Shakespeare wore jeans, they were probably white.) The blue dye was part of a nineteenth-century marketing decision. Makers said the stuff was "blue denim," denim being the name for a wool cloth that had much more prestige than cotton.

By the time Levi Strauss came along (1873), making and selling blue jeans was about as bold an idea as making white paper. Even so, it was still a good idea. Originality is given too much importance; most departures from the tried and true are merely reappearances of the failed and rejected. Levi Strauss started with an ancient cloth dyed in a well established color and then he added one new detail. He riveted on buttons and snaps to strengthen the weak spots where threads tended to break, a small idea but a powerful one. By 1873, the industrial revolution had brought such fabulous advances in textile production that city folk were not much interested in coarse medieval-style cloth. But Levi Strauss managed to see that the old cloth's durability still appealed to the poor and hard working. So instead of embracing the new textiles he made the old pants even more durable.

Until quite recently Levi Strauss was entirely family owned; first by Strauss and his family, then by the Haas family. Walter Haas married a grandniece of the founder and took over the company. During the 1960s, however, the company's sales began to expand dramatically and eventually the financial rewards of selling some stock became irresistible. The Haas family still holds 45 percent of the corporate shares, more than enough to insure continued power.

The growth in popularity of Levi's blue jeans is hard to explain. Sure, they are great pants, but over the past three decades sales have increased about twenty-five times and Levi Strauss has become the world's largest manufacturer of brand-name clothing. This growth was not based on any new brilliance at the factory. No new weave, no modification à la riveting was at work. Levi's jeans had simply become caught up in a world-wide fad. Today the terror that grips the hearts of the Haas family is that the fad will end, the pants will only be sought by customers who really need durable clothing, and the grossly swollen Levi Strauss company will collapse. So, the company which began as a super-conservative enterprise now has to hustle every hour to remain leader of the pack.

## HALLMARK CARDS

**Auctioneer's price:** $1,050,000,000.
**Owner:** Donald Joyce Hall.

Although the best advertising simply puts forth the information a consumer needs in order to make a wise purchase, the most memorable advertising manages to short-circuit consumer judgement and turn an ordinary product into an extraordinary money-maker. No company was ever more successful at this second kind of advertising than Hallmark Cards.

Originally brand names played no role whatsoever in greeting card sales. People selected a card on the basis of design and message. In fact, storcs mounted the cards on numbered boards, so it was impossible to discover what the card's brand name was. Customers made their selection and reported the number to a clerk who then produced a fresh card from out of a drawer.

Despite these difficulties Joyce Hall began to advertise his cards in the 1940s, using the diabolical slogan, "When you care enough to send the very best." This line probably would have been less intimidating if the consumer were buying an item for himself. Many people are willing to say, "I don't care, I like it," but matters change when it comes to gift-giving. Buying to suit another's taste is more challenging, especially if the differences between products are slight. Then Hallmark came along with a little guidance and the not very subtle claim that giving any other card meant a lack of concern on the part of the giver.

The first sign that the ad campaign was working came when stores complained that customers were ripping cards off their mountings to see if they were Hallmark. Stores couldn't believe it. Surely customers were interested in the card, not the maker. They finally faced up to what was happening and got rid of the mounted displays. From there on out customers had no excuse for not caring enough to buy Hallmark, and sales grew like tadpoles beneath a lily pad.

Today Hallmark is one of the largest privately held companies in the world. It has 20,000 card shops of its own, a second line of greeting cards, Ambassador, and the vast Kansas City Crown Center Redevelopment Corporation.

Joyce Clyde Hall founded the company and thought up the slogan and advertising campaign that raised him beyond rich. Until his death (in late 1982) the family owned three-quarters of the company. (The other quarter was held by employees.) The family still owns over half of the company outright, but Hall left a sizable chunk to nonprofit enterprises that are controlled by the family. Hall's heirs were his son Donald, who runs the company, and his two daughters.

## FEDERAL EXPRESS

**Auctioneer's price:** $710,000,000.
**Owner:** Frederick W. Smith.

Every television viewer knows about the Federal Express overnight package delivery business. These advertisements are quite unlike other television commercials because they are aimed at the business market. Most consumers never ever have to use the company's service, but so intense has the competition for office business become that every night ordinary consumers watch Federal Express, Emery, Airborne, Purolator, and even the post office fight for money that the viewers don't plan to spend on any of them. Are they kidding? Ten to thirty bucks to send a short letter to somebody! Most people are just not in that much of a hurry. Yet everybody is familiar with the ads.

For most people the Federal Express revolution begins and ends at the TV screen, but the company's founder/owner, Fred Smith, is the kind of fellow who sparks revolutions and legends at every turn.

> In college Smith's economics professor graded the Federal Express idea "C." While a student at Yale, Smith wrote a term paper in which he set forth his whole organizational scheme. The professor will look foolish forever because instead of investing in the idea he dismissed it. Because we all like horse laughs on academic know-it-alls, this story will be told whenever Federal Express is discussed, however, there may be another side to it. Smith was late in getting the paper in, he wrote it in one night, and the major customer he proposed to serve, the Federal Reserve banking system, has never signed up for Smith's scheme. So maybe the paper only deserved a C, maybe it was even a "gentleman's C." (The paper was lost long ago, so we shall never know the truth of it.)

> Smith bet his birthright on the company. When he was four years old, Smith's father died and left his son four million dollars. The interest on that sum can provide a very tidy living. A lazy man would have bought a beach house and moved no further. A prudent one would have invested three million in gilt-edged securities and perhaps taken a flyer with one million. Smith bet the whole pile on his idea. For a project involving so many airplanes and delivery vans his money wasn't even enough to start it sparking. He found other investors who raised the kitty to $72,000,000. If the company had failed he would be known, to the few who knew him at all, as the foolish young man who had squandered his inheritance before he was thirty.

Smith met a payroll by playing blackjack in Las Vegas. Federal Express began its overnight delivery service in 1972, and only started showing a profit in 1976. OPEC's increase in the price of jet fuel forced Smith to scramble for more money. He found that his investment sources were going dry, a payroll was coming due, and the company appeared to be headed for bankruptcy. Smith was in Chicago's O'Hare airport waiting for a plane to Memphis when, on a desperate impulse, he flew to Vegas and parlayed the few hundred dollars he had on him to $27,000. He met his payroll and, with the extra time his winnings granted him, he found more backers.

The central idea behind Federal Express was so advanced that even today it sounds futuristic. The key idea in Smith's term paper was "hub and spoke" organization. We are more

Federal Express sorting room. Photo: Courtesy Federal Express Corp. Photo by Bill Speidel.

familiar with network organizations, like the one used by the postal system in which each local post office picks up, sorts, and distributes batches of mail. Federal Express works in quite another way. While he was at Yale, Smith realized that the jet plane had made it possible to organize a one-stop sorting system that would serve the whole country. All Federal Express packages are flown to Memphis, Tennessee, sorted, and then flown to their destination. It doesn't matter if the package is going from Washington, D.C. to Boston or from San Francisco to Seattle, they all go via Memphis. It takes a minute or two to be persuaded that this method really is a good idea, but it is. Instead of needing many planes flying out of each city, the company only needs one. The planes begin arriving in Memphis around 11:30 at night. For the next hour and a half the Memphis airport is one of the world's busiest as over seventy planes land. At 2 a.m. they start taking off again with their new cargos. Under this scheme a package going from San Francisco to Boston is handled as easily as one going from San Francisco to Salt Lake City.

Because he needed so many other investors Smith holds only 11 percent of his company's stock. He is the largest shareholder, but not the only significant one. However, he is firmly in control. Along with his stock he holds the titles of chairman of the board, president, and chief executive officer.

The package delivery service most people know from experience is the United Parcel Service. Its six million packages per day is better than twice the number of parcels handled by the U.S. Post Office. It is owned by its employees. Usually worker ownership reflects a last desperate effort to save the jobs at a dying steel mill or coal mine, but the United Parcel Service is thriving. Its auctioneer's price would be well above one billion dollars, perhaps over two billion.

Stock in the company is awarded as bonuses to middle-level and senior management. Most of the employees—the ones who drive the trucks, sort the packages, and arrange for parcel pickups—participate in a profit-sharing plan that lets them receive dividends but gives them no control over the stock. Direct shareholders are also restricted. All sales of stock must be approved by the company and it disallows sales to outsiders. Sales to a co-worker would probably also be disallowed if it was thought the employee's holding was growing too large. When an employee retires he must sell his stock back to the company. If United Parcel were failing, this scheme would be cited as proof that universal ownership stifles individual initiative. As it is, ideologues can only still their lips and stamp their feet.

## H&R BLOCK

**Auctioneer's price:** $557,000,000.
**Owner:** Bloch family.

Ten percent of all individual tax forms filed with the federal government are filled out by H&R Block. The company has offices in every city with a population above 5,000. And because taxes are collected everywhere, H&R Block has expanded abroad. It has offices in Canada, Australia, and New Zealand. It is impossible to get through the tax season (Jan. 2–April 15) without hearing about the company. Temporary offices sprout like dandelions; its labor force jumps from just over 2,600 employees to over 45,000; the air is full of commercials for the service. Block's advertising is famous for being dull and its spokesman, Henry Bloch, is about as exciting as the 1040 form itself, but who wants to put his money in the hands of a man with flashy tastes?

Henry Bloch and his younger brother, Richard, stumbled into this line of work. Shortly after World War II they began providing bookkeeping services for small businesses in Kansas City. As part of the work they prepared a company's tax forms and tossed in free tax preparation for the employees. In those days a low-cost tax preparation service would have seemed a weak idea because the Internal Revenue Service prepared forms free for anybody who asked. In 1955, the IRS stopped being so helpful and Block advertised that it would prepare anybody's taxes for $5. They made $250,000 that tax season and suddenly the Bloch brothers knew what they wanted to do with their lives.

Henry and Richard had discovered the great secret of their success, the mass market tax business does not consist of ferreting out clever deductions and secret loopholes. Their service is more basic. If you pay close attention to what the ads offer, you will catch the term "tax preparers." Block is not an advisor, not a planner, not a strategist. The company has nothing to recommend about tax shelters. It fills in forms. The median family income of Block's customers is only $20,000. The law's really super tax breaks go to families with much more income. Block gets its business from people whose taxes are a little too much for them to want to handle, but not so complicated that they expect major savings through shrewd accounting.

Block is one of the strangest corporations going. For nine months of the year it loses money, but for the three months of the tax season it does enough business to turn an annual net profit of over $40,000,000 almost all of it in cash. The Blochs have sold a lot of the company stock to the public, but the family still owns over a quarter of it and holds the senior positions. Henry's son, Tom, is being groomed to take charge of the business. Currently he is vice-president in charge of the tax operations divisions. (What other divisions could there be? In an effort to get some year-round income, the company has been buying a few other professional service businesses, most notably the Hyatt Legal Services chain of cut-rate law clinics.)

## CANNON TOWELS

**Auctioneer's price:** $547,000,000.
**Owner:** David H. Murdock.

According to a marketing survey, Cannon's name is recognized by 90 percent of the adult public. Abraham Lincoln's name does not do as well. The company that invented looms for making terry cloth has dominated the towel business since the 1920s. It still makes about half the towels sold to American consumers and a fifth of the bedsheets.

For most of its history the company was owned by the Cannon family. In 1906, James Cannon founded the company. His youngest son, Charles, took control at the start of the '20s and ran the business for fifty years; however, his firm hand appears to have poisoned prospects for continuing family control. He fired his son William, and his grandson William, Jr. from the mill, weakening the sentimental ties they may have felt for the business. In 1981, when an outsider first offered to buy the company, a stock analyst said, "The company does not appear to be interested in being bought. The company has the financial means and management to do what it wants." So observers were surprised when members of the Cannon family said, yes, they'd sell their shares.

The name of the buyer was almost as surprising as the discovery that, while building a family empire, Cannon had failed to build a family. David Murdock was a Los-Angeles-based deal cutter whose operations usually concerned west coast real estate. When he did invest in business he usually just bought a stake in the operation. It seemed quite out of character for him to become the sole proprietor of a textile business based in North Carolina. It was true that Cannon's assets were undervalued and Murdock used Cannon itself as collateral to secure loans for the purchase, but the world is full of good deals. Why did Murdock take this one?

Actually it is not quite as strange a buy as it first looks. While Cannon Mills is known to the public as a textile business, it is also a large real estate owner. When James Cannon started his mill he bought land for the factory and founded a town where the employees could live. Most city founders would have named the place Cannon City or perhaps Cannonville, but James preferred Greek and chose Kannapolis. (In the town itself, residents claim the name is Greek for "City of Looms," but this assertion is nonsense.) The fire department and police are paid by Cannon and the company still owns 1600 houses, all painted white. Originally the town was built to look like any other drab mill town, but Charles Cannon visited Williamsburg in the 1930s and was so impressed by it that he turned Kannapolis's business district into a colonial facsimile. Today the town has a population of 40,000, one-third of whom work for Cannon. When Murdock bought the company he gained both a giant textile operation and a medieval barony. What real estate man could resist?

## THE A & P

**Auctioneer's price:** $425,000,000.
**Owner:** Haub family.

In his account of travels through the back road "Blue Highways" of America, William Least Heat Moon quotes a Tennessee grocer talking about what happened to his store, "Then them supermarkets down in Cookeville opened and I was buyin' higher than they was sellin'. With these hard roads now, everybody gets out of the hollers to shop or work. Don't stay up in here anymore. This tar road under my shoes done my business in."

Less remote parts of America underwent that process fifty years ago. Easy transportation took the competitive edge from the neighborhood shopkeeper and passed it to the best organizers. The leader of the pack was the A&P. It already had over seventy years' experience in business based on discount volume, was already spread across most of the country, and advertised nationally, even sponsoring a radio program.

The standardized form of cash and carry grocery store called the A&P Economy Store began to appear in 1912, replacing earlier Great Atlantic and Pacific Tea Company stores that gave credit, delivery, and premiums. The economy stores proved so popular that during the boom of the 1920s new A&Ps began opening at the rate of over 1,000 per year. By 1930 there were 15,709 stores. Self-service was introduced to A&P in 1936 and was an immediate hit. Two years later only 5 percent of the stores were self-service, but they accounted for nearly half the profits.

The business practices that supported this kind of standardization are so common today that we don't give them a second thought, but in the 1930s the economic power of a national giant to crush small retailers was news. Congressman Wright Patman of Texas held hearings revealing the way A&P got millions of dollars from suppliers in discounts, allowances, rebates, and fees. These favors amounted to a tiny percentage of the business A&P brought the producers, but was enough to make competitors buy higher than A&P was sellin'.

The organizers behind this system were two brothers, George and John Hartford. In 1859 their father, George Huntington Hartford had gone into the tea business with George Gilman. They bought tea by the ton straight off the China clipper ships and sold at half the price of their rivals. Gilman retired in 1878 and the Hartfords had full control of the operation. The brothers took charge early in the century and continued past World War II.

The investigations into A&P instilled a previously unknown sense of prudence into the Hartfords. In 1942 an antitrust case was brought against the A&P and after seven years of litigation the company was fined $175,000. As soon as that case ended another suit was brought, this time with the declared intention of breaking up the company. That case ended with an out of court settlement in which the company signed a consent decree agreeing not to operate in restraint of trade. Since consent decrees imply no admission of guilt they are often considered meaningless wrist slaps, but the fear of the lord had gone into the A&P and it never again pioneered a retailing revolution. The A&P is still found coast-to-coast, but it is no longer the leader in any region.

Brother John died in 1951, while the second antitrust case was underway. George lived to 1957 and died at age 94. There were about 150 heirs to the business, but none of them seemed interested in running the company. The only Hartford of the next generation to become at all well known was art patron Huntington Hartford, the son of a third brother, Edward, who had stayed out of the grocery business. After George Hartford died, the stock was sold to the public.

Public stock offerings made it possible for some other incredibly rich family to buy control of the company. Just over half of the A&P's stock is now owned by Germany's largest grocery chain, the Tengelman Group. Despite the conglomerate name, the "group" is a family operation. The chief executive officer at Tengelman is Erivan Karl Haub. He owns half the corporation's stock and, for tax reasons, one of his sons owns the rest. Supermarkets reached Europe only after World War II. For most of its history the Tengelman Group was a candy company.

The triumph of the supermarket was once thought to have forever ended the profitability of conveniently located higher priced stores, but during the 1960s residents of suburbia began patronizing small stores that sold milk, bread, and other fast-moving items. Prices were well above those in the supermarket; for success the stores relied on location, long hours, and high-demand merchandise. The largest group of these convenience stores is the 7-Eleven chain, with over 7,000 members.

7-Eleven stores are master sellers of the sort of impulse items displayed around the cash register in grocery stores. Their biggest selling item is cigarettes. They are America's largest seller of candy bars, canned beer, and Playboy magazines. Many of the stores also sell gasoline. 7-Eleven follows the fads. When electronic games became popular the stores installed them.

The Southland Corporation, 7-Eleven's parent company, is owned by the Thompson family. It began in 1927 when Joe C. Thompson opened an icehouse in Dallas. Storing ice was always too much trouble for supermarkets to fool with and icehouses were a common urban sight into the 1950s. Thompson had found a niche where he could grow. He added milk and bread as a kind of pick-up business with his ice buyers. The present 7-Eleven business was organized in 1961. Thompson's sons run the corporation: John P. is chairman of the board, Jere W. is president, Joe, Jr. is executive vice-president. They own 16 percent of the stock.

Most surprising of all is the company's auctioneer's price ($1,100,000,000). Fifty years after the supermarkets were thought to have killed convenience stores, the Southland Corporation is worth nearly three times the A&P.

## CRAYOLA CRAYONS

**Auctioneer's price:** $115,000,000.
**Owner:** Binney family.

Looking into the story of Crayola's ownership is like hunting up the third grade teacher you once loved and discovering she has all the complexity of a grown woman. Crayola crayons have been a part of nearly every American childhood this century. They were the consolation on rainy days when it was impossible to go outside, and they served as the party refresher at friends' houses when other games grew dull. Eighty percent of all crayons sold are Crayola brand. Current sales are 1.8 billion Crayola crayons each year.

So why did Crayola agree to a million dollar settlement in a price-fixing case brought by the Federal Trade Commission (FTC)? The FTC said it had entered into a conspiracy with other crayon makers to overcharge for the crayons sold. The baby boom had ended, sales were flat, the company was stagnant. It wouldn't be a particularly shocking story if the company made toothpicks for cocktail sausages, but in the case of something remembered and loved from days of innocence the news is dispiriting.

Crayola is made by Binney & Smith, a family-owned company that ran out of interested family. The company was founded late in the last century by Edwin Binney and a cousin of his. Originally the company specialized in carbon black, a sooty material used in paints, inks, and a variety of other chemical mixes. Only later, in 1902, as a sideline, were crayons added to the business.

Binney had four children, only one son. (In those days it was only the sons who were thought eligible to carry on the family business.) Edwin Binney, Jr. might have taken over operation of the company, but he died before his father. He contracted a mysterious disease, perhaps while traveling through the Panama Canal, and died in 1929. His son, Edwin Binney III, was just reaching school age. A few years later, in 1934, the founding Binney died and left his estate to his children, to be held in trust during the remainder of his wife's life while she enjoyed its income. This arrangement was not unusual, but it stagnated the firm. His wife lived twenty-six more years, until 1960, when she was ninety-four. During that time Binney & Smith's product line declined until Crayola was about all that remained. With the postwar baby boom it was nearly impossible to botch the crayon business.

Eventually even crayon sales ceased to boom and the company turned to price fixing. Although straying from the path of propriety is never to be encouraged, it is common enough and can sometimes spur a resolve to amend one's ways. After it was charged by the FTC, Binney & Smith did become a more successful company. A host of new products were added to the company line, many of them using the name Crayola. Ten years ago it was not entirely clear that Crayola crayons would last out the century, but now the survival of the name seems certain.

The shake-up reduced the grip of the Binney family on the company. Their stock holdings declined from over 50 percent to just under a third. Although no longer in senior management positions, many of the members of the board of directors are grandchildren of the founder:

Edwin Binney III—art patron and educator. He collects Indian and Persian art, none done in crayon.

George P. Putnam—his mother, Dorothy Binney, married the publisher George Putnam. Putnam later left Dorothy for the famous flyer Amelia Earhart. The present Putnam is retired and living in Florida.

Douglas B. Kitchel—son of another of Edwin Binney's daughters. He operates ski resorts.

This diversity of interests and last names suggests that, while Crayola is likely to be part of every childhood in the twenty-first century, the Binney family's role does not look as if it can survive much longer.

## FREDERICK'S OF HOLLYWOOD

**Auctioneer's price:** $20,700,000.
**Owner:** Frederick Mellinger.

Frederick's of Hollywood is actually the fruit of a man named Frederick. He is not from Hollywood, however, and his original firm, founded in 1946, was called Frederick's of Fifth Avenue, as though he were competing with Saks Fifth Avenue. Frederick Mellinger was a New York kid with an idea for a mail-order firm that specialized in provocative women's underwear, so he set up business in his home town. But New York, especially Fifth Avenue, meant taste and sophistication, and Frederick was after the most tasteless market in clothes. In 1947, he wisely moved to Hollywood, the capital of pubescent dreams. His first successful item was black panties, previously a movie fantasy, suddenly a mail-order item.

The 1950s-look came straight out of his catalogs. In 1949, he introduced the padded bra. The next year he came out with a bra that forced the breasts up and together, giving the wearer cleavage and a look that dominated the next two decades. Padded girdles came next. Super-high heels (five inches) were introduced in 1953, the same year that Frederick imported America's first bikini swimsuit (originally a French item.)

By 1955, Frederick's had established nearly all of the fantasy female characteristics that women denounced in the late 1960s. The only major detail to follow was the cheap wig that came in 1959. During all the years when he was giving form to his dreams, Mellinger was denounced as scandalous, shocking, and sinful. His father, an immigrant tailor, told him his work was "shameful," but by the end of the 1960s his inventions were considered so natural and ancient a part of American culture that women who complained were ridiculed as bra-burning crazies.

His mail-order business has grown so that now he has about one million subscribers. There are over 140 stores in shopping malls around the country, plus the main store on Hollywood Boulevard. Although stock in the firm is traded publicly, the Mellinger family still holds 60 percent of the shares. (Besides

Frederick, the family includes one wife, Harriet, and two kids, David and Susan.)

For many decades Frederick had the mail-order market pretty much to himself, but recent years have brought some competition. The most notable rival has been Victoria's Secret, a San Francisco company, that aims for a wealthier clientele than Frederick draws. Victoria's was founded in 1977 by a marketing psychologist named Roy Raymond, with an investment of $80,000. It was sold in 1982 for over one million. The current owner is Leslie Herbert Wexner, founder-owner of The Limited stores and Lane Bryant shoes.

# 8

# ART

## A RECURRING SYMBOL

**Auctioneer's price:** $180,000,000.
**Owner:** Stone family.

A Bible commonly has a cross on the cover in order to reaffirm its Christian content. When the president appears on television the American eagle is displayed on a seal, associating the man with the state. Symbols like these are the visual equivalents of words. They have understood meanings and can be manipulated in traditional or novel ways. Great art has always used symbols and great artists have created many new ones, but lately artists have surrendered this creative role to businessmen.

The modern preference for originality over tradition permits artists to copy techniques, but not content. The emphasis on abstract painting frowns on the introduction of meaning. The rise of copyright laws have made it dangerous to be too generous in helping yourself to another artist's idea. But ordinary people still like their art to be meaningful and when artists won't provide society with symbols people turn to whoever will.

No group is more eager to satisfy public taste than the producers of consumer goods, so when public symbols disappeared from fine art they began appearing on consumer items.

Because it would be unacceptable to have a profound symbol like a crucifix on a lunch box, manufacturers turned to pop symbols like Mickey Mouse and Superman. Corporations are richer than most artists, so copyright provisions are no problem. Users just pay a royalty.

By the late 1970s the use of copyrighted symbols had become big business. *Star Wars*, James Bond, the Peanuts characters all brought fortunes in royalties to their creators. Then somebody asked a bold question. Why wait for the appearance of a popular symbol? Why not invent one yourself?

The answer was Strawberry Shortcake, a symbol without

Strawberry Shortcake. Photo: © 1984 American Greetings Corp.

any tradition behind it. Strawberry Shortcake is a Raggedy Ann–type little girl who wears a granny bonnet and sits atop a plump, red strawberry. She symbolizes the money to be had when you aim at the little girl (ages 3 to 8) market. Cute friendly symbols à la Raggedy Ann had almost disappeared when Strawberry Shortcake was introduced. They had been replaced by aggressive brats like Lucy, in Peanuts. Of course, a symbol nobody ever heard of has pretty limited appeal, so Strawberry Shortcake was introduced in the spring of 1980 with a $2,300,000 ad campaign. (Got that? Advertising a symbol found on products rather than simply advertising the product.) Each succeeding year the advertising has doubled: 1981, $5.5 million; 1982, $12 million; 1983, $25 million. The number of companies using the symbol has gone from three to sixty-five and sales in 1983 approached one billion dollars. Over 1,400 products carry the symbol, including:

> ***Clothes:*** belts, boots, costume jewelry, halloween costumes, pajamas, purses, raincoats, sandals, scarves, shoelaces, socks, sweaters, swimsuits, underwear.
>
> ***Decor:*** bedspreads, Christmas ornaments, clocks, clothes trees, curtains, lamps, lounge chairs, pictures, toy chests, wallpaper.
>
> ***Eating:*** baking pans, breakfast cereal, bubble gum, drinking glasses, lunch boxes, plates, spice racks, TV trays.
>
> ***Party things:*** balloons, cake decorations, favors, greeting cards, paper plates, party hats, ribbon, wrapping paper.
>
> ***Toys:*** board games, coloring kits, doll carriages, dolls, figurines, records, roller skates, story books, tricycles.
>
> ***Et cetera:*** boxes, bubble bath, cellophane tape, eyeglass frames, luggage, music boxes, potholders, sleeping bags, stationery.

This bonanza is the creation of American Greetings, a greeting card company that lived for decades in the shadow of Hallmark. In fact, it was this low prestige that led it to the creation of licensable symbols. Hallmark could afford to sign up the Peanuts characters while American Greetings had to hustle. In 1972, American Greetings introduced a card character called Holly Hobby that proved popular enough to earn a few hundred thousand dollars after three years. It was enough to encourage a search for a new character and Strawberry Shortcake resulted. That second success led to the creation of a new company division called Those Characters from Cleveland. The company now grinds out symbols with the zeal of James Joyce coining words. New "friends" for Strawberry Shortcake come out every year. Another little girl symbol called Herself the Elf was introduced in 1983. Ten bears, called Care Bears, with icons drawn right on their stomachs, were also introduced in 1983 with double Strawberry Shortcake's initial advertising budget.

A children's symbol created by a corporation over forty years ago was Bozo the Clown. Bozo was invented by Capitol records as a character and voice for children's records. Typical of Bozo's adventures was an underwater sea dive in which he met a fiddler crab playing country music. Cornball humor like that never goes out of fashion and Bozo is still part of many a childhood. Capitol records sold all Bozo rights in 1954 to Larry Harmon, an actor who played Bozo on television. At the time of the purchase Harmon was not quite thirty and Bozo rights have provided him with a very tidy living. A dozen TV stations still carry the show.

## A PUBLIC MUSEUM

**Auctioneer's price:** $25,500,000.
**Owner:** Norton Winfred Simon.

Although anyone is allowed to open a business and call it a museum, we do not usually think of nonprofit operations as having owners. The Pasadena Art Museum, for example, was founded in 1924 as a nonprofit corporation and seemed like a typical public institution; however, fifty years later, control passed into the hands of Norton Simon.

Simon is the Grand Acquisitor of American capitalism. Starting with $35,000 in the depression year of 1931, he formed a company that grew like a python, swallowing other companies whole. Hunt Foods, Canada Dry, Wesson Oil, McCall's, and many other famous firms were consumed by the corporation. Simon quit his company when he was sixty-two, in 1969, but he did not retire to a Florida bungalow.

For decades Simon had been collecting masterworks of art and he had grown eager to find a satisfactory way of displaying them. His collection (auctioneer's price is about $100,000,000) includes works by Rembrandt, Raphael, Poussin, Manet, Degas, Picasso, Matisse, Rodin, and many other of the world's greatest artists. The public did not often see any of his collection, for Simon did not lend his paintings to exhibitors.

In 1974, the Pasadena Museum of Modern Art, as it was called then, had taken its nonprofit status a little too seriously and was in bad financial shape. It had built a new $5,500,000 building it could not afford and was in danger of bankruptcy. Suddenly Norton Simon appeared at the museum's door offering to put up $850,000 to end the debt crisis.

Simon attached a few conditions to his money. The museum was immediately renamed the Pasadena Art Museum, the better to conform to the nature of Simon's own collection. (In October, 1975, when Simon's control was uncontestable, he changed the name to the Norton Simon Museum of Pasadena.) Most important, the museum's board of trustees had to be cut from thirty-five to ten members and Simon wanted the right to name seven of them. The old board obligingly voted itself out of existence.

With his new power, Simon then showed the old board what it had done. The building was closed for changes. Most of the staff was fired; even the volunteer guides were dismissed. The museum's auditorium, restaurant, and classrooms for visiting schoolchildren were abolished. The policy of almost always lending art works to other museums was replaced by a policy of never lending. Public support for the museum was actively discouraged and membership dropped from 4,500, at the time of Simon's arrival, to under 500 members. Many of the museum's paintings were removed from the walls and replaced by the works in Simon's own collection; however, Simon did not donate his works to the museum. They are still his property and under his full control. He began raising money for the museum by selling paintings in its permanent collection.

In many ways the museum is much improved. Simon's collection is greatly superior to the old museum collection and the improvement in the exhibition is widely recognized and appreciated. However, the place has become more of a monument to Norton Simon than an institution to benefit the city and people of Pasadena. The chairman of the new board is Simon's wife, the actress Jennifer Jones, and nobody expects her to challenge the operation.

Another great privately dominated museum is the J. Paul Getty Museum of Malibu. Before his death in 1976, Getty was often described as America's richest man. He built and controlled this museum in the final years of his life. The building is a replica of the villa at Pompeii owned by Lucius Calpurnius Piso, father-in-law of Julius Caesar and one of the richest men in the Roman Republic. Piso was a patron of the arts and Getty felt he had much in common with the man. The museum has an endowment worth over one billion dollars, eight times the endowment of the New York Metropolitan Museum of Art. The Getty only opened in 1974, but with an endowment like that it is certain to become one of the world's greatest museums.

The greatest collection not housed in a museum is thought to be that of Armand Hammer. Portions have been exhibited many times, in such places as the High Museum (Atlanta, Georgia); Albright-Knox Art Gallery (Buffalo, New York); Denver Art Museum; Museum of Fine Arts (Houston, Texas); Los Angeles County Museum of Art; Oklahoma Art Center (Oklahoma City); Smithsonian Institution (Washington, D.C.); Corcoran Gallery (Washington, D.C.).

J. Paul Getty Museum. Photo: Julius Shulman

Thesc great collectors are often described as modern Medicis, the merchant patrons of art who financed the Renaissance. While these modern collectors are at least as rich as the Florentine family and are as fond of art, they differ in one great way. The Medici most loved the art of their own day. The great modern collectors concentrate on works of the past. The Medici bought art from artists; modern collectors buy from other collectors. The difference is by no means trivial and suggests that none of these patrons will be remembered 600 years from now, the way we remember the Medici.

## THE MOST COSTLY PAINTING IN AMERICA

**Auctioneer's price:** $5,830,000.
**Owner:** H. Wendell Cherry.

In May, 1981 an early self-portrait by Pablo Picasso was auctioned in New York for $5,300,000. It is the custom in the big auction houses to add on a 10 percent purchase fee which, in this case, raised the price by more than half a million dollars. That final cost is listed above as the auctioneer's price because it is impossible to predict what the painting will bring the next time it goes on the block. This work was auctioned during the 1960s for $360,000 and again, in 1975, for $650,000. Nobody then was predicting an 815 percent rise in the price.

The work itself is called, "Yo Picasso," and was painted in 1901, when Picasso was twenty. Its style shows how strongly the young artist was influenced by the post-impressionists of that time. Only a little later, when he entered his Blue Period, did Picasso move from being a member of movements to being their leader. Thus, the crowd at the auction was startled to see such an early Picasso become the most expensive twentieth century painting ever sold.

The buyer, Wendell Cherry, was in the audience bidding against a European collector who was bidding by telephone. When the bidding passed three million dollars a rush of excited chatter swept across the floor, but was quickly silenced by the auctioneer. Finally, as the price reached 5.3 million, everyone's breathing seemed to have stopped. The bid from the floor was reported on the telephone, pause, and then the woman speaking into the phone shook her head. A howl of excitement rose and no amount of gavel pounding could quash it. Cherry quietly held up his bidding paddle and the sale was recorded.

Cherry was not well-known as a collector. His name was not even listed among the collectors in *Who's Who in American Art.* He is a founder and the president of the Humana Corporation, a company founded in 1964 to sell mobile homes. A few years later it expanded into the lucrative nursing-home business. One acquisition led to another and today Humana owns sixty-four hospitals, over fifty-five medical office buildings, and forty-five medical care centers. More medical care centers, more medical office buildings, and still more hospitals are under construction. Humana is also erecting a $40 million corporate headquarters in Louisville. About the only dark spot on the company balance sheet is that Humana no longer has any trailers to sell.

## A DALI COLLECTION

**Auctioneer's price:** $5,600,000.
**Owner:** Albert Reynolds Morse.

One of modern art's most appealing collectors is a Cleveland man who makes his living from the machinery business. Reynolds Morse is not an artist, not a critic, not even a giant of commerce, but he knows what he likes and has the self-confidence to stick with his opinion.

Reynolds likes Salvador Dali. He bought his first work in 1943 and forty years later has over 1,000 prints, more than 100 drawings and watercolors, and 93 oils, all by Dali. He has privately published a book displaying the oils in his collection and for a time operated a special museum in Cleveland. The material is now housed in St. Petersburg, Florida.

In the world of art critics and scholars, Dali's reputation is thin. His influence on other painters is negligible and shrinking further. Morse is not Dali's only enthusiastic supporter, but Dali's general reputation makes him a poor investment.

Morse is no investor. He is an aficionado who buys what he likes and is undeterred by the tastes of others, not even by Dali's taste. Dali has told Morse several times, "Oh, don't buy that one. Let me show you something that is more important," but Morse follows his own desires. In the days before the romantic myth of the artist as solitary genius was combined with the financial myth of art as a sound investment, men like Morse were taken for granted as the major customers for art. Today they are rare. Only a few people have the courage to spend money continuously in ways the experts say is foolish.

When Morse began looking for a suitable place to display his collection he discovered, quite literally, that he could not give it away. He contacted several universities to report his willingness to donate his entire collection, but they were not interested. Then a Florida attorney approached Morse and asked about establishing a self-sustaining museum. The museum is now open to the public, and during the St. Petersburg tourist season (winter), it receives about 750 visitors a day.

The paintings have been willed to the state of Florida upon the death of Morse and his wife, whenever that shall come. In the meantime Florida spent $2,000,000 developing the museum facilities. The state also agreed to provide $200,000 a year for five years while the museum worked to become self-sustaining; however, annual appropriations of that money have fallen short. The entire Morse collection is on display. When the museum opened (1982), Morse donated twenty-five works to it and has contributed several more each year. Thus, slowly, ownership is being transferred from Morse to the museum.

Salvador Dali Museum. Photo: Courtesy of Salvador Dali Museum

Some other notable collectors with special tastes are:

***Jean Brown:*** her collection in Tyringham, Massachusetts is known as the Jean Brown Archive. She documents modern art movements. Because much of contemporary art is transitory, the documentation is often all that is left. For example, the "Happenings" of the '60s don't happen any more, but Jean Brown's archive has written records of the events.

***Gerald Cantor:*** this New York stockbroker with offices in the World Trade Center has a major collection of the works of Auguste Rodin.

***Wilhelmina Holladay:*** has established an archive in Washington, D.C. on women's art. Her own collection specializes in women's art from the Renaissance to the present.

***James Burnett Ivey:*** a newspaper cartoonist himself, Mr. Ivey has a collection of over 2,000 political cartoons from twenty countries. He displays them in a tiny museum in Orlando, Florida, near Disneyworld.

***Paul Ritter MacAlister:*** his collection is one of the strangest, concentrating on the American eagle as represented in art. He is past eighty and living outside Chicago. Before he retired he was a prominent interior decorator.

***Robert Gore Rifkind:*** a Beverly Hills attorney whose specialty is German Expressionism. He has 6,000 prints and 3,500 books on the subject. In 1978, the West German government awarded him the Order of Merit, First Class for his support of German culture. Like Morse, Rifkind grows irksome when reminded that, among art critics, German Expressionism doesn't have much of a reputation. He asks what would be the reputation of the School of Paris if "in the 1930s the French government had declared all the contemporary French artists degenerate, confiscated their works from museums, disparaged them publicly, destroyed tens of thousands of their major works, and forbidden them to work from the mid-1930s until after the Second World War."

## FABERGÉ TREASURES

**Auctioneer's price:** $4,000,000.
**Owner:** Malcolm Forbes.

During the last decades of the Russian monarchy the tsar developed a taste for the jeweled what-nots made by the great goldsmith, Peter Carl Fabergé. Most famous of all Fabergé's designs were the Easter eggs that were given annually to the tsaritsa from her loving husband. When the revolution came, many a fleeing nobleman discovered an unexpected advantage to Fabergé's work—it fitted neatly into pockets—and much of this treasure was suddenly scattered about the globe.

The basic idea of Fabergé eggs was defined in the first one, given in 1886 by Tsar Alexander III to his wife Maria Feodorovna. It was 2½-inches long and at first looked quite simple. Its exterior was made from polished white enamel. Inside, however, was a golden yolk and when the yolk was opened it revealed a gold hen with ruby eyes. The hen could be opened by lifting the beak, exposing a tiny diamond replica of the imperial crown. A still smaller ruby pendant hung from the crown.

The tsar's later eggs continued this theme of lavish ornaments with surprises hidden inside. The closest any of them came to being practical was the 1903 egg given by Tsar Nicholas II to his mother. This egg, nearly a foot tall, included a small clock ringed by tiny pearls. Every hour on the hour a gold grillwork at the top of the egg popped open and a golden rooster with diamond eyes emerged flapping his wings and crowing the hour.

The ordinary Russian aristocracy could not afford such baubles and over half of the Fabergé eggs are miniatures, often under one inch long. Fabergé also made other decorative objects, including animal sculptures (many of them now belong to the Aga Khan), cigarette cases, boxes with the tsar's portrait, and *art nouveau* works like a small golden basket containing lilies of the valley made with gold stems and pearl buds.

Readers may recall having seen many of these items on display in New York's Metropolitan Museum. They were not the property of the museum itself, but were on long term loan. That entire collection plus many other Fabergé items belong to Malcolm Forbes, owner of the largest collection of Fabergé work outside of Russia. To see it, a visitor need only go to the ground floor of Forbes's building at Fifth Avenue and 12th Street. Forbes had hoped that this public display would win him a tax deduction, but the IRS said no. (Weep not; Forbes does all right. One year, with an income above $50 million, his federal tax bill came to $8,000.)

Forbes himself lives like a man who admires the movie *Citizen Kane*, but somehow missed the point that Kane was not a role model:

- In the film Kane reluctantly inherited a newspaper empire; Forbes reluctantly inherited ownership of a successful magazine founded by his father, Bertie Forbes. (BC, as he was called, had begun as William Randolph Hearst's favorite financial writer.)
- Kane tried to launch a political career, but failed. So did Forbes.
- Kane consumed his wealth in flamboyant ways—building a castle, founding a private zoo, collecting art and bizarre trinkets. Besides collecting Fabergé eggs, Forbes has a castle in Morocco, the world's largest collection of nineteenth century toy boats, a real boat valued at two million dollars, an enormous toy soldier collection displayed in diorama style, several huge land projects, and, of course, the magazine.

The great mystery of the movie was the motivating force behind Kane's odd mixture of energy and whimsy. There are several clues in the film—Kane often justifies himself by saying something is, or will be, "fun"—but only at the end does the story reveal Kane's lifelong quest has been for the secure sense of fun he knew as a boy while playing on his sled, named Rosebud.

When people seek to explain what drives Forbes, they talk about his father (quoth BC, "I never met a rich man's son who was worth a damn,") or about tax write-offs, but then they pause. More seems to be at work than just the mechanics of Freudian theory or the IRS's system of odd rewards and perverse punishments. Forbes himself favors one special word in explaining his taste: fun.

Rosebud, where are you?

## A CENSORED ART COLLECTION

**Auctioneer's price:** $620,000.
**Owner:** Saki Karavas.

British art is not quite as rare as British music, but neither is it so common as a day in spring. A tour of the sculptures and monuments in Westminster Abbey shows that, when it comes to things visual, British taste has favored junk for quite a long time. Thus, it should not be surprising that when an Englishman actually does do interesting work a museum dedicated to his art is likely to be in America rather than Britain.

Saki Karavas owns one of America's most eccentric museums, one devoted to an English artist, who, of course, was banned in his homeland. Mr. Karavas owns the Fonda de Taos Hotel in Taos, New Mexico. Guests and the curious can pay $1 to visit his office where ten paintings by D.H. Lawrence are on display. The author of *Lady Chatterly's Lover* was famous for many things, but never a rich sense of humor, yet probably even he would have seen that you could write a thoroughly absurd "Saturday Night Live" sketch about a hotel manager working at his desk while all about him curious tourists are looking at nudes in sensuous paintings.

Lawrence turned to painting only upon reaching middle age. His work is sometimes compared to that of the Mexican artist Orozco, although the paintings seem less powerful (at least to this author's untrained eye). Lawrence's pictures of voluptuous nudes seem to mix a little Gauguin, a little Reubens, and a touch of Picasso's harlequins. When they were exhibited in London in 1929 they were declared obscene and seized. "At the age of 40," Lawrence lamented, "I had the courage to try to paint a picture without copying. Then it became an orgy."

Scotland Yard gave Lawrence a choice of shipping the pictures abroad or having them destroyed. He chose to take them out of the country. This ban is still officially in effect. British galleries have expressed an interest in showing them, but first the sentence of death has to be removed.

One of the few places in the world Lawrence actually seemed to enjoy was his ranch beneath the Sangre de Cristo mountains, 20 miles from Taos. Lawrence died soon after the scandal of his art show. His wife Frieda, however, returned to the Taos ranch with D.H.'s ashes and many of the paintings. She died in 1956 and shortly after that Mr. Karavas bought them. He values them, quite optimistically, at $1,500,000.

A second museum devoted to a British artist, this one unquestionably of the first rank, is the Turner Museum in Denver. Turner's will called for the establishment of a Turner Museum in London, but naturally no such institution was ever founded in Britain. The museum's founder and owner is Douglas Graham, an unusual millionaire who answers the phone himself and sends hand-written business correspondence. Graham wisely concentrates on collecting prints rather than oils; Turner oils are for billionaires. The most expensive painting ever sold anywhere was Turner's "Seascape: Folkstone," auctioned in 1984 for a total price of $10,023,200.

## TIFFANY LAMPS

**Auctioneer's price:** $315,000.
**Owner:** Walter Chrysler, Jr.

During the first decade of this century America's wealthiest homes included vases, boxes, and windows from the Tiffany Studios. Most remarkable of all were the firm's lamps. Electric lights were new in those days and the lamps were a response to the problem of having to hide the brilliant glare of the new bulbs.

Tiffany lamps were a brilliant expression of American decorative aesthetics. Technically they were perfect. Their creator, Louis Comfort Tiffany, spent years experimenting with sand and discovered how its impurities could give glass different colors. Eventually he was able to produce glass, which he called Favrile glass, in any color and intensity without using stain, paint, or enamel. He also discovered an acid process that gave the glass a radiant quality that seemed nearly miraculous.

His lamps were also practical. Tiffany knew his customers and their tastes. He had been a successful interior decorator whose clients included Mark Twain and Cornelius Vanderbilt. Useless baubles were not for these men. They didn't mind decoration, but the decorated objects should be functional. One Tiffany lamp, for example, held eighteen lights. The lamp was designed to look like a bouquet of lilies. Each light was inserted into a bronze stem and the shades were transparent amber glass that shone with a golden iridescence. The artistic idea behind this lily lamp was similar to one that inspired Fabergé to copy lilies of the valley in gold and pearls, but in the final analysis the Tiffany item was to be used while Fabergé's was to be looked at.

The Tiffany style was part of a movement called "art nouveau" which praised simplicity and imitation of nature. When cubist and other ideas of abstract art took hold, Tiffany designs fell out of fashion. Then came the collectors, notably Walter P. Chrysler, Jr. Chrysler's father made his pile in the automobile business, but the son has always been more interested in art than industry. His taste is especially broad and his collection covers the whole spectrum of artistic masterpieces.

He was the first important collector to buy Tiffany works, apparently for the straightforward reason that he had seen Tiffany lamps in his home as a boy and he liked them. The lamps and other works from the Tiffany Studios can be seen in the Chrysler Museum at Norfolk, Virginia. The museum is managed through a foundation established by Chrysler.

Wisteria Lamp by Tiffany. Photo: Courtesy of the Institute of Glass, The Chrysler Museum, Norfolk, Virginia, gift of Walter P. Chrysler, Jr.

## THE MOST VULGAR STATUE IN FRONT OF A MUSEUM

**Auctioneer's price:** $4,500.
**Owner:** Leonard Slye.

Instead of creating, vulgarity strips established symbols of their meaning, impoverishing a thought or memory or tradition. Vulgarity can sometimes work like a broom. Traditions do become overblown and most of the great artists who rebelled against one tradition while establishing another were denounced in their own day as vulgar. Most people who are criticized as vulgar, however, do not turn out to be Beethovens or Wordsworths. They remain as they first appeared to be, cheapeners of culture.

Sometimes vulgarity arises out of a form of blindness or ignorance, as with a child snickering at a dirty joke. There is a lack of deep acquaintance with the subject at hand, so a fuller more profound thought is impossible. Other vulgarisms arise from a monstrous vanity that reduces all symbols to personal references. The gaudy display of self-engrandizement at Lyndon Johnson's pyramid in Austin, Texas is probably the strongest example of this kind of crudeness. Other presidents, the flag, indeed every symbol of the nation is introduced somewhere in the building and stripped of all meaning beyond, "Glory, glory, LBJ."

Most shocking of all is the cheapening of a symbol the vulgarizer has himself created. The master of this form is Roy Rogers, born Leonard Slye. He appeared in nearly 90 cowboy films made by Republic Pictures and 101 half-hour television shows for CBS. Roy billed himself as "The King of the Cowboys," although readers who grew up in the 1950s may recall a rumor that there had been another election and Roy was voted out in favor of Gene Autry.

On the edge of the Mojave desert, in Victorville, California, Roy has raised a monument: The Roy Rogers and Dale Evans Museum. Roy has erected a crude fiberglass statue of Trigger that dominates the parking lot. By making the statue inappropriately huge (21 feet tall) Trigger is reduced to the status of one more giant billboard, like Bob's Big Boy or the Golden Arches, trying to snare the loose change of passers-by.

Inside the museum things don't get a whole lot better, although the mementos may be enjoyed by old fans. Trigger is stuffed and on display. So is Dale Evans' horse, Buttermilk, and Roy's faithful dog, Bullet. In the "Hall of Christ," a tableau of the Last Supper reduces one of the most sacred events in Christian religion to the level of a silly dinner party. In front of the tableau an invitation reads, "Jesus of Nazareth requests the honor of your presence at a dinner to be given in his honor." Most Christians will be taken aback at the reversal which says Jesus would be honored by *their* presence. Most orthodox believers will also argue that it wasn't Jesus who threw parties in his own honor, but apparently such sensitivity to humility is not part of Roy's baggage.

# 9

# FOOD

## AMERICA'S FAVORITE CANDY BAR

**Auctioneer's price:** $3,600,000,000.
**Owner:** Mars family.

The best-selling candy bar in America is Snickers. It is made by Mars Inc., America's biggest candy maker. (About a decade ago its sales moved ahead of the old champion, Hershey.) After Snickers, Mars's other big sellers are M&Ms, Three Musketeers, and Milky Way. The popularity is based partly on quality—inflation has upped the price and reduced the size of a candy bar, but Mars has not diluted the recipe—partly on advertising. Mars spends about $1,500,000 per week promoting its candy.

Mars is America's largest private corporation. The thought that so huge a business could be based almost entirely on candy bars amazes many people. (Mars also makes Uncle Ben's rice and Cal-Kan pet food.) Candy bars do have most of the characteristics of contemporary America's most successful food products. They are cheap, sweet, and can be eaten quickly and privately. These last characteristics are surprisingly important. Today the social role of eating is often bypassed in favor of speedy consumption. Candy bars, especially Mars-style bars that are thick and gooey, are quickly eaten and hard to share.

The company is wholly owned by the Mars family—Forrest

Mars and his two sons, Forrest, Jr. and John—and nobody expects its shares to be sold publicly in this century. Forrest senior's two sons are co-presidents of the company, show no sign of wanting to reduce the family hold on the business, and won't reach retirement age until the end of the 1990s.

This branch of the family gained control of the business only after a bitter internal struggle. Forrest Mars's parents were divorced and he was raised by his mother. When Forrest came of age, instead of taking him into the family candy business, his father sent him to England with best wishes and a copy of the Milky Way recipe. Forrest founded a separately owned company in England; he was free to make whatever he wanted, but the best-selling products came from his father's recipes. Milky Ways were a hit and, later, so were Snickers bars. After his father's death there was an in-family fight in which Forrest beat out a stepsister and, in 1964, merged his British company with the American firm.

These battles have not made Forrest Mars a friend of publicity. He is semi-retired now and lives mostly in Las Vegas, commuting a few times each year to his company's headquarters outside Washington, D.C. The Las Vegas connection and his isolation has led to his being dubbed, "The Howard Hughes of candy," but Hughes was a recluse only in his later years. Originally he was famous and quite visible. Forrest Mars has always been out of the public eye. He is the only American billionaire who is not listed in *Who's Who in America*. He has given only one interview in his life, to a trade magazine. It took five years to arrange and Mars immediately regretted his act. No future interviews are anticipated. Any employee caught passing information about the Mars family to the press loses his job on the spot. A check in the *Personal Name Index to the New York Times* failed to turn up his name. Mars's demonstrated taste for obscurity would not be surprising if he were a member of the Chinese Politburo, but is unusual in the land that invented public relations.

The candy bar market is in the firm grip of giants; newcomers, eager to cash in on the national love for chocolate and

Wally Amos. Photo: Famous Amos Chocolate Chip Corporation

sugar, have to try other types of food. A recent success has been the chocolate chip cookie. According to marketing studies, chocolate chip cookies have found an astonishing niche. The NPD Group, a market research company, found that the people who most frequently eat the cookies are health food fans. They don't eat many Snickers, but chocolate is indeed the food of the gods, so the cookies have been moving into health food meals. (Yes, I know it is amazing, but that is what they found.)

The rise of the chocolate chip cookie is generally credited to Wally "Famous" Amos, owner of the Famous Amos Chocolate Chip Corporation. He began the company in Hollywood, California in 1973. Amos spent fourteen years before that as a theatrical agent and when he opened his first store, on Sunset Boulevard, he opened it like a movie premier, with a press party where ragtime music, cookies, and champagne were served. The entertainment community is full of health food fans and Amos was off. His tasty recipe includes pecans with the chips.

The east coast chocolate chip king is David Liederman, owner of David's Cookies, begun in 1979. Liederman is a lawyer who worked as a chef in France and published a book, *Cooking the Nouvelle Cuisine in America*. Besides cookies, David makes a great bagette, France's traditional long thin loaf of bread. His is the cookie to eat while reading Proust.

## THE MOST POPULAR BREWERY

**Auctioneer's price:** $3,240,000,000.
**Owner:** Busch family.

Augie Busch, Jr. has lived long enough to see his family become the lords of St. Louis. Much of the city's downtown, excluding the monumental arch, belongs to Busch while his giant holding corporation, Anheuser-Busch Companies, brews nearly one-third of all beer sold in the U.S. Their biggest brand is Budweiser.

The company began in 1875. Back then, St. Louis was an old French city that had prospered through fur trading in the west. By 1875 the fur business was mostly a memory, and the power of the founding French families was well past its prime. German immigrants had been pouring in for decades and brought a social change, much like that in Boston, as Irish immigrants overwhelmed the old Puritan families. As in Boston, the old St. Louis families sneered at the newcomers or else pretended they did not exist, so the founding of a German brewery by Adolphus Busch was ignored by the Chouteaus, Papins, and other exploring families of the west.

By the turn of this century, when the present patriarch was born, the Busch family was growing rich beyond reckoning, but socially they still stood so low they were even banned from the local country club. Money has its ways, however, and the Busch family founded its own country club. By now Busch owns the baseball team (Cardinals), the stadium, the civic center, the old farm that once belonged to General Grant, and a variety of other properties in the city.

Their civic success has been based on developing a national beer market. A dozen years ago Busch had "only" 18 percent of the national market and almost every large town had its own brewery. During the '70s, new powers of marketing and shipping favored the large standardizers over the distinct regional beers and local brewers began to close. In 1970, many shrewd observers thought Schlitz beer would be the big winner in this trend toward national brands, but in the mid-1970s Schlitz changed its recipe and brewing process and lost many customers. It finally went back to the old ways, but not until the Busch operation had moved irretrievably ahead. Another key to Busch's success may have been its advertising. Most commercials emphasize the social side of drinking beer. Budweiser is different. Their images tend to be more isolated, usually without reference to any drinking at all, and their slogan, "This Bud's for you," stresses individuality rather than group feasting. (Another Busch beer, Michelob, does not follow this approach.)

Busch is currently headed by the patriarch's son, Augustus Busch III. The family still holds about 15 percent of the giant's stock and has enough millions in annual income to assure a perpetual welcome at most country clubs.

The success of national beers has resulted in the disappearance of many favorite local brands. Some former regional giants do persist, although sales have declined. Ballantine, Falstaff, Jax, Lucky Lager, Narragansett, Pearl, and Regal are all proud names that now survive by costing less than the national competition. All of these beer companies have been bought by Paul Kalmanovitz, a Polish-born American who came to this country in 1926. His method of rescuing these old brands is to cut the staff and advertising pretty sharply, then rely on nostalgia and low costs to produce sales. If business gets too bad, the brewery is treated as real estate and its land is sold or developed according to potential. Kalmanovitz is an old man, approaching eighty, and has no children. These fine old beer names are not expected to survive long after his death.

One regional beer that grew and prospered during this time of standardization is Coors of Denver. The company was founded in 1873, two years before Busch got started, and all voting stock is still held by the Coors family. (They also hold 35 percent of the nonvoting stock.) Adolph Coors Company is run by two brothers, Joseph and William Coors, and two of Joseph's sons, Jeffrey and Peter Coors. While the market for other regional beers was shrinking, Coors became a national beer. During the early '70s Coors was fighting hard to remain a regional beer and imposed a number of rules on wholesalers in order to limit the beer's distribution. In 1975 the Supreme Court ruled, in effect, that it was unconstitutional to deny Americans the right to drink Coors just because they lived far from Denver. This kind of federal interference in commercial decisions, even dumb decisions, is contrary to Joseph Coors's very conservative politics, but he obeyed the law. Thanks to the Supreme Court, the company has become a successful national firm.

The decline of distinctive beers has brought some rebellion. Imported beers have become more popular as customers searched for stronger flavors. Their sales have quadrupled since 1975. Another solution to the problem of increasing blandness has been the formation of new local breweries devoted to tasty beers. The most successful newcomer has been the Anchor Brewing Company in San Francisco. Fritz Maytag, heir to the appliance company fortune, owns and directs the business. The troubling question about such an operation is, can it grow and keep producing tasty beer at the same time?

## A GOOD WHISKEY STILL

**Auctioneer's price:** $901,000,000.
**Owner:** William Lee Lyons Brown.

Not all bars are fancy enough to serve Wild Turkey or broadly stocked enough to include J.W. Dant or cheap enough to have Rosy O'Grady, but a bar is hardly a bar if it doesn't have Jack Daniel's Tennessee sour mash. By the same standard, St. Patrick's Day isn't St. Patrick's Day unless you've slipped Old Bushmill Irish Whiskey into your coffee, and a rock queen is no

Photo: Jack Daniel Distillery

rock queen if she doesn't perform while waving a fifth of Southern Comfort.

As it happens, all of these drinks come from the same company: Brown-Forman Distilleries, founded in 1870 by George Garvin Brown to distill liquors for "medicinal" purposes. (If you believe that claim, you probably also believe all marijuana smokers are seekers of wisdom.) The company now offers many famous brands. Besides those just named there is Martell brandy, Noilly Prat vermouth, Bols liqueurs, and Korbel champagne.

TV watchers may have noticed the difference between two widely advertised Italian wines. One is Cella and its commercials feature "Aldo Cella," a short fat man with all the style and zest for life of a spaghetti stain on the shirt. He obviously has a cousin in America, and just as obviously the cousin drives a cab. The other wine is called Bolla and in its ads we see "Franco Bolla," a tall thin man of prestige and dignity. If he has any relatives in America you can be sure they are emissaries from the Vatican. Which type are you? A Cella drinker or do you prefer Franco's style? Ha—once again Brown-Forman got you. They import both wines and simply split the market between the two types. Cella and Bolla are America's most popular imported table wines. (Cab driver Aldo is a step ahead of aristocratic Franco in sales.)

The descendants of George Garvin are obviously onto a good thing and they have kept it in the family. Company president William Lee Lyons Brown is the largest single stockholder and the family, as a whole, owns about a third of all the corporation's shares. William Lee's brother, Martin Brown, is president of the Jack Daniel Distillery, a wholly owned subsidiary of Brown-Forman. (Pay no attention to the line in Jack Daniel's label that says "Lem Motlow, Prop[rietor]." That's just a bit of history.) Another brother, Owsley Brown II, is a senior vice-president of the corporation. Cousin Robinson S. Brown, Jr. recently retired after many years of directing the company. His son, Robinson S. Brown III, is rising fast in the corporation. Still another cousin, Owsley Brown Frazier, is also a senior vice-president and has an enormous holding of stock in the company.

As well as any, the Brown family illustrates that if you play your cards properly you can sell off over 50 percent of the family corporation, get all the money that such sales bring, and still have the power and prestige that comes with ownership.

A second great family fortune based on distilled liquor is the Seagram wealth. Seagrams began making Canadian whiskey and the Bronfman family, which still owns 40 percent of the shares, is Canadian. Brothers Edgar and Charles run the corporation in New York and Montreal. (Seagram's auctioneer's price is $3,200,000,000.)

The best-selling single brand of spirits in the United States is Bacardi rum. The descendants of the company's founder, Don Facundo Bacardi, still control all thirteen corporations that comprise the worldwide Bacardi network. The two corporations bringing the rum to the American market are Bacardi Corporation in Puerto Rico, the distiller, and Bacardi Imports, the distributor. From 1862 to 1960 Bacardi was based in Cuba, but then Fidel Castro nationalized the company and the Bacardi family fled abroad. Castro's action cost them $76,000,000, but still they prospered, for although they had lost their Cuban assets they had escaped with something more valuable. To this day, only members of the family know the company's secret formula for the world's most popular rum.

## THE LARGEST COCA-COLA BOTTLING COMPANY

**Auctioneer's price:** $800,000,000.
**Owner:** John Lupton.

By chance, or was it through astrological design, the two most famous symbols of American culture and life were born on the same day, May 8, 1886. On that day the Statue of Liberty was unveiled and Coca-Cola was formulated. The statue immediately became the symbol of how America wished to be seen. It took a little bit longer, but eventually Coke became what the Kansas newspaper publisher William Allen White called, "The sublimated essence of all that America stands for." Perhaps on the centennial anniversary of the two events, the statue's torch should be replaced by a Coke bottle.

Most surprising about Coca-Cola is that its greatest fortunes and longest family loyalties have come from bottling rather than from manufacturing. Of course, the main company (auctioneer's price: $6,440,000,000) is worth more than any of the bottlers and it is also true that many fine old southern families have a tidy income from Coca-Cola stock bought long ago, but the history of Coke's ownership is strange. Originally the company was owned by John Syth Pemberton, the man who formulated the drink, but he soon died and after a bit of bouncing about, the company was bought by another Atlanta druggist, Asa Candler. He built Coca-Cola into an empire, but in one of the great unexplained twists of commercial history, he then gave the company away to his children and retired. His family promptly sold it. The family no longer owns a significant amount of stock. The chief stockholder is thought to be Robert Winship Woodruff, but his 3,500,000 shares—while enough to make him very rich—is not even 3 percent of the company.

It is in bottling that private and family ownership has survived. Just about every valley between Savannah and Seattle seems to boast a family-owned bottling company. Sometimes the family is nationally distinguished—the bottler in Fayetteville, Arkansas is the family of former Senator J. William Fulbright—but usually the bottlers are simply local lairds descended from some shrewd fellow who bought a bottling franchise decades ago. Bottling franchises are sold in perpetuity and are passed from generation to generation.

America's largest bottler is John Lupton, the grandson of one of the original financers of the Coca-Cola Bottling Company. Lupton now owns the major bottling companies in Texas, Arizona, and Colorado.

The idea for bottling Coke was said to have occurred to one Benjamin Franklin Thomas, a Chattanooga lawyer who served as chief clerk in the quartermaster's office during the Spanish-American War. The story is that Thomas was sweltering in Cuba, drinking a bottle of pineapple pop, when he thought to himself, "Not bad, but Coca-Cola is better." A gleam flickered across his eye.

Back in Chattanooga, in 1899, Thomas persuaded a lawyer friend, J.B. Whitehead, to join him in a bottling venture. They traveled to Atlanta and persuaded Asa Candler to sell them bottling rights to almost the entire country for $1. (Shrewd as he was, every now and then Candler did something that strikes today's mind as incredible.) Not everything came so cheaply, however, and to raise new capital one-quarter of the bottling company stock was sold to a third Chattanooga lawyer, John Thomas Lupton. Lupton had married into money and worked at his father-in-law's patent medicine firm. Their most famous product was "Cardui," a medication for "female disorders." The present Lupton's position is a direct result of this early foot in the door.

Success has spawned many myths about Coca-Cola:

- *It began as a patent medicine.* It was never promoted as a cure-all or hawked at medicine shows, but curative powers were often implied. The drink was initially formulated as a pick-me-up, to be sold in pharmacies and the original name for its syrup was Coca-Cola Syrup and Elixir. An advertising slogan in 1893 captured the spirit of those days. Coca-Cola was proclaimed, "The ideal brain tonic," brain tonic being an archaic expression for mind blower, stimulant, or consciousness expander. The famous slogan, "The pause that refreshes," introduced in 1929, is a somewhat understated expression of the claim that Coke is a pick-me-up.

- *Coca-Cola contains cocaine.* Once it did, but no longer. Coke's formulator, John Pemberton, was a pharmacist in Atlanta, Georgia. For years he had sold an alcohol based tonic called, "French Wine Coca–Ideal Brain Tonic," but the temperance movement was sweeping through the southern Bible Belt and Atlanta went dry in 1885. Pemberton developed a new tonic based on a number of powerful nonalcoholic stimulants: the kola nut from West Africa, cocaine from Central America, raw sugar, and caffeine. The cocaine was always the most criticized part of the formula and in 1902 it was dropped. The syrup now includes spent coca leaves, that is, coca with the cocaine removed.

- *If you pretend you found a bug in your bottle, Coke will always settle.* In the early years of the century, there were a few people who traveled about the U.S. threatening different bottling companies with lawsuits over roaches supposedly found in their bottles. Local bottling companies did sometimes pay up at once, for fear of scandal. In 1915, however, the Coca-Cola Bottlers Association was formed, largely to protect themselves from the scam, and since that time such claims have usually been fought vigorously.

- *It took a court order to let rival companies call their drinks "colas."* For many years Coca-Cola vigorously defended its name against imitators like Koca-Nola, Coca-Kola, Coke Ola, Toca-Cola, and King Cola. Pepsi Cola had been around since 1893, but until the 1930s it never seemed important enough to worry about. Then it hit on the marketing device of selling twice as much drink for the same price as Coca-Cola. Pepsi was taken to court in 1938, but Coca-Cola suddenly abandoned the case. Pepsi-Cola had planned to inquire into a $35,000 payment made to the head of Cleo Cola just before he agreed to drop "Cola" from the product name. In the Pepsi settlement, Coke agreed not to press the suit and Pepsi agreed not to pursue its inquiry. This settlement ended the monopoly on the name "Cola" and in 1941 the company officially began calling its product "Coke."

Two other prominent owners of Coca-Cola bottling companies are:

***Arthur Montgomery:*** The great nephew of an earlier Arthur Montgomery who, in 1903, invested in the Atlanta bottling plant. The present Montgomery now owns the Atlanta franchise.

***Crawford Veazey Rainwater:*** His father, Charles Veazey, was an associate of Lupton's partner, J.B. Whitehead, and took over Whitehead's position when he died in 1906. Rainwater headed the Pensacola, Florida bottling company until his retirement in 1981.

## AMERICA'S LARGEST MAKER OF FRENCH FRIES

**Auctioneer's price:** $720,000,000.
**Owner:** Simplot family.

The number one frozen vegetable in America is the potato. This fact might seem puzzling to anybody who thinks of potatoes from an agricultural point of view. They are not fragile roses that must be treated tenderly lest they perish before tomorrow's dawn. Potatoes are durable and they don't become much more so by freezing. From a cook's point of view, however, they are a big advantage. The rise of the frozen potato is, therefore, the story of the abandonment of all the peeling and slicing that chef's assistants hate.

The problem of preparing massive numbers of potatoes is especially acute in institutions that have thousands of meals to fix. During World War II, the army got around the difficulty by using dehydrated potatoes. Jack Simplot got rich in a hurry off that business. Back then he was a young Idaho businessman looking to get ahead on potatoes. Food processing was becoming important for other crops, why not the potato? In 1941, he opened a dehydrating plant in Caldwell, Idaho, on the Snake River. It was one of the most remote spots in the United States, but it managed to supply 75 million pounds of potatoes each year to the armed forces. Of course once the war ended demand dropped considerably. The army had many fewer mouths to feed and the returning vets had no nostalgia for meals of powdered eggs and powdered potatoes.

Simplot thought he might recover this lost business if he could develop a frozen potato. Every reader knows that potatoes, especially french fries, surround us, so it is hard to recall the time when french fries were not considered the natural accompaniment to any entrée sold at any restaurant from steak houses to burger joints to sea food houses. Yet there was such a time. In those days onions and onion rings were a favorite side dish of the short order cook. Simplot succeeded beyond his greediest dreams. Today the J.R. Simplot Company of Boise, Idaho, is the world's largest producer of frozen potatoes. Its warehouses can house 50 million *tons* of potatoes at a time and the company still has to rent more storage space. It is the major supplier of frozen french fries to McDonald's, the company that made french fries more popular than hot dogs.

At the end of World War II, however, Simplot didn't know what lay ahead. He knew only that if you froze a potato it turned black. It wasn't until 1948 that he solved that problem and not until 1950 that steady commercial production was possible. Housewives immediately took to the idea of easy-to-fix french fries, but in the institutionalized kitchens at hospitals, restaurants, schools, prisons, and hotels, the old peel-and-slice method

French fries traveling through processing plant. Photo: J.R. Simplot Company

had become routine. Nobody there was eager to make life easier for the employees.

Then, in the mid-1950s, America was hit by a potato famine. It wasn't as devastating as the one that swept Ireland a century earlier, but potato prices soared. Simplot seized the opportunity to persuade institutions to buy frozen potatoes from him. When the fresh potato famine ended his customers were persuaded and did not leave him.

There was only one more break needed in this rise from lowly vegetable to the national side order. Shortly after the potato famine, Ray Kroc began developing his McDonald chain. He insisted on easily prepared, perfectly consistent food. Frozen french fries were just what he was looking for and when Simplot and Kroc met, the fate of the American taste bud was determined.

Simplot, now in his mid-seventies, is still chairman of the board. His two sons, Don and Richard, are vice-presidents and serve on the board of the company. The stock is privately held by the family. If it were publicly owned, the history of the company might be quite different. A public corporation probably wouldn't have chosen to spend years developing the frozen french fry when success was uncertain and there was no known market for the product. If it weren't for Simplot's persistence, we would probably be eating a lot more onion rings these days.

## AMERICA'S LARGEST WINERY

**Auctioneer's price:** $585,000,000.
**Owner:** Gallo family.

In the early 1970s television watchers were astonished to see British actor Peter Ustinov urging a new line of wines made by, "my friends, Ernest and Julio Gallo." There was some doubt that the Gallo brothers were really friends of Mr. Ustinov and little but scorn for the idea that Ernest and Julio could make a wine worth drinking.

Back in the '50s and early 1960s, comedian Lenny Bruce used to joke about, "Your honest Gallo drunk." The phrase cut to the soul of Gallo's reputation—no frills, no flavors, no fancy stuff, just booze. The Gallo brothers were young men when Prohibition ended and they began making cheap ports and muscatels. The company seemed aimed directly at winos. In the '50s the Gallos introduced a couple of popular "fortified" wines called Thunderbird and Ripple. The jokes about those brands turned on the assumption that the consumer was not yet on skid-row, but headed that way.

So audiences were quite unprepared to see Peter Ustinov suggesting that a sophisticated new line of wines was being produced by his friends the Gallo brothers. Gallo was expanding again, this time into the table wine market. A table wine is meant to be taken with food. It is not a super-wine to be part of a great dinner, but neither is it drunk simply to get drunk as quickly and cheaply as possible. Most of the wine in Europe is table wine and most of it is awful. It quickly became apparent

Ernest and Julio Gallo. Photo: E&J Gallo Winery

that Gallo table wines really were better than most of the European lines.

Wine sales expanded very rapidly in America during the 1970s, so much that today it is hard to remember how unusual it was in the 1960s to see people serving wine. This growth has been an important countercurrent to the breakdown of social eating. You do not hurry through a meal that includes wine. Increasing sales are always accompanied by increasing attention to prices and that tendency naturally favored Gallo. The countervailing pressure came from Gallo's reputation for fermenting junk. The company had to overcome the "What me drink Gallo?" sentiment and, by and large, it has succeeded.

Gallo is America's largest wine maker, accounting for over

one third of all California wine sold. Its huge wine batches are blended in lots of 250,000 gallons. Its plant looks like an enormous chemical factory, which of course it is. The company is entirely owned by the Gallo family. The two brothers, Ernest and Julio, are now in their seventies and still running the company. Ernest is in charge of sales and manufacturing. Julio oversees the vineyards and the wine making. Their children are much less interested in the wine business and the future role of the family in management is uncertain.

## A FAST-GROWING FAST FOOD CHAIN

**Auctioneer's price:** $490,000,000.
**Owner:** David Thomas, Jr.

While it is difficult to come up with a good and original idea, it is seldom really necessary. Perhaps the most characteristically human form of thought is plagiarism. It is through this method that children learn the clichés of their elders and television programmers fill out their schedule. Many a business success has turned on the idea, "Let's copy that." Those who sneer fail to realize just how difficult successful imitation is. In order to copy something aptly you have to understand what you are imitating. If you don't, you are bound to do something inappropriate.

It is obvious that in developing McDonald's fast food business the late owner/founder, Ray Kroc, had a good idea, one any businessman would be proud to borrow, but not every would-be fast food entrepreneur realizes just what Kroc did. They think in traditional restaurant terms, about food and menus, while Kroc saw that the way to become the Rockefeller of restauteurs was to eliminate all the qualities that drew people to restaurants (good food, pleasant service, choice) and replace them with advertising and more advertising.

Ordinarily there is a limit to advertising's power. If a campaign is energetic enough, people will give a product a try, but then independent judgment comes into play. Customers start responding to the experience rather than to the publicity. This humble reality should have doomed McDonald's, but its advertising was aimed at children whose experience with enjoyable restaurants was still too meager for them to bring any judgment to bear on the matter.

The McDonald's publicity agents managed to spread a story that a child had asked Mrs. Santa Claus where she had met her husband. The reply came, "At McDonald's." Anyone young enough to be moved by that fable is too young to judge restaurant quality.

McDonald's advertising wisely avoided discussion of factors like taste, variety, and service, preferring slogans about the "All-American Meal" or deserving "a break today." Now that a generation has grown up with McDonald's the advertising can include young adults, though the ads still avoid talk of food, service, or choice.

Many would-be McDonald's imitators did spring up, but they couldn't challenge the original. They preserved McDonald's bus-terminal atmosphere, but overlooked the emphasis on childish judgment. Often enough they even called for actual judgment. Ashamed to imitate McDonald's exactly, they served pizza, or roast beef, or chicken, or tacos, or whatever seems different. Of course, this attention to the food missed the point of McDonald's. The ghost of Ray Kroc just laughs.

One imitator who has not missed the point is David Thomas, Jr., owner/founder of the Wendy's chain of hamburger stands. The first Wendy's opened in 1969 in Columbus, Ohio. In 1972, Thomas began selling Wendy's franchises. He sold only to established business people able to open many Wendy's restaurants at once.

Thomas took the appeal to childish judgment even further than McDonald's. The chain is named for his daughter and the chain's symbol is a cute little all-American girl, a stylized drawing of the original Wendy. Its advertising slogan, "You're Wendy's kind of people," tells you nothing about the food and discourages wondering about it. Think about yourself instead.

The Wendy's menu is quite similar to the one at McDonald's, but the decor is a bit more cozy, a bit more imaginative. Unlike most would-be imitators of McDonald's, Thomas has not chosen to copy McDonald's shake-a-leg ambiance. Wendy's is still a fast food place with customer lines and small menus, but the addition of a salad bar helped increase the take your time (not just a break) atmosphere. By competing against McDonald's style rather than its menu the Wendy's chain has become the first outfit to look as though it might be able to give McDonald's a run for its customers.

Owning a fast-food franchise can often be profitable, but it seldom brings power. The franchisee has to agree to maintain certain standards and is dependent on the home company to provide the product and advertising approach that makes money. When times are hard or the home company sees new opportunities it can turn on the vassals with the eagerness of a crocodile feeding on chicks. One family that has managed to avoid these pitfalls is the Rieses. Joseph Riese, his brother, Irving, and son, Dennis, own the National Restaurants Management Company. It holds twelve separate food franchises in New York City. With an auctioneer's price of about $90,000,000 and half a million customers a day, the company is larger than many of the businesses that sold them the franchises.

The Rieses' technique is to put franchises side-by-side, so that anyone in an area who is hungry will see only them. Then they locate in places where people are in a hurry. Most of the restaurants around New York's travel points belong to them; they dominate Grand Central Station, Penn Station, and the Port Authority Terminal areas. They also have most of the restaurants in Times Square, near Macy's department store, and around the Empire State Building. Pick a restaurant, or its neighbor, or the one two doors down. The Rieses own them all.

Their franchises are: Bagel Eateries, Brew & Burger, Chock Full O'Nuts, Chicago Restaurants, David's Cookies, Godfather's Pizza, Haagen Dazs (ice cream), J.J. Mulligan, Lindy's, Martinson's Coffee Shops, Pete Smith's Hall of Fame, Roy Rogers.

## POULTRY BARONY

**Auctioneer's price:** $488,000,000.
**Owner:** Franklin Parsons Perdue.

Despite all the hamburgers, the coming meat is chicken. Consumption has been increasing for years. Its price is much better than beef and by the end of this decade chicken is expected to surpass beef as America's major source of meat protein. Trends like that one suggest two things: (1) America's standard of living is moving toward the Third World's; and (2) the biggest chicken farmers are getting richer than the old cattle barons.

The idea of a chicken baron may sound silly, but we've got one. Frank Perdue raises chickens from egg to grocery freezer. He has a fully integrated operation, meaning that he does it all from breeding to blending the food to wringing necks and dressing the remains. He uses over a million tons of chicken feed every year, so much soy and corn that Perdue Farms holds a seat on Chicago's commodity exchange. The grain is converted into meat. Perdue runs through five million birds a week.

Perdue Farms is one of America's largest privately held corporations and is the largest private poultry operation. It is based in Salisbury, Maryland with other chicken complexes operating in Delaware, Virginia, and North Carolina. Perdue's family has been living on Maryland's Eastern Shore region for over 300 years. The house Perdue lives in has belonged to the family for nearly 200 years. Chicken farming, however, is relatively new to the family. Perdue's father decided to go into chicken farming, initially for the eggs. In 1940 he switched to raising broilers. Frank didn't enjoy growing up among chickens and did not plan to join his father's business, but he did.

Small scale chicken farming is about the most demanding work a person can undertake. Vacations become something to be read about in books, only there is no time to read. Wives and children are recruited into tending the birds. When a chicken farmer is not working, only one subject is proper food for thought, chickens—specifically, how to increase production or cut costs. The answers usually lie in doing some more work yourself or recycling something being wasted. Perdue seemed to be thinking straight. In 1958 he began grinding his own feed. Ten years later he bought his first processing plant. In 1970 he started advertising on television. Brand name chickens was a novel idea back then. Most people just bought chicken, but Perdue's ads worked. He now sells 5 percent of the chickens in the country, an amazing feat for so diversified an industry. He recently began making chicken hot dogs and already accounts for about 10 percent of the nation's hot dog sales. With that kind of success, can chicken salami and chicken burgers be far behind?

## NUTRASWEET

**Auctioneer's price:** $472,000,000.
**Owner:** Searle family.

The ancient lamentation of worldly Puritans says, "Everything I enjoy is either immoral, illegal, or fattening." Much of the gross national product is devoted to evading this conflict between desire and its consequences. Laws and morality are more easily outdistanced than is metabolism, so the largest pots of gold are likely to go to the discoverer of a means of preserving the pleasures of rich food while stripping them of their caloric side-effects. From time to time someone hits upon a food additive that tastes sweet and contains little or no calories. "Yahoo," the finder shouts, "Pleasure without penalty," and off to market he runs.

There seems to be some dread bookkeeper watching over this process. It is as though every credit on the pleasure page calls for a balancing notation on the debit side. Sweetness without calories? The bookkeeper reluctantly bypasses the obesity column and then his crafty eye sees the all purpose column headed, "Carcinogen," and he makes a check. Just to be vindictive he also adds a check in the column headed, "Lousy aftertaste," thus reducing the original appeal of the substance. Both cyclamate and saccharin got this treatment.

A new substance called aspartame, brand name NutraSweet, has evaded the familiar debits of sweeteners. It is not fattening, not known to be cancer causing, and has no vile aftertaste. The only drag on its popularity has been its price. Aspartame costs more than twenty times the price of saccharin, so food containing this new sweetener is usually a blend of aspartame and saccharin.

Aspartame was originally synthesized in Britain by Imperial Chemical Industries, but its sweet taste (200 times sweeter than sugar) was only discovered when James Schlatter, a chemist at G.D. Searle & Co., got some aspartame on his fingers and boldly licked the stuff off. He might have had bad luck and discovered that aspartame worked like cyanide. Instead he smacked his lips and smiled.

The discovery of aspartame's sweetness touched off a long series of tests in search of the place where the bookkeeper made his debit mark. Inevitably some problems were found; the most important is the chemical's instability. It breaks down when mixed with fluid acids and, surprise, soft drinks are strong acids. No rules have been introduced yet, but this problem delayed federal approval a long time and there is still speculation that diet drinks with NutraSweet might ultimately have to be dated, like dairy products. The additive is also off-limits to sufferers from a genetic disease known as phenylketonuria (PKU). But by and large the Food and Drug Administration was impressed by aspartame and, after years of hesitation, approved its use.

The decision brought a sigh of relief from members of the Searle family which still owns 30 percent of the corporation's stock and presides over the board of directors. The current Searle leadership is the fourth generation of the family. The pharmaceuticals concern that introduced the first contraceptive pill blossomed under the direction of John Gideon Searle, star member of the family's third generation. When the fourth took over, in 1966, Searle was the most profitable of the major drug companies; by 1977 it was the least profitable. Daniel Crow Searle, eldest of his generation, oversaw a plan to diversify company activities and acquired a series of losing investments in animal medicine, hospital supplies, and diagnostic equipment. William Searle, Daniel's brother, was the number two man in the company, but he spent a lot of time managing the football squad at his *alma mater* in Ann Arbor, Michigan. By 1977, the boys had to admit they were not doing a great job. Day to day running of the company was turned over to outsiders. Daniel is still chairman, however; his brother-in-law, Wesley Dixon, is vice-chairman and William is on the board of directors.

The new management was considered an improvement, but the introduction of aspartame is what put fire back into the profit column. (The auctioneer's price above is just for the aspartame portion of Searle's business. You can see how important the line is to the whole company by comparing that price with the auctioneer's price for the entire firm, $1,920,000,000. It already accounts for over one-quarter of the company's worth.) By autumn of 1983, the sweetener was turning up in soft drinks, cereals, packets for mixing into coffee and tea, and an increasing number of dry food mixes like cocoa and gelatine. Demand for NutraSweet exceeded all predictions and outstripped the company's ability to produce it.

This success meant that some consumers were eating a lot more NutraSweet than anyone anticipated and soon complaints of headaches and dizziness began to be voiced. The Food and Drug Administration continues to support aspartame, but the doubts persist. People remember that cyclamate and saccharin were also approved only to be condemned later. Besides, it goes against all our Pilgrim fathers' teachings to hope there really can be pleasure today and no price to pay tomorrow.

## BIGGEST HEALTH FOOD BUSINESS

**Auctioneer's price:** $297,000,000.
**Owner:** David B. Shakarian.

There are people who are willing to try any mind-altering drug, but are fearful of the poisons in sirloin steak. If you can explain that paradox, the intricacies of the 1960s hold no mysteries for you. David Shakarian does not pretend to understand the whole '60s sociology, but he sure benefited from it.

Shakarian is the founder and chief executive officer of the country's largest chain of health-food stores, the General Nutrition Corporation (GNC). The company's stock is sold publicly, but the Shakarian family still owns 82 percent of it. The company began in the 1930s as a yogurt stand in Pittsburgh. In those days it was called, "Lackzoom."

Only 5 percent of the public ever buys health food, but during the early 1960s health food did become more visible and more available, moving from downtown locations to suburban malls. It became part of the diet of people you knew rather than people you read about. Shakarian both profited from and led this change. Today he has over 1,000 stores around the country, mostly in shopping centers.

The biggest difficulty faced by his stores is summed up in the term, "health food." The beasts of the field eat just for their health, but most people still eat to be sociable, to find pleasure, and to escape the tiresome daily routine. Sweets, intoxicants, and hearty staples are what people prefer. When it comes to proper diet we talk a lot about balance and nutrition, but we put our money where our sweet tooth is. Even Shakarian's customers look on his stores as chiefly a kind of specialty drug chain. Half his sales are for vitamin and mineral supplements.

Shakarian has overcome many of these limitations by emphasizing price and location. Health-food markups are often enormous, sometimes 1000 percent, a fact that has given the industry the reputation for being something of a scam. General Nutrition's markups are about 45 percent, typical for a moderate volume business. Shakarian also keeps his costs down by making most of what he sells. Even shampoos, fruit juices, and vitamins are made by General Nutrition.

A second strength Shakarian has always enjoyed is that although most people have no interest in his wares, some people are wildly enthusiastic about them. Shakarian is an Armenian refugee, a survivor of the genocide that the Turkish perpetrators still deny ever took place. He was the first person to import yogurt into America. Even though yogurt was unknown to most Americans it is a staple of near Asia. Armenians, Turks, Soviet Georgians, and Lebanese all love it, so there were some eager customers and Shakarian's one stand grew to six by the outbreak of World War II.

In Armenia yogurt is just seen as food, but Shakarian soon realized that many of his customers were eating it because they felt it was good for them. To serve these people he began adding various other health foods to his menu. During the war, Shakarian introduced a mail-order service, the best way to serve customers who, in absolute numbers form a good market, but are too scattered to be reached by a store. Then when the '60s brought a new scorn for the hollow values of affluence, Shakarian was well poised to serve people who dismissed all uses for food save the primal one that it keeps you fit. His business grew like yeasty dough.

## BEST-SELLING BIRDSEED

**Auctioneer's price:** $242,000,000.
**Owner:** Leonard Norman Stern.

Birdseed sounds as if it must lie at the chicken feed end of the pet food business, but one of America's greatest fortunes is based on birdseed, fish food, and related pet accessories. After all, pets have to eat and if you can seize most of the market, there is obviously plenty of money to be gained. But how do you go about getting a grip on such a market? Superior quality helps with some foods, but who can judge among birdseeds? Advertising and packaging matters, but when quality is not an issue, advertising has to find a way to overcome judgment if a market is actually to be monopolized. To date no such genius of advertising has appeared.

There is another way to become king of a market. Consider these excerpts from some recent indexes to *The Wall Street Journal*:

> A.H. Robins Co. and its Miller-Morton Co. unit filed antitrust suit in federal district court against [Hartz Mountain], charging it dominates pet-care market in U.S. (2/10/78)
>
> [Hartz Mountain] Agreed to let distributors and retail sellers

of pet food handle products made by company's competitors, Federal Trade Commission revealed (8/29/79)

Hartz ex-sales aide is indicted for perjury concerning alleged payments of bribes and procurement of prostitutes by firm (10/1/82)

Hartz owner Leonard Stern made a prime target of a big grand jury investigation into charges of commercial bribery, antitrust violations, obstruction of justice and perjury (1/17/83)

Rumors about Stern's business methods have persisted for years. When Miller Morton, makers of Sargeant's flea collars, brought their antitrust suit Hartz settled out of court by paying $42,500,000. The settlement prevented many of the rumors from being placed on the official record.

The sequel to the film *The Godfather* gave the sentimental, we are all to blame, explanation for the spread of corruption and brutality in a group of people. Immigrants arrive at the bottom of society and find they must choose between fighting back or being exploited. That explanation offers no insight into the success of the Stern family or the Hartz Mountain Corporation. (The corporation is a subsidiary of Hartz Mountain Industries, which includes many real estate holdings. The auctioneer's price above is for the subsidiary only.) After World War I, Leonard Stern's father, Max, immigrated to America from Germany. He was down and out, but hoped to find success in America. He brought 12,000 canaries with him, thinking of going into business. He sold the lot within six months and was off to a successful career in the pet, pet food, and supplies business. When he died in 1982, age 83, he was mourned as an honorable man who had come to America in search of opportunity and found it.

When talk turns to his son the question "why?" pops up a lot more than the word "honor." No references to the immigrant experiences of Don Corleone are going to explain what drives Leonard Stern. One thing is obvious: a lot of money is at stake. Stern has plenty of cash, but there's more to be had.

Leonard Stern dominates 75 percent of his market. His chief rival in the birdseed business used to be French's, but they abandoned the effort nearly a decade ago. That decision meant money in Leonard's pocket and for some people the bottom line *is* the bottom line.

Just what is Leonard Stern up to? Rumors have for years said that Hartz uses a number of "anti-competitive" practices: *requiring retail and wholesale dealers to handle them exclusively,* a lawyerly way of saying that if a store tried to sell both Hartz and competitive products, the squeeze was put on them; *price discrimination*, charging different dealers different rates for the same items; *kickbacks*, payments made for buyers who handle large accounts; *threats* to people who propose to tell what they know; *pandering,* arranging for prostitutes to be readily available to important buyers at trade shows. Some of the stories told about Stern sound like sour grapes or paranoid fantasies. Some sound like exaggerations or fabrications, but others are routine, grubby, and full of sleazy similarities as they are repeated time and again around the country by one alleged witness or victim after another. And all for the sale of birdseed.

## BEST-SELLING JAMS AND JELLIES

**Auctioneer's price:** $179,000,000.
**Owner:** Smucker family.

America's leading producer of jams, jellies, and preserves is J.M. Smucker. This bit of information seems to surprise many Smucker's customers even though they themselves swear that it is the only jelly to buy. Most elites in America consist of large numbers of people who believe themselves to be one of a very small number of people and Smucker has done a splendid job of creating the impression that it is hard pressed to survive. Their advertising slogan, "With a name like Smucker's it has to be good," makes a subtle appeal to the snob in each of us. Yes, one supposes, those jerks out there probably are put off by something as simple as a funny sounding name, but I'm not that stupid. Another thing about Smucker's is the price. It costs more than most jellies and jams, so shoppers have to say to themselves, "It's worth it." Undeterred by the higher price or the strange sounding name, customers proudly join the elite consumers, unaware that a full third of all jellies and jams sold are Smucker's brand.

Smucker is in the hands of the third generation of Smucker family leadership and a fourth generation is expected to take over soon. The current chairman and chief executive is Paul Smucker. His grandfather, Jerome, founded the firm. Paul's son, Timothy, is the company president and another son, Kim, is treasurer. The family still controls 30 percent of the stock.

The Smucker family is quite smart about their business. Overall sales of preserves are declining because many people don't eat leisurely breakfasts anymore. Smucker's sales, however, are slowly increasing. They have expanded their line as well, adding peanut butter. They wisely chose to stick with their quality image by offering a "natural" peanut butter instead of one of the processed easy-to-spread versions. If they had gone head-to-head with makers like Peter Pan and Skippy, surely they would have failed to find a niche in the market and would have damaged their quality reputation at the same time.

A bolder introduction was "Goober Grape" which mixes peanut butter and jelly right in the jar. Everybody loves, but nobody admires, peanut butter and jelly sandwiches. With this product Smucker is coming close to the line. Parents may say to themselves, "Well, at least it's Smucker's peanut butter and Smucker's jelly," but in the presence of such unabashed junk food they may, at any moment, break through the snobbery of brand appeals and see jellies and jams for what they are. Sure Smucker's tastes great and is better than most rivals, but when you come down to cases this goo is one of the world's least vital dietary substances.

If you really want the best in jams and preserves, Sarabeth's Kitchen makes a startlingly superior product. At this point we aren't talking, "Costs a few pennies more." Sarabeth's orange-apricot marmalade sells for over $7 a jar. Besides her own two stores in New York and her mail-order business, a number of gourmet shops across the country carry the jams. Even with a national distribution the business is small. Owner Sarabeth Levine still works in the kitchen herself, making preserves according to the recipe her aunt taught her. She began her business working in her home kitchen and selling marmalade to Bloomingdale's. Business grew and in 1981 she opened a store with a larger kitchen. Business grew some more. Now she has five other regular spreads besides the marmalade and she is talking about getting a larger kitchen. Growth means more money and more people enjoying the jam, but at some point a businesswoman who says, "The secret is in the cooking," has to wonder what the effect of using larger pots is going to have. Fig preserves (called "Miss Figgy") taste one way when cooked in a small kitchen, another from a large vat.

## DANNON YOGURT

**Auctioneer's price:** $91,000,000.
**Owner:** Antoine A.P. Riboud.

Three billion cups of Dannon/Danone yogurt are sold each year. Because none of the cups go to China, that means there is enough for everybody else on earth to get one. This kind of popularity might seem to run against the trend that is so evident in the finances of food—people prefer sweet, tasty solids to sour, bland, and runny food—but, of course, the world's most popular yogurt is not quite like the item invented by Turkish goatherds.

A Spaniard who later moved to France, Issac Carasso, invented commercialized yogurt. He added flavors, sweeteners, and enough milk particles to give the dish a custard-like solidity. His product was called Danone and was a hit both in Spain and France. Issac's son, Daniel, came to America and began his own company, Dannon, making a similar commercial style of yogurt. (The name "Danone" was given in honor of Daniel, when he was a boy.) Dannon and Danone were separate companies under separate ownership. In 1959, Issac sold the American Dannon to a giant food conglomerate called Beatrice Foods.

Meanwhile, back in France, a completely unrelated individual named Antoine Riboud was taking charge of a glass bottle company he had inherited from his mother. Riboud's idea was to expand by taking control of the companies that used his bottles and he turned his small business into France's largest food company, BSN—Gervais Danone. (The auctioneer's price for that company is $3,100,000,000. The price at the top of this entry is just for the American, Dannon Milk Products, division.) Riboud is now Europe's largest beer producer and the world's largest producer of dairy products. His brands include Evian mineral water (more popular in France than Perrier) and Kronenbourg beer. In 1972 he bought up Danone. It looked like the original Danone and Dannon had met similar but separate fates, swallowed up by local food conglomerates.

The separation seems to have chafed at Riboud's soul. He has exported some items to America and imported others (he has the French franchise for Canada Dry), but he had not done much buying here. Yet, in 1981, he bought Dannon from Beatrice Foods. For the first time Danone and Dannon were part of one organization under one ownership.

## TABASCO SAUCE

**Auctioneer's price:** $60,000,000.
**Owner:** McIlhenny family.

There are *no* empty Tabasco bottles, or so says an old joke. If you are in the Tabasco business, however, the joke cuts too close to the truth to be funny. Market research shows that over half of America's homes hold a Tabasco bottle. The trouble is most people seldom uncap the bottle and when they do they pour out its content with all the generosity of the Ayatollah on a Fourth of July. Yet even at glacial rates of consumption, 50 million two ounce bottles are sold annually in America. (Another 30 million are sold abroad.) That's quite enough to keep the conservative Tabasco family rolling along.

In a world where even so apparently a perfect food as Grape-

Nuts is forever being "improved," the constancy of America's native pepper sauce is amazing. Tabasco is more than 100 years old and is still made by the family that invented it, is still prepared in the same place it was first made, and the original recipe is still followed.

The *family* is the McIlhenny's: Edmund McIlhenny was a banker in New Orleans whose career was ruined by the Civil War. When the war ended he went to his wife's old home. It was in ruins and so was its garden, except for a few red peppers that hadn't seemed worth looting. McIlhenny seemed to have the tough mind of Scarlett O'Hara, for he soon devised a formula for a hot sauce made from the garden peppers. Edmund died in 1890 and the company was put under the care of his eldest son, John Avery. In 1906 John went to work for Theodore Roosevelt and his two brothers took over the Tabasco operation. They ran it until World War II. In 1949, Walter McIlhenny took charge and still directs the company. Walter is the son of John and grandson of Edmund McIlhenny. Three other members of the family also hold leadership positions in the company.

The *place* is Avery Island: readers of Tabasco labels know it says, "New Iberia, La.," but that is because New Iberia (nine miles to the north) held the closest post office when Edmund McIlhenny began his business. McIlhenny's wife, Mary Avery, was born on this remote island at the edge of the Louisiana bayou. Most of the swampland is flat, but Avery Island is one of five islands that rise a hundred feet above the Gulf coast. These islands are the peaks of enormous salt deposits which, from top to bottom, are larger than Mount Everest. This area is abundant in wildlife—mostly birds, alligators, and deer. Ned McIlhenny, one of Edmund's sons, was a devoted naturalist and made Avery Island a refuge for snowy egrets. The McIlhenny family still owns the entire island and, besides making Tabasco, they mine salt and receive about 100,000 tourists each year. There are also some oil wells on the island; because of Ned McIlhenny's conservationist attitudes, the rigs are well concealed.

The *recipe* for making tabasco:

Mash peppers, picked when they are bright red
Add salt, from the island mine
Let age—about 3 years

Blend with strong white vinegar—stir for 4 weeks
Strain and pour into bottles

The tabasco peppers are a specially bred strain of Mexican red peppers. They were developed on Avery Island by Edmund McIlhenny. Because they are much hotter than the jalapeno peppers used in Mexican cooking, they are never consumed straight. Most of the peppers are now grown in Central America, but the seeds are still selected on Avery Island and the mash is still converted to Tabasco sauce there.

## OLDEST NEW ORLEANS RESTAURANT

**Auctioneer's price:** $6,300,000.
**Owner:** Roy Guste, Jr.

"Let me see," says the customer.

The waiter stands patiently. He holds no pad in his hand and will write nothing down once the customer starts to order. Even though there are five other people at the table the waiter simply remembers what is said.

"I think I'll have . . . ," the customer hesitates again.

The waiter shows not a sign of irritation. He has been at the restaurant for many years, beginning as a busboy. His father before him was also a waiter here. Management and staff positions in the restaurant are hereditary.

"Ah, I know," says the customer at last, "I'll start with the oysters Rockefeller and the gumbo, followed by pompano *en papillote* with soufflé potatoes, and for dessert my wife and I will share a baked Alaska."

The waiter has absorbed the order, total bill before taxes and gratuity $43.75, and casts his eyes to the next person at the table. There is a long pause. The customer is embarrassed. The menu is entirely in French and contains no hint of a translation.

Such is the daily scene at Antoine's, the oldest restaurant in New Orleans and reputedly the oldest restaurant in America that has been in continuous operation. Its specialty is Creole cooking, a blend of French cooking style and southern American materials. Indeed, Antoine's is one of the places where Creole cooking was invented. The older Louisiana food style is Cajun, which is related to Creole cooking but is not the same thing.

Antoine's was founded in 1840 by Antoine Alciatore, a French-born immigrant to New Orleans. He was trained in French cuisine and opened a restaurant soon after reaching the New World. This same kind of behavior is common today as refugees from around the world flee to America and set up restaurants. Today's immigrant can often find the foods they used to prepare in the old country, but in 1840 it was not so easy to import foods from around the world. Antoine was forced to cook local foods which he prepared in the French manner. (Similar pressures in San Francisco led to the creation of chop suey.)

In 1885, ownership of the restaurant passed to Antoine's

Antoine's Restaurant. Photo: Antoine's

son, Jules, and he directed it for the next forty-five years. Jules had been sent back to France to study cooking, so he was in a fine position to continue the Creole tradition. It was Jules who invented the restaurant's most celebrated dish, oysters Rockefeller. The name was given it because the sauce is so rich.

The restaurant has stayed in the family and is now owned by the fifth generation, descended through a female line. Roy Guste was also trained in France before taking charge of Antoine's. The present look of the restaurant is not so different from its turn of the century appearance—high ceilings, spare furniture, rich place settings—but the business Guste operates is quite different from the one that faced great-grandpère Jules. Along with regular customers (who reserve their waiter along with their table) and distinguished transients, are the throngs of tourists. New Orleans may be the only city in America that people visit simply to eat in as many different restaurants as possible.

The tourists line up every evening, starting at 6 p.m. A lot of restaurants encourage this waiting because it runs up the bar tab, but Antoine's customers form a line that stretches out into the street of the French Quarter. Sober and stoical, the tourists wait until a table in one of the fourteen dining rooms becomes available. Then they too can relax for a few hours over a gargantuan meal. The spirit of the experience is summed up in a little note on the menu, "Si on vous fait attendre, c'est pour mieux vous servir, et vous plaire." Translation: no fast food here.

## AMERICA'S BEST BUTTER AND CHEESE COW

**Auctioneer's price:** $25,000.
**Owner:** Earl Waltemeyer.

One of the saddest triumphs of food technology is Rocky Hill Favorite Deb, the most productive Jersey cow in history. In a single year, running from June, 1978 to June, 1979, she gave 35,880 lbs. of milk and 1,923 lbs. of fat, an average of 102 lbs. of milk products per day.

Holstein cattle are even more productive than Jerseys. Their best cows give 55,000 lbs. in a year, but Holstein milk is thin gruel when compared to Jersey milk. Holstein milk is not rich enough in proteins and fats to be much good for making cheese or butter.

Because of economies of transportation, America's dairy industry has evolved in two directions. The great liquid producers (mostly Holsteins) are kept on farms near large population centers. Their milk can be trucked daily into metropolitan stores and quickly consumed. Farmers in less populous areas raise the breeds whose milk is richer in milk solids (mostly Jersey and Guernsey cows) and most of their milk is turned into butter or cheese, items more easily stored and shipped over long distances.

Rocky Hill Favorite Deb was born in northern Alabama and when she set her record was still at the farm of her birth. Earl Waltemeyer bought her after she set the new record and brought her to his farm just outside of Philadelphia. That metropolitan setting is not the Jersey cow's usual home, but Favorite Deb is now treasured more for her ovaries than her milk.

The technology of test-tube infants and surrogate mothers is well advanced in the veterinary world. Favorite Deb is artificially inseminated and then the fertilized eggs are implanted in more ordinary cows. It would be grossly inefficient, from an economist's point of view, for Favorite Deb to give birth to her own offspring when she could be ovulating instead. Rocky Hill Favorite Deb's reward for giving so much rich milk was her transformation into a queen bee.

# 10

# TRANSPORTATION

## A TANKER FLEET

**Auctioneer's price:** $1,250,000,000.
**Owner:** Daniel Keith Ludwig.

One of the perennial candidates for the title of "richest man in America" is almost completely unknown to his countrymen. Ludwig's name is famous in Brazil because he once wasted $780,000,000 there trying to build a lumber kingdom in the Amazon. He bought a slice of jungle territory larger than the state of Connecticut, then built three thousand miles of roads, established a town of 30,000 residents, spent $200,000,000 getting a prefab pulp mill up the river, but he finally folded his hand. Red tape and jungle rot ate up his billion and cried, "Please, sir, I want some more." It was a rough game, but Ludwig still had a couple of billion left in his pocket.

Ludwig's surviving fortune is based on tankers. He owns fifty ships weighing seven million tons. Tankers are ugly things with none of the romance or pioneer daring of the great sailing vessels, but they matter as much to our civilization as the sails did to theirs. Because of Ludwig's ships, oil found on the flip side of the globe is burned in America. The size of Ludwig's wealth has a certain absurd aspect to it, but he didn't get to be so rich by doing nothing. He is the father of much that is modern in shipping.

It was Ludwig who introduced supertankers, ships of 500,000 tons or more. Ludwig was also the man who developed the system of launching a ship sideways; without that idea large ships could only be launched in very wide waters. It was Ludwig, again, who discovered the technique for financing oil-carrying ships that was to make himself and others, men like Aristotle Onassis, stupendously rich. Ludwig was also an early backer of containerized freight.

He was an eighth grade drop-out who began working for a ship chandler in Port Arthur, Texas. One authoritative guide to matters nautical describes a ship chandler as a "shop which is full of things that are eaten and drunk on board ship; where you can get everything to make her seaworthy and beautiful." To work for one, the same source reports, a man "need not pass an examination in anything under the sun, but he must have Ability in the abstract and demonstrate it practically." Ludwig had Ability, so while other boys his age were still in high school learning algebra, Ludwig was learning what it took to keep a ship running.

Later he drifted back north and got a marine engineer's certificate working on the Great Lakes. He tried developing his own fleet and, for a while, owned a group of tugboats. His great break came when he was almost forty. In 1936, he chartered some oil tankers and then went to the banks with his charter agreements. Because the business was already guaranteed it took no special courage for the banks to agree to provide money to build the ships. This idea—first the customers, then the ships—reversed tradition and common sense, but it worked. It permitted a man of only ordinary financial means to become well-off, then rich, then superrich, and finally richest of all.

During World War II, Ludwig built tankers for the navy. It was a small operation, his total output was less than the tonnage of one supertanker, but it gave him a toehold to pull himself even higher in the industry. After the war he got a lease on Japan's destroyed Imperial Navy Yard. Japan has not been allowed to reestablish a navy, but the rebuilding of the Japanese merchant marine has been dramatic and Ludwig was an important part of it. The 1970s were particularly fine for Ludwig. The oil crises kept his ships full and in great demand. These days, however, the energy boom is in dry dock and, by multibillionaire standards, times are lean.

Ludwig does not raise money by selling shares in his companies. He has never sold stock in any enterprise he controlled and his ships are his own. When he takes a financial bath, as in Brazil or another time when he tried to construct a huge ship-repair yard in the Bahamas, it is his money that goes down the drain. And when he does well, the pennies from heaven all fall into his personal umbrella.

## LOVE BOAT LINERS

**Auctioneer's price:** $450,000,000.
**Owner:** Ted Arison.

"Let temptation be your guide," is part of the advice offered in the introductory pamphlet given to passengers who have booked a voyage aboard Carnival Cruise Lines. The slogan has done well by the cruise company's sole owner, Ted Arison, who began in 1972 with one partner, one ship, and a $7 million investment. Today he has four ships, no partners, and every month the cruise line grosses more than twice seven million dollars.

Sounds good? Yes, but there are ways to make it better. One thing you can do is register your corporation outside the country. Carnival is legally listed as a Panamanian corporation and does not have to pay U.S. income taxes, although none of the four ships actually sails to Panama and Arison works in Miami. The line's tax-sheltered income permits quite energetic expansion. Three more ships are planned. The $170,000,000 ship *Holiday* is expected to be ready in mid-1985.

The ships sail from Miami and Los Angeles every weekend and steer south. Because they are soon beyond U.S. territorial limits, the sale of tax-free liquor begins and the roulette wheels start spinning. All four ships have casinos.

Arison's father also made millions from shipping, but Arison was driven by a compulsion to make it on his own. He organized a cargo company when he was twenty-eight and was ruined by the time he was thirty, a great age to go broke because it leaves lots of time to try again. Arison soon had another cargo company going and shortly after he turned forty he made the stock available to the public. He sold out completely and became a multimillionaire. This little fund served as kindling capital for the cruise line fortune. (Nobody ever got a hundred million without first having ten million he was willing to burn.) After a tottery start, Arison found his feet and since 1975 all his ships have been fully booked for every cruise.

## WINNEBAGO

**Auctioneer's price:** $158,000,000.
**Owner:** John K. Hanson.

The old (pre-spring, 1974) attitude toward energy was best summed up by a news clip shown on national TV shortly after the first gas lines appeared. A reporter described a prototype electric car that didn't need any gas at all. Just plug it into your garage wall socket every night and recharge the battery with free energy. When the news film ended, anchorman Walter Cronkite appeared to disavow the story just broadcast. Looking somewhat abashed, Walter explained that actually it took fuel to produce electricity, so the electric car did not run on free energy. That moment of disavowal marked the end of the old innocence, when even a presumably educated reporter could think that energy was free.

Many promises, worlds, and ways of life were destroyed when that innocence collapsed. Transportation was especially hard hit. One of the worst sufferers of the destroyed dream was the Winnebago recreational vehicle company. In the years before the first oil crisis Winnebago Industries was considered a sure giant of the future. Its founder and owner, John Hanson, was listed as one of America's newest superrich. But Winnebagos got about 5 miles to the gallon of gas.

Winnebagos are something of an ultimate in one branch of the American dream. They wed the love of home and the love for the automobile into a single unit, producing a home you can drive. Beds, kitchen, and TV are all stretched out behind the cab. Passengers can move from the front seat to the living quarters at will. It seems like a perfect idea, or it did until people began using the word "energy" with about the same frequency as "coffee."

Riding this roller-coaster of public expectations was John Hanson. He began as an undertaker and also sold some furniture, then, in 1959, he organized a move to bring a California trailer company to Forest City, Iowa. The business failed in six months and Hanson took it over. At first it was one more company in the camper/trailer business, but then Winnebago began making the single unit motor-homes that made the company famous. In 1971, when Wall Street decided the Winnebago was the car of the future, Forest City became home to a couple of dozen millionaires and Hanson was one of the richest men in the country.

Hanson seemed eager to keep his company in the family. In 1971, when the Winnebago enthusiasm was at its peak, he made his son, John V., the company president and his son-in-law, Gerald Bowman, became the company's chief executive officer. By 1977, when Hanson reached sixty-five and went into semi-retirement, the end of energy innocence had brought Winnebago into hard times. In a search for more effective leadership, Bowman was reduced to the rank of senior vice-president. But Hanson still seemed family-oriented. He established a fund putting his stock into a family trust; however, two years later, as another oil crisis was approaching, Hanson overthrew the family organization. He returned to take over as chairman of the board. Bowman and John V. were out of the business entirely and the family trust was abolished. Today John Hanson and his wife Louise hold 45 percent of the company's stock.

Recently Winnebago has become profitable again. Hanson says, "You can't take sex, booze, or vacations away from the American people." It sounds true, but recurring oil crises have made a lot of people nervous about their ability to hang onto the final part of that trinity.

## LEARJET

**Auctioneer's price:** $157,000,000.
**Owner:** Gates family.

In the early 1960s, William Lear caught the public's fancy by developing a jet plane small enough to be used as a private aircraft. The first Learjet flight was on October 7, 1963. At that time jet travel was only just coming to dominate commercial air travel in the United States and the idea of private jet travel still seemed like something from science fiction. Skeptics said there was not enough demand for so expensive a luxury and they swore Lear would fail. They were right too. By 1967 Lear was running out of money; he sold his company for $30,000,000 to Charles Gates. The company is now called Gates Learjet.

The Gates money was based on tires, rubber, and engine belts, one of those sizable fortunes made by taking routine things seriously. Gates knew nothing about airplanes. His initial impression was that he had made a terrible mistake in buying Learjet. In 1971 he offered to sell the business to the Northrop Corporation for $1 plus responsibility for the company's debts. Northrop refused. Gates saved himself by hiring an experienced man, Harry Combs, to direct operations. Combs had been flying since 1928 and later showed his love and knowledge of flying by writing a splendid biography of the Wright brothers entitled *Kill Devil Hill*. By 1976, Learjet was showing a profit.

A casual study of this book might make the turn around seem surprising because midway through this success came the first oil crisis and so many other transportation firms suffered catastrophically during that period. A closer look, however, shows a split. Transportation for the middle class was badly hit. Cheap transportation did much better. Transportation for the rich did not exactly boom, but it was able to hang on and even grow. Many people, especially those in energy-related businesses, grew richer than ever precisely because of the oil crisis. For them, luxury transportation companies seemed a natural purchase.

The Gates family does sell stock in the jet plane portion of their business, but they still hold just under two-thirds of the

The Gulfstream III. Photo: Gulfstream Aerospace Corporation

shares themselves. Gates's one son is an architect and he has made it clear that he has no interest in running the family business. For many years the long-term fate of the Gates's family operation was in question, but recently a way to keep the company in the family has been found. Gates has a daughter and she is interested.

The largest most luxurious executive jet is the American Gulfstream III with a range of 4,660 miles, speed of Mach .85, and a price of about $14,000,000, depending on options. The company that makes it, Gulfstream Aerospace Corporation, was created by Allen Paulson when he bought American Jet Industries and the Gulfstream division of the Grumman corporation. In 1983, Paulson began selling stock to the public, but he still holds over 70 percent of the company.

## THE BUICK OF BICYCLES

**Auctioneer's price:** $100,000,000.
**Owner:** Frank V. Schwinn.

You'll often see phrases like "The most respected name in the bicycle industry," "the aristocrat," "most profitable in the industry," when you read about Schwinn bikes, yet Schwinn accounts for only 10 percent of bike sales. They are at the upper end of the price scale, so owning a Schwinn is what many a bike rider aspires to rather than achieves. The reputation is also helped by Schwinn's decision never to sell bikes under a private label. Many bikes are sold without the brand name of the manufacturer. A bicycle may, for example, simply carry the name of the store that sold it. The biggest private-label company is Murray Ohio Manufacturing. It sells more bikes than Schwinn, but most of their bicycles carry some other label, so the Murray name is not so widely displayed. Some Murray bikes are even made for Schwinn and are sold under the Schwinn label.

The past fifteen years have been a boom time for bicycle makers. In the early 1970s, enthusiasm for environmentalism and aerobics led to a quite unexpected rise in bicycle sales. In 1972 and 1973, for the first time since World War I, more bikes were sold in America than cars. The 1974 oil crisis did not help bicycle sales much. People were not yet ready to trade in their Chevy for a Schwinn; that crisis sold more motorcycles than bikes. In 1977, however, there was a small surge in bike sales when President Carter suggested imposing extra taxes on gas guzzling automobiles. Then, in 1979, came the second oil crisis, this one following the overthrow of the Shah. Now there was a great rise in bike sales. In five years, bicycles had gone from being unacceptable to becoming a practical alternative to the car. During those years there was also a great reversal in the nature of bike riders. Up through the end of the 1960s most bikes sold in America were for children. Today most are for adults.

This kind of growth and market strength make the Schwinn Bicycle Company a tempting attraction to conglomerates, but the company is entirely owned by the Schwinn family and they don't want to sell. The business was founded in Chicago in 1895 by Ignatz Schwinn. The present chairman of the board is Ignatz's grandson, Frank, and a fourth generation is ready to take over.

## THE CLASSIC MOTORCYCLE

**Auctioneer's price:** $48,000,000.
**Owner:** Vaughn Leroy Beals, Jr.

Since 1948 there has been only one American maker of motorcycles, Harley-Davidson. It is the classic "hog" machine favored by Hell's Angels. It is the brand name tough guys have tattooed on a bicep. It is the one that bikers yearn to own. It is also in serious trouble.

Harley-Davidson has brand loyalty—company executives like to point out that nobody tattoos "Honda" on his arm—but other bikes have the customers. Motorcycle magazines report that in tests the Japanese bikes are faster, handle better, and stop better. The Harley price also makes it a poor value.

This sad decline is generally blamed on the AMF corporation, the leisure-time company ("we make weekends") that bought Harley-Davidson in 1969. When they took over, Harley had a virtual monopoly on heavy-duty motorcycles. When they sold the business in 1981, Harley's share of the market had fallen to 31 percent. AMF was run by bottom-line men who preferred short-term profits over longer term development.

In the case of Harley-Davidson, AMF milked the company for a dozen years, getting less milk as time passed. When different models, particularly the lighter-weight ones, grew uncompetitive they were dropped from the line. An unexpected boost to sales came in 1974, after the first gas shortages appeared, but that special interest did not last forever. It favored the lighter machines anyway. By the beginning of the 1980s it was apparent, even to AMF, that for Harley-Davidson to survive it was going to need some new investment in equipment and technology. Instead of making the investment, AMF sold the company.

The buyer was Vaughn Beals and a group of investors, including two sons of one of the founders. (Harley-Davidson was founded in 1903 by William Harley and three Davidson brothers. It remained privately held until 1965.) Beals began work as an aeronautical engineer, then came to AMF. He was concerned with Harley-Davidson almost the whole time it was held by AMF. Initially he was deputy executive and after 1977 he was in charge of the division. Because AMF management did not do well by its motorcycles, this background does not speak well for Mr. Beals; however, it is generally believed that it was the management above Beals's level that followed so disastrous a policy.

At the time of the sale there was a bit of a stir; in 1981 conglomerate sales of their parts to the management was still a new phenomenon. Yet the longer lasting puzzle is why Beals would want to buy it. He, more than anybody, knew of the company's problems, although he waxed optimistic. "If this works," he said, "the investors will do well . . . and if it doesn't work you will have no one to blame but yourself." By August, 1982, he had found someone else to blame, the Japanese.

Harley-Davidson petitioned the government for relief from Japanese competition by seeking greatly increased tariffs on Japanese motorcycles. To most people's surprise, the government agreed and in early 1983 America raised the tariff 1000 percent. Japanese motorcycles will face special, but declining, taxes through 1987 in order to give Harley-Davidson a chance to pull itself back together.

## AN AIRLINE

**Auctioneer's price:** $45,000,000.
**Owner:** Edward J. Daly.

During the 1960s, students discovered that if they didn't mind loose scheduling, they could fly to Europe on charter planes at marvelously low costs. A leader in the field of super-charters was World Airways.

In 1975, American television audiences were treated to perhaps the most eloquent news footage ever shot of an army in collapse. A plane landed at Da Nang, South Vietnam. As it sped down the runway motorcyclists and runners on foot dashed for the aircraft. It was the South Vietnamese army in full rout. Terrified men were throwing away their guns and racing for the last flight out before the North Vietnamese army arrived. *Me first* was stamped on every brow. The plane was a World Airways charter.

In that news footage a passenger could be seen trying to keep the mob from storming the plane. He was Edward Daly, chairman, president, and owner of World Airways. Daly bought the airline in 1950 with a down payment of $50,000 and he still owns over 80 percent of its stock.

The fact that the owner of an airline could be the man riding in the hold of his company's most dangerous flight suggests we are confronting both an unusual airline and an unusual owner. World Airways carved out a special niche for itself in the world of regulated air traffic. It sidestepped many regulations by providing charter service to passengers and the military at super-low costs. (Charter flights were relatively free of price regulation.) Daly had found a way to be bigger than most charter companies while still not having to compete head-on with the major companies. Then came the Airline Deregulation Act of 1978.

It is odd that deregulation is generally considered a "conservative" policy. Ordinarily a conservative politician is one who favors the established distribution of power. Deregulation, however, changes the entire environment of operation and is almost always revolutionary in its effects. In Daly's case, the change destroyed the market niche he had created for himself.

There was little to be done except scramble to find a new place. World began offering scheduled flights from its base in Oakland. Its big innovation came in 1979 when it offered scheduled transcontinental flights for $99. In a way, this step was in keeping with the old days when World attracted business by offering low rates, but the new element in the battle was that the other airlines could slash prices to match. Thus began the most visible characteristic of the age of deregulated air traffic, ruinous price wars. World did not have the finances to challenge the giant airlines directly and in March, 1982, Daly tried to cry uncle. He urged the Civil Aeronautics Board to resume price regulation. Of course he was laughed at. He sounded like a condemned Robespierre calling for restoration of the monarchy.

March 2, 1982, was the day the internal strains deregulation was putting on companies became visible:

- Braniff International announced that in the face of a cash crisis it was cutting the next paycheck of its employees in half. This drastic move was said to be a one-time event, but within the year Braniff had gone into bankruptcy.
- Continental airlines held an emergency meeting of its board of directors to avoid bankruptcy. Later, in 1983, it did declare itself bankrupt.
- Edmund Daly announced that World Airways would collapse within the week if it did not get pay concessions from its employees and debt concessions from its creditors.

Perhaps because it was the most flagrantly in trouble, World outlasted Braniff and Continental. Everybody knew Daly wasn't kidding, so he got concessions. Daly cut his own salary drastically, to $26,000, bringing his pay well below that of many commercial pilots.

Then, at the end of 1982, there was a coup at World Airways. The board of directors began changing top personnel and rewriting the corporate by-laws in ways that weakened much of Daly's authority. Daly soon denounced the changes and, because the directors can be voted out by the stockholders, Daly's 82 percent vote should guarantee him the power to find more suitable directors. But because of the airline's serious debt problems, open warfare in top management might frighten Daly's creditors into pressing for their money. He does not want to see a crowd of creditors rushing toward him, each with *me first* written on his forehead. The powers of ownership do not count for much during times of revolution.

## CUSTOM-MADE CARS

**Auctioneer's price:** $5,500,000.
**Owner:** Stephen Blake.

Luxury automobiles aren't what they used to be. Once luxury models were the avant-garde of the industry, but today America's luxury car company makes a Studebaker designed in 1961. It sounds like a joke for late-night TV, but, oddly enough, it's true. The Avanti was designed in 1961 by Raymond Loewy. It was Loewy who designed most of the 1950s Studebakers and who later designed the Exxon logo. The Studebaker-Packard Corporation began selling Avantis in 1962, but then stopped making cars altogether in 1964. Most people barely noticed the change, but to Studebaker loyalists (and there were such people) the closure was painful.

Under capitalism, if you are popular enough, the lost can live again. The rights to the Avanti were bought by an auto dealer in South Bend, Indiana who preserved the business by converting the Avanti into a luxury car. Customers could order specific carpeting, upholstery, and paint. From order to delivery took six months and the customer usually had to make a trip to South Bend to settle all arrangements. The look of the car persisted in the low sleek tastes of the early 1960s. Of course, the technology was also early 1960s and as time passed the brakes, suspension, and steering systems were increasingly old-fashioned. Avanti customers became like old Studebaker customers. They were intensely loyal to the car's style and not much concerned with the general run of opinion.

One of the most enthusiastic Avanti owners was Stephen Blake, a real estate investor in Washington, D.C. He bought one in 1972 and loved it. In 1976, the original owner of Avanti Motors, Nate Altman, died and Blake began calling Altman's brother to ask about buying the company. For years he was told *no* in angry tones, but finally the answer was *maybe.*

Blake's background in automobile making was nonexistent, so it took him a while to find backers, but he got them and did buy the company. He immediately introduced changes—upgrading the technology, improving the efficiency of the assembly, increasing the number of dealers, and raising the basic price from $25,000 to $30,000. He also commissioned a design for a convertible and the hardtop Avanti is also being redesigned. These ideas all sound reasonable enough, but in the process the company is abandoning its initial purpose of preserving the finest old Studebaker.

The Avanti. Photo: Avanti Motor Corporation

## FUGAZY LIMOUSINES

**Auctioneer's price:** $888,000.
**Owner:** William Denis Fugazy.

Limousines are ceasing to be the exclusive vehicle of the very rich. Travel by taxi used to be ritzy enough to suit most tastes, even on special occasions. In most cities, that is no longer true. Taxis are still preferable to mass transit, but they are hardly elegant, spacious, or even particularly comfortable. For special occasions like weddings, important engagements, and anniversary outings, travel by taxi strikes an increasing number of people as too seamy, so quite ordinary people are calling limousines.

The man who stumbled into this line and now offers limousine service in New York, Los Angeles, Detroit, and several other large cities is William Fugazy. He is a deal maker whose finger gets into many pies. He promoted the second and third Floyd Patterson-Ingemar Johannsen heavyweight championship fights of two decades ago. He loves to be seen with celebrities and has photos on the office wall of him with Sinatra, him with Jackie Gleason, him with Gerry Ford, him with etc. Celebrity followers always seem a little sad, but they make a lot of contacts and if you are a deal cutter, contacts are life.

Fugazy inherited a family business begun in the nineteenth century. William's grandfather, Louis, had a bank in Greenwich Village, New York, the Banco Fugazzi. It died with him, but a sideline, the Fugazy Travel Bureau, founded in 1870, survives today with franchised offices nationwide. The generation following William is expected to continue the business. One of his sons, William, Jr., is vice-president and general counsel to the firm and a daughter, Denise, also works for the company. Auctioneer's price for the whole business is about $60,000,000. (The price above is just for the limo fleet.) All stock is held within the family.

It was William who got the company into limousines. In 1963, he was offered a deal on a group of Lincoln Continentals and decided to accept. Now his fleet has grown to over seventy limos and Fugazy Continental Limousines is a full division of

Fugazy International. William is prominent in Catholic circles and building on those contacts he secured the contract to provide twenty limousines for the visit of Pope John Paul II to New York.

Deal makers are easy to satirize because their eye is so often on the main chance, but their interests force them to be alert to what is going on in the real world. They tend to identify changes in tastes and desires before anybody else. In Fugazy's case, he was the one to see that the growing wealth of the rich and the declining quality of traditional services to the middle class combined to make a steady business in limousine travel. Discovering such a change is not as monumental as writing *Catch-22*, but acting on the discovery has altered the flavor of important moments in private lives and that accomplishment is nothing to blush about.

## WORLD WAR II INVASION CRAFT

**Auctioneer's price:** $43,200.
**Owner:** Ben Olson.

While most of the largest transportation fortunes are based on meeting people's everyday needs, smaller businesses have found success by solving local transportation problems. In the last half of the nineteenth century, the "Dells" or small canyons, of the Wisconsin River was a popular and stylish summer resort. The place then went into a long decline and never has become stylish again, but after World War II Herman Breitenbach had the smart idea of showing tourists through the Dells in amphibious vehicles built for the army to assault beaches.

Anyone who ever saw a halfway decent World War II movie remembers these transports. They turn up in the scene where the heroic platoon is riding in some kind of armored barge toward the battle. Everybody is nervous, especially the kid from Brooklyn, but the war seems like a dream: it is still so far away. Then suddenly the front of the amphibious craft drops down, light is everywhere, the platoon is running forward, men are falling, and the war is no longer a dream's distance away.

The army's landing craft were called DUKWs, pronounced "ducks." Today the Wisconsin Ducks corporation operates thirty-one of the vehicles, twenty-six of them to take people around the Wisconsin River and five more as tour shuttles for the town. They also own twenty non-operational ducks that are in various states of disrepair and serve mainly as sources for spare parts. None of these ducks were used in the war; they were built as training vehicles and as preparation for the invasion of Japan. Although amphibious six-wheel-drive vehicles are perfect for zipping up and down the terrain, they do have one limitation. The landing craft were designed for short term use—a few trips between ships and shore and then they were abandoned on the beach. Forty years of operation was in nobody's design plans. Maintenance on them is steady and extensive. Tires especially suffer.

Breitenbach sold his operation in 1956. Ben Olson, the senior owner, and his partners dominate the Wisconsin Dells tourist business now. Very few businesses based on World War II surplus materials have been so successful, so practical, or so unconcerned with singing the praises of military technology.

Touring via landing craft. Photo: Wisconsin Ducks, Inc.

# APPENDIX

## AUCTIONEER'S PRICES

| | | | |
|---|---|---|---|
| $11,800,000,000 | E.I. du Pont de Nemours & Co. | 1,920,000,000 | G.D. Searle & Co. |
| 6,440,000,000 | Coca-Cola | 1,840,000,000 | Metromedia |
| 5,630,000,000 | Ford Motor Company | 1,690,000,000 | Wang Laboratories |
| 3,600,000,000 | Mars Inc. | 1,560,000,000 | Levi Strauss |
| 3,324,000,000 | Anheuser-Busch Companies | 1,300,000,000 | Hearst Corporation |
| 3,200,000,000 | Seagram's | 1,250,000,000 | Daniel Ludwig's tanker fleet |
| 3,100,000,000 | BSN—Gervais Danone | 1,100,000,000 | Southland Corporation |
| 2,400,000,000 | Loews | | |
| 2,250,000,000 | Phibro-Salomon | 1,080,000,000 | Irvine Ranch |

| | |
|---|---|
| 1,050,000,000 | Hallmark Cards |
| 1,000,000,000 | Electronic Data Systems |
| 901,000,000 | Brown-Forman Distilleries |
| 851,000,000 | King Ranch |
| 800,000,000 | Coca-Cola Bottling Cos. of John Lupton |
| 720,000,000 | J.R. Simplot Company |
| 710,000,000 | Federal Express |
| 672,000,000 | Commodore International |
| 617,000,000 | *New York Times* |
| 599,000,000 | TeleVideo Systems |
| 585,000,000 | Gallo Wine |
| 557,000,000 | H & R Block |
| 551,000,000 | Hyatt Hotels |
| 548,000,000 | Freedom Newspapers |
| 547,000,000 | Cannon Mills |
| 490,000,000 | Wendy's International |
| 488,000,000 | Perdue Farms |
| 483,000,000 | Twentieth Century-Fox |
| 472,000,000 | NutraSweet (aspartame) |
| 450,000,000 | Carnival Cruise Lines |
| 450,000,000 | Gucci |
| 445,000,000 | A.C. Nielsen |
| 425,000,000 | Great Atlantic and Pacific Tea Company |
| 419,000,000 | Nike, Inc. |
| 412,000,000 | Lefrak Organization |
| 405,000,000 | Estée Lauder |
| 345,000,000 | Tandon Corporation |
| 322,000,000 | *TV Guide* |
| 297,000,000 | General Nutrition Corporation |
| 263,000,000 | Harry Winston |
| 255,000,000 | Jordache |
| 250,000,000 | Grand Ole Opry |
| 242,000,000 | Hartz Mountain Corp. (division of Hartz Mountain Industries) |
| 236,000,000 | Las Colinas, Texas |
| 196,000,000 | ComputerLand |
| 180,000,000 | Strawberry Shortcake |
| 179,000,000 | J.M. Smucker Co. |
| 167,000,000 | Empire State Building |
| 158,000,000 | Winnebago Industries |
| 157,000,000 | Gates Learjet |
| 142,000,000 | *Parade* magazine |
| 115,000,000 | Binney & Smith |
| 114,000,000 | Genentech |
| 112,000,000 | *The National Enquirer* |
| 110,000,000 | North American Watch |
| 102,000,000 | Loews theaters |
| 100,000,000 | Art collection of Norton Simon |
| 100,000,000 | Schwinn Bicycle Company |
| 97,800,000 | Johnson Publishing Company |
| 93,500,000 | Star Wars |
| 91,000,000 | Dannon Milk Products |

| | |
|---|---|
| 90,000,000 | National Restaurants Management Company |
| 83,000,000 | Bantam Books |
| 78,400,000 | *The New Yorker* |
| 69,800,000 | Del Amo Fashion Center |
| 60,000,000 | McIlhenny Company |
| 60,000,000 | Fugazy International |
| 58,000,000 | Dow Jones News/Retrieval Service |
| 56,300,000 | Lindblad Tours |
| 55,000,000 | Trump Tower (atrium and office space) |
| 53,000,000 | The Los Angeles Raiders |
| 49,500,000 | Thomas Nelson Publishing |
| 48,000,000 | Harley-Davidson Motor Company |
| 46,100,000 | Oil of Olay subsidiary of Richardson-Vicks |
| 45,000,000 | The Los Angeles Dodgers |
| 45,000,000 | World Airways Inc. |
| 42,500,000 | Binion's Horseshoe Casino |
| 40,000,000 | *Southern Living* |
| 40,000,000 | Dungeons & Dragons |
| 35,600,000 | Godiva Chocolatier |
| 35,000,000 | The Daily Racing Form |
| 32,000,000 | Trinchera Ranch |
| 28,000,000 | Mammoth Lakes Ski Resort |
| 25,500,000 | Norton Simon Museum of Pasadena |
| 25,000,000 | Harfred Inc. |
| 20,700,000 | Frederick's of Hollywood |
| 20,600,000 | South of the Border |
| 15,900,000 | Kloss Video |
| 15,200,000 | Ringling Brothers and Barnum & Bailey Circus |
| 13,300,000 | Energy Conversion Devices, Inc. |
| 12,900,000 | Secretariat |
| 12,400,000 | Philadelphia Seventy Sixers |
| 11,000,000 | Boston Bruins |
| 10,000,000 | Wharton Econometric Forecasting Associates |
| 9,400,000 | Steuben Glass |
| 8,700,000 | The Pleasure Chest, Inc. |
| 8,500,000 | Casa Pacifica |
| 6,650,000 | Microsoft BASIC |
| 6,300,000 | Restaurant Antoine |
| 5,830,000 | "Yo Picasso" |
| 5,600,000 | Salvador Dali Museum collection |
| 5,500,000 | Avanti Motors Corporation |
| 4,900,000 | Carson & Barnes circus |

| | |
|---|---|
| 4,000,000 | Collection of works by Peter Carl Fabergé |
| 4,000,000 | Elias Sports Bureau |
| 3,150,000 | Bronco Bowl |
| 2,640,000 | Scott Instruments |
| 2,500,000 | Space Services Inc. |
| 2,150,000 | Santa Catalina Island |
| 950,000 | Louisville Redbirds |
| 895,000 | The laser patent |
| 888,000 | Limousine fleet of Fugazy Continental |
| 877,500 | *Soldier of Fortune* magazine |
| 850,000 | *Sequoia* presidential yacht |
| 810,000 | Robert Trent Jones design company |
| 620,000 | Collection of paintings by D.H. Lawrence |
| 560,000 | Solzhenitsyn's Retreat |
| 315,000 | Collection of Tiffany lamps |
| 89,800 | All Star Baseball School |
| 75,000 | Oldest house in America |
| 43,200 | Fleet of World War II DUWKs |
| 35,000 | "Pepsi Challenger" bicycle |
| 25,000 | Rocky Hill Favorite Deb Jersey cow |
| 18,000 | Rubik's Cube |
| 12,000 | Oscar's Velvet Brahma bull |
| 10,000 | Linda Wells's letter-writing business |
| 4,500 | Statue of Trigger |

# INDEX

# Index

# Index

# INDEX